AMERICA:
Through a veil of tears

Thanks for the new lease of life

AMERICA:
Through a veil of tears

Les Kay

Published by Les Kay
lesdkay@yahoo.co.uk

A CIP catalogue record for this book is available from the British Library.

ISBN 978-0-9572645-0-2

Book and cover design by Clare Brayshaw

Prepared and printed by:

York Publishing Services Ltd
64 Hallfield Road
Layerthorpe
York YO31 7ZQ

Tel: 01904 431213

Website: www.yps-publishing.co.uk

Dedication

To my closest of friends, my confidante, my beloved son.
Cai ap Leslie.
Often remembered, never forgotten!

The author

Les Kay, a Marine Archaeology graduate of Bangor University, has devoted much of his life to travel, and even more to raising his son, Cai ap Leslie. His travels have taken him far and wide, often through adversity, and always with a sense of adventure. The subsequent tales of derring-do have long since enthralled friends and family, whose encouragement finally led him to consider recording events more formally. His first attempt at writing was to be a humorous account of high adventure and motorcycle mayhem across the Americas with son in tow. So much more than words has been invested in this first book, and much has been gained. No-one could have foretold the events that created this story, nor the poignancy of the words that followed.

Prelude

Like the majority of proud fathers, I claim the birth of my son as one of the happiest days of my life. Having scant regard for the relationship with my own father, I swore to create something better with Cai. All I really wanted to do was to share his life with him, nurturing and caring, relishing the good times, overcoming the bad. I didn't bargain for how much it would change my life, how much fun it could be. He gave me a new lease of life, invigorated me, and in turn took me into the realms of my second childhood. We could be as bad as each other, mischievous kids always looking for fun and excitement, always off on mini-adventures.

Rarely looking back with remorse, I wholeheartedly endorse the institution of parenthood, frequently blessing those days as the best days of my life. For twelve years I'd been a single father, he was the light of my life, my focal point. That isn't to say we didn't have our moments, but they merely served to strengthen the bond between us, and form a deeper understanding of each other. We became far more than father and son, we were friends, confidantes, partners in crime. Our relationship was criticised by few and admired by many, seen as something special, unique.

We had a penchant for the same things, wild and exciting things mainly. Our strength was our mutual love of thrilling past-times; travelling, climbing, scuba diving, kiting, and eventually motorcycling. Being brought up with motor biking parents, his thrill of them started at an early age. At three years old, he'd sit on the tank of my bike, twisting the throttle back with glee, always wanting to go faster. I guess it was inevitable he'd take up the mantle of biker when the chance finally came. True to form, he had his first bike on the road on his seventeenth birthday, the minimum legal age. He took to it like a duck to water, riding the twenty-five miles back and forth to college whatever the weather, joyful of the freedom it gave him. Frequent rides together honed his riding skills, his overall competence grew with a succession of more powerful bikes. But what he hungered for most was to be let loose upon the world, he'd heard too many stories of the glorious adventures to be had riding through foreign lands. Tales of riding far off the beaten track, of warm welcomes from poor peasants in lonely mountain villages, enthralled him. That was the way he'd like to see the world, straddling his machine, riding mountain ranges, across continents, reaching regions where tourism doesn't exist.

I'd always wanted to take him on a prolonged journey, circumstances had never given me the opportunity though, and we'd never had longer than six weeks travelling together. With a gap year between college and university forthcoming the perfect opportunity arose, and so we got to planning. I tried to keep it sensible, six months touring South America – a creditable trip by any stretch of the imagination. Cai pushed for more, he wanted to do the whole of the Americas, and who was I to argue? The idea was too thrilling to disregard. So we settled on a ten month period to traverse the entire American continent, an estimated distance of thirty thousand miles. There wasn't that much to plan other than visas, neither of us wanted a set itinerary, decisions would be made as and when they were needed. Bikes would be bought in the States, our gear could be prepared and taken over with us, all we'd have to do is strap it on and ride away.

Our intention was to leave the highways behind and strike out on tracks and trails, camping wild wherever possible. Cai pretty much bowed to my superior knowledge of motorcycle touring. The bikes would need to endure the rigours of off-road riding, so we narrowed the choice down to a shortlist of four. All were 650cc, single cylinder, Japanese Enduro style bikes. So soft luggage was selected, to save weight, it could also be fitted onto whichever bikes we chose. As for tools, there was no need to encumber ourselves with unnecessary weight, experience had taught me that any of the models shortlisted required the same range of spanners, with only a few other auxiliary bits of equipment. Basic mechanics had been a part of Cai's introduction to the delights of biking, and was a bit of a forte for me; we wouldn't be relying on the availability of local mechanics. For camping we were already well equipped; a small lightweight tent and our sleeping mats and bags weren't exactly new, but they were good quality. That only left our personal gear, which had to provide protection for our own safety and from the elements. There was no stinting in that regard, we'd face soaring temperatures in desert climates, prolonged bouts of driving rain, and the freezing conditions of high altitude riding. Despite the rising costs, decent quality gear was bought, supplemented by bits and pieces from on-line auctions. Rather than worry about cost, it merely served to enhance our growing excitement.

I wasn't a high flying business man, there were no rich relations waiting in the wings with bundles of cash to bail us out. To raise the funds I was selling everything, house, furniture, electronic goods and a vast array of sports equipment. To make ends meet until the house was finally sold, a loan was secured against the value of my house. It was all or nothing, such was my commitment to the forthcoming, ultimate, adventure of our lives. We'd be on a tight budget at first, which meant relying on used machines. By scouring available local sources, a combination of used bike dealers and private advertisers, we'd have to make the most of what was on offer at the time. Exactly which locality remained undecided. It could be the making or breaking of our initial funds, a lengthy delay in rented accommodation could easily break the bank. Then came our lucky break, in the form of a family contact in Ojai, close to Los Angeles. It was an old university friend of Cai's aunt, not anyone either of us had ever met, or even heard of before. But we had a base, somewhere to hole up while we found bikes, and an address to use for all the legal requirements of registering and insuring our bikes.

There was nothing left to organise. In the last few weeks we lived in a house devoid of even the most rudimentary luxuries of life. A friend was to lodge temporarily, for however long it took to sell the place. They'd take care of our beds when the time came, the rest of the household goods had been sold and taken away. It was a spartan existence, but short lived and worth the inconvenience. We were itching to go. All there was left to do was bid farewell to a host of friends and family. A farewell party was the answer, all and sundry were invited for a night of drunken debauchery. By invitation only, fancy dress was obligatory, and we decided on a Hollywood character theme, we were heading for Los Angeles after all. We were graced with the presence of Bruce Willis, Hunter S. Thompson, Marilyn Monroe and Scarlett O'Hara. Three Cleopatras draped themselves provocatively around the garden, while two King Kongs had to battle it out over one Fay Wray. Alice fell down a rabbit hole, to be rescued by the Universal soldier, totally ignored by Fred and Ginger, who danced the night away oblivious to the surrounding chaos. Cai himself carried off a perfectly camp rendition of Johnny Depp as Captain Jack Sparrow from Pirates of the Carribean. As for me, I went all out for a full character portrayal of Robin Williams as Mrs Doubtfire. It proved to be a night well worth remembering, the perfect send off for the daring duo.

Chapter One

July 3 2007, the day before American Independence Day! By 7am it was a hot, sunny Californian day, everything had been organised, and we were ready. We'd spent the last week viewing motorbikes. There were far fewer than expected, but we'd found a pair of bikes. Brand new, matching, 2007 model Kawasaki KLR 650's, one red and the other black. Once the rental car had been returned, we'd be free to pick up our new toys. But they were so much more than that. They were to transport us the length and breadth of the American continent. They were our trusty steeds, our life for the next ten months. They were also more than we'd hoped for and more than we budgeted for, much more! We'd been expecting to buy a couple of second hand machines, dependent on what was available at the time. Damned if it wasn't worth it though, we were both so excited! For the last eighteen months, we'd been planning this, so often it had felt it would never happen; bugger any doubts, today was the day, the start of our greatest adventure yet.

We looked a right couple of posers; there was no mistaking we were a partnership. Our jackets, trousers and luggage matched perfectly, same make, style and colour, even the same size. Now matching bikes as well, but we felt elated, pleased to look the part, cheesy or not! Throughout the journey to the bike dealers our conversation was a contagious babble of likely routes, possible hazards, mainly bikes and bears. How fast can a Grizzly accelerate? Will a KLR outrun it? We even joked about who was the fastest runner, obviously the slower would be Grizzly breakfast. 'Hey Cai, you reckon you can outrun your old man?' No doubt about it, we were flying high; full of ourselves full of life, more than ready to meet the challenge of riding around the Americas. Thirty thousand miles, no sweat – what an adventure, bring it on!

Having spent over $9000 on our bikes we felt OK to take liberties. I phoned the dealership and got them to pick us up from the car rental company. The salesman was more than pleased to oblige. It was only ten minutes away after all. While we waited, the choice of bikes had to be settled, and we both preferred the red one, purely for aesthetic reasons. Before leaving home an agreement had been made; I'd have first choice of bikes, simply because it was me funding the trip. Cai's mood was so infectious, he was buzzing and didn't really care which colour he had. The red one was mine for the taking, but how could I insist, how could I deprive him solely on the basis of colour? Seeing his face light up when I let him have the red one really made it worthwhile. Isn't it lovely being a generous guy with your nearest and dearest? It certainly is when their appreciation is so obvious, their delight so contagious.

The dealership had the bikes ready to wheel out. We kitted up and waited for our sparkling new machines. Making a quick visual check, everything seemed fine, there was plenty of fuel in each tank; and the gleaming newness of the machines made it hard to notice anything but their pristine condition. At least we were sensible enough to ride them round the car park, checking the controls to ensure they all worked and were adjusted to our satisfaction. Well, what more is there? The documentation included a dealership checklist, they'd been thoroughly checked in the workshop, we only had to familiarise ourselves with any differences in the controls.

Whilst the bikes were fuelled ready for the run back to Ojai, we weren't. Hunger dictated the need for a lunch break; only a mile down the road we made a stop. A crappy fast food joint was our last chance for sustenance before entering the Los Angeles freeway system. We didn't give a damn about the quality of the food, we only wanted to fill our bellies and get back on our bikes. We really felt the business, and laughed at how good it felt with everything matching. At least no one would be able to mistake we were together! This was a trip of equals, none of your traditional father and son hierarchies. Our bond was so much more than that, more than close friends, more than travel buddies. Shit man, we'd grown up together, Cai from a babe, me from an irresponsible adult. Happy as pigs in shit we were! The new bikes felt great, better than either of us had at home, so with beaming grins and a flick of the switch we were all

revved up and ready to rock. Cai su'
wasn't about to argue. I trusted his s
navigation skills bettered his. So '
do so.

Once hitting the freeway
a relaxing ride up the Pacif.
only straight forward route thro
pleasant travelling the day before i.
frantically busy roads; they were packed a.
in our new engines for five hundred miles me.
speed of 4,000 rpm, allowing us only 60mph in .
a bother, we both had many miles of experience b.
were happy to take our time and plod along at that spee.
been riding over fifty miles a day for nearly two years, to ana
college. He was used to tackling one of the busiest roads in Nor..
Wales, it was just another ride for him. The incredible heat couldn't
diminish our enthusiasm either, neither of us had ever had a brand
new bike; we were ecstatic, full of energy, just raring to go!

Jeez, but the traffic was busy. The sun was scorching hot, so
we took our time to adjust to the extreme conditions. They weren't
too bad really; it was only the initial intimidation, so many lanes
of traffic! Once amongst it though, it was easy, concentrate on
the relevant vehicles. There is no point worrying too much about
something two lanes over unless you're both heading in the same
direction. We settled down quickly, flowing through the traffic,
allowing others a bit more leeway than they generally allowed us.
Things were cool, we made easy progress, I rarely lost sight of Cai
for more than thirty seconds or so. Cruising down the second lane,
I moved over. Cai drew alongside me, he had the cheesiest grin you
could imagine. An emphatic hand signal showed clearly everything
was AOK. Hey, this was our dream come true, we were doing it!
Look out the Americas, here we come! I acknowledged his signal,
grinning like a Cheshire cat myself. I thought he might want to take
the lead; no, he only wanted to share the thrill with me. What a
lovely feeling.

Highway 55 took us through the busiest part of the city, I
expected to lose sight of Cai now and again, so it wasn't of any
great concern. I rode through a really congested patch of traffic,
a camper tailgating, trying to squeeze me out the lane, so my full
concentration was needed. By the time I'd dealt with the immediate

ed for Cai, no sign of him! I reduced speed a little
…e out behind, expecting him to appear over a slight
…. I slowed even more and made my way near to the
…er. Still nothing. I decided to pull in. As I did so, another
…owed me, calling out his window, 'your buddy's come off,
…, he has people taking care of him.' Oh, fucking hell, NO!
…t, safe or not, I turned right around and rode like the fury
…the hard shoulder, the wrong way.

Cai was laying in the middle of the freeway, his head being held
…a guy doing his accident first aid routine. Cars were queued up
…ehind, squeezing past anyway they could. It didn't matter, my bike
was hurriedly parked at the side of the freeway. Whether it caused
more congestion or not I did not care. His bike barely damaged, I
assumed Cai's injuries would not be too severe either. The poor
lad was laid there, his head being held immobile, pointing straight
at the sun. With his full bike kit on the sweat was pouring off him.
His first words, while I tried to shield his eyes, were to let me know
a truck had hit him from behind. 'What truck? Turning around to
the onlookers, 'Where's this fucking truck driver?' He wasn't there,
he hadn't even stopped! I was furious, but more aware of Cai's
immediate needs; I needed to ensure he was OK, ensure help was
on its way.

Time took on a new meaning. It seemed hours before the
ambulance appeared, so much happened and I never once thought it
would be the last moments I would spend with my son. Cai wanted
to assure me the truck driver was not at fault, the bike's engine
had cut out, he'd tried moving to safety, the truck just ploughed
straight through him. He was in so much pain, I could only do my
best to assure him it would be fine, and that medics were on their
way. I undid his jacket, against the orders of the guy holding his
head. I felt so angry at him, who the hell did he think he was? Being
very careful I carried on, pointing out that the intense heat was not
helping Cai remain calm or comfortable. An off duty nurse helped
shield his eyes; he was cooler, but he was reaching out for me. The
pain was obviously too much for him, he wanted me to hold him,
desperate to have me close. I pressed myself to him, desperate to
give comfort. Again, I was rebuked by the guy holding his head,
I can't even remember what I said. I was grateful he was there to
help, but wished he would shut the fuck up! If Cai needed to be
held I would bloody well do it, without causing him more problems.

Consciousness began to slip away; my concern increased, I spoke to him constantly trying to keep him focused. With relief I heard someone announce the ambulance had arrived.

America's emergency services, the gallant heroes, took nearly half an hour to turn up. Their headquarters were just up the road, the tailback of traffic was abysmal though, and when they did show up they proved to have zero public relations skills. I'd have thought the paramedics would be better at handling people, they had their hands full caring for Cai and I was happy to give them the space, despite a strong reluctance to move from Cai's side. I assured him I'd be at the hospital as soon, or soon after, he arrived; he was in the best hands he could be, I'd only be in their way! With a trauma centre within a couple of miles, it was a quick journey, they'd only just taken Cai in when I pulled up outside. I had to waste time though, as the front entrance was the only way open to me. Due to delaying tactics and false promises by the hospital care worker, I never saw Cai conscious again. They refused to let me in to see him, promised I would be allowed as soon as I signed the relevant forms; then said it wasn't possible!

Yes, I was annoyed, I felt deceived! 'Of course you need to see your son sir, just sign these forms, then you can join him'. Well actually no, they lied, I still wasn't allowed go through. I knew that if Cai were conscious he would want me to be there with him, but they would have none of it, finally claiming he was under sedation, so there was no way could I get to be with him. How I wished to force my way in, I was furious, tried my damnedest to be forceful without threatening. The person in charge of emergency services actually threatened to cite me, unless I stopped my demands. All the way through dealing with the administration of the various services, I was stunned at how impersonal and officious they were. Nary a thought for anyone, just doing their job! If you made it more difficult, 'Stand aside sir, or we'll have you removed'! The anger those people instilled in me has been one of the hardest things to deal with. They made the whole episode so much more traumatic, especially discovering he'd been conscious for some time after reaching the hospital. I was swamped with administrators and do-gooders, a constant stream of officials and support workers; they couldn't do enough to help, except allow me in to be with Cai. It certainly wouldn't have helped him if I'd been issued with a citation. No sirree. It didn't mean I had to stomach the waves of people, their constant diatribe; I needed my head space. I needed to calm myself down, to be there for him when he needed me.

Time warp! I've no idea how long passed, I'd sat, eyes closed, lost in a thoughtless vacuum. As if in a deep trance my mind was blank, I could only feel an all encompassing fear and love for Cai. No other way could I be with him, emotions filled me, yet all I could do was reach out metaphysically, send him my love and support. For about three hours they operated, informing me of which procedure they were attempting at each step of the way. At some point I phoned our new found friends in Ojai, Alasdair and Lauren Coyne. I needed someone to phone Cai's mum, my cell phone couldn't be used for UK calls. I guess I didn't believe he would die, assumed he would pull through. Maybe he'd need a couple of months recovering, then we could continue, he'd be desperate to ride again by then. Surely it wouldn't put him off! As I learnt more I grew more concerned, they successfully removed his spleen and repaired a ruptured diaphragm; they hadn't even got close to operating on his smashed hip. Oh, my poor lad, the bike must have landed on his mid section, pulverising his body. What a massive amount of damage, surely that frigging truck was hammering down the freeway? Why couldn't it have been me? Why didn't I insist on the red bike? If only...then I could take his place, his pain, save him from the horror he was going through!

Tannoy announcements alerted the resuscitation team, they were called to the department I knew Cai to be in. I was petrified, on the verge of complete panic. He couldn't die, he just couldn't! Shortly after another call went out, and then another, all for the same theatre. Now the waiting was unbearable, desperation took over, my whole being screamed. NO! NO! again and again. This really could not be happening, not to Cai, not my son, he was everything to me; never has anything seemed more unreal. This isn't what life should be about, he's a great guy, so full of life; how can it end so unexpectedly? We'd only just started our trip of a lifetime! But it was true, the third attempt to resuscitate him failed. I was stunned and could only think that I had to phone people, to let them know. Maybe that would make it more real. But how do you relate something that you're fighting so hard not to believe? Like me, Alasdair struggled to take it in, that wasn't the direction it had been going in; he'd assumed it was a situation of repairing the damage, not fighting for his life.

Only then did they allow me to see his body, 'You are free to touch, hug or even kiss him Leslie'. I was too devastated for sarcasm, too shocked to voice my feelings. And there was my most beloved son, lying still on a hospital trolley, pale, covered to the chin. He did not look as though he were in a restful sleep; he did not look like I could shake him awake. It wasn't my son, just a lifeless shell, devoid of life or meaning. It still didn't stop me using it as a focus for my thoughts, my words; they had to be voiced somewhere. One clear thought shone out above all else, I desperately wanted there to be somewhere for Cai to continue his existence. As I leant over to hug him I felt nauseous, the stench of antiseptic overwhelmed me. It proved to be a smell that lingered, for weeks it crept back, a nasal flashback guaranteed to make the eyes water. Oh, how I scrubbed myself trying to wash it away! Each time my mind took me back to the image of Cai laying there, dead, the end of everything I valued. The feelings of hopelessness were beyond imagining, only time would reveal the magnitude of despair, the depth of grief. Christ, how could I possibly hope to deal with this? One thing for certain, there was no way I was going to stay in the Ronald McDonald charity home for distressed relatives, however much the bloody social workers tried to insist. I needed to get away, be alone, my bike was outside, and that was my only means of escape. No way was I waiting to be picked up and taken back to Ojai, I needed out of that damned hospital, immediately!

How the hell it took me four hours to ride to Ojai I don't know, in fact I know too little of those first few hours. Vague memories of riding through darkness, getting very cold and the road in front illuminated by my headlight, are my only recollections of those hours. I was in a daze, oblivious to people's concern for me jumping on the bike and vanishing. It was the only solution at the time. I couldn't have dealt with other people, didn't want to, I had to give myself time for it to sink in. Holy shit, it was too much to comprehend, every conscious thought fought against the information! No way did my head want to accept it; it was my worst nightmare. In all my days as a father, it was what I'd most feared. I'd always rejected the slightest thought of Cai dying; it was way too scary. Don't even go there! What parent would like to contemplate the death of a dearly loved child, especially a vigorously healthy one? Whatever process my mind needed to begin absorbing this news, it acquired on that ride back. I rode completely on autopilot, it took ages to leave the city lights of LA. Maybe I rode round in circles, maybe I lost an hour between drags on a cigarette. Nothing mattered, anything could have happened, I cared not one iota!

I know I stopped and bought some cigarettes, I'd only given up a week ago, 'Sorry Cai, I hope you understand.' The rest is a blur. In the blink of an eye (or was it an eternity?) I was riding down the track to Alasdair and Lauren's house. They sat on the doorstep, fretting over my prolonged ride back. Time didn't exist though, everything was a void! I doubt if I talked much sense that night, I'm surprised I managed to talk at all; how did I manage to stop crying long enough? But through the tears, the wracking sobs, the story unfolded. Communication helped a lot, explaining the details reinforced it in my own mind, gradually sinking in to my deeper consciousness. It had to be real, I could still smell the hospital antiseptic from Cai's body!

Chapter Two

Returning to North Wales tore me apart. For me the events were based where I was, not at home. Home represented a surge of concerned people, a torrent of visitors, another onslaught of emotions. With the utmost sincerity everyone's hearts went out to me, everyone grieved with me, but I could have done without facing people, without their heartfelt sentiments. I felt touched by the support; the number of people expressing their deepest regrets, their shock and horror at the turn of events. It needed to be done, but every time I saw anyone who knew me, I cringed. The last thing I wanted was to face yet another person, another pained and awkward moment; yet I knew how important it was to allow people to express their emotions, however difficult. Too many times I felt my presence was purely for the benefit of others, rather than myself. Maybe that is the ultimate responsibility of losing a loved one, being there for their friends and family when they die. It's pleasing to have stayed accessible for everyone, and it is pleasing to have shared those emotional times, even with virtual strangers. How could I deny anyone their expressions of sorrow? Seeing the pain in their eyes really did touch me, however awkward I felt. But it wasn't where I wished to be, what I wished to be experiencing.

Ironically in our last weeks in Wales Cai and I had driven behind a funeral cortège. It initiated a conversation concerning the huge expense undertaken in the western world to mourn the loss of loved ones. We both felt it a luxury not afforded most peoples of the world, that it was a shame to expend such resources when the bulk of the world's population were left wanting. Instead of flowers and expensive tributes we asked for donations, which were in time used to fund a third world environmental project; a subject close to Cai's heart. I gave the eulogy in the crematorium. I needed for people to understand the situation immediately before Cai's accident, his happiness, the bright shining smile, that he was riding high, fulfilling his dream. That was how I wanted folks to remember him, it was all I had left of him to share with them. Hundreds attended the funeral and the wake, it was a fitting tribute to a popular young guy, a guy with the world at his fingertips.

Blurred days flowed into blurred weeks; the only thing that changed was the countdown before departure, before returning to the States. Inebriation was the ready solution to my emotional difficulties. It seems my whole social network pulled together and catered to my every need, and it did make time go quicker. Most days were seen through a drink- and drug-induced haze, numbing the pain served a purpose, allowed me time to take stock. Only three weeks were spent at home, and even that was too long. I couldn't have coped there alone, yet needed to escape, needed to cut myself off from that world, the one I'd always shared with Cai. Isolation was really what I needed, the time and space to deal with myself. Not to lock myself away from others, but to set myself free. I knew how concerned people were for my safety, though others weren't my concern, I needed to cater to my own needs.

No-one was surprised when I declared my intentions, without exception they understood, yet it still worried them, needlessly. I knew I could ride my bike under the greatest duress, none could ever prove as great as the ride back to Ojai after Cai's accident. Travelling was second nature, maybe a touch lonely at times, but cope-able. Travelling by motorcycle, for weeks alone, is near perfect headspace; it's like meditation, definitely therapeutic. Nothing else made sense, whether it was to honour memories of him, for me to run away, or to allow myself time to heal, it all had the same result. I had to get away! Flying home over the Rockies I'd vowed to return. There was a shiny new motorbike waiting in Ojai, and one way or another I had to do something with it. But my primary reason was to ride those mountains, to see wild bears, elk, bison; at least those things we'd enthused about together. Whichever way I looked at it, the only thing that had any meaning in life was the dream we'd shared. It was all I had left.

Chapter Three

On August 8 2007, I eventually set off into the Californian wilderness, alone and more than a touch apprehensive. By 2 p.m. the heat was unbearable, it almost seared the lungs to breathe deeply. Despite wearing my lightweight desert gear, I was sweating profusely, even at 80mph. Riding with my jacket open at least allowed a through wind, some respite; stopping I was instantly awash with sweat. Route 33 carried me from Ojai, through the Sespe wilderness, to California's central valley. Despite the overbearing heat, this section provided the perfect distraction as well as cooling interludes of shade, as I passed under looming crags of rock. The entire panorama exudes desolation, tinder dry mountains and valleys blackened by wildfires, evidence of the precarious nature of the region. What a lovely twisting, turning mountain road though. After each bend another loomed invitingly, rarely was the bike upright. It was good being able to lose myself in the ride. All my awareness focussed on the next section of tarmac and the machine I sat astride. Road position, the correct gear, speed, angle of lean, they're all sub-conscious actions; my conscious mind left free to roam.

The central valley area is a high altitude plain. It is very arid and naturally barren, though south of Maricopa intense agriculture stretches to the distant, mountainous horizon. It is a veritable oasis, rows of crops, green and resplendent, their soaked foliage sparkling in the sun. Water is constantly pumped through a maze of pipe work, huge jets spray continuously to maintain the vitality of the crops; the alfalfa, vines and orange groves that dominate the landscape. The road ploughs straight through, boring and monotonous, with a thick overlaying heat haze. Worse is to come! From Maricopa there is no lush vegetation: there is no vegetation, the stench of crude oil precedes an abundance of small scale oil wells. The only sign of movement is the slow churning of the rigs. It is a desolate, inhospitable furnace. Neither the scenery nor road offer much in the way of respite. It is so oppressive I struggle to remain emotionally buoyant, wavering on the lip of an abyss, the fierce heat sapping my limited reserves.

How simple life was supposed to be, Cai and me riding along in unison, high as kites! Not now though, just me, in the depths of despair, teetering on the brink of sanity. Only days before that sanity had been sorely tested, my rationale lost to uncontrollable emotion. I never understood what a panic attack was before then. Alone, reading, a stray thought brought on a few tears which lead to a veritable deluge. Unable to control the desperation I'd felt, I'd started to panic. Struggling for breath, I'd staggered around, unable to grasp the simplest coherent thought, totally overcome by fear. My body had shaken uncontrollably, a vibration had risen into my chest, pounding so ferociously my heart had threatened to give out under the strain. No longer able to stand, I'd slumped onto the sofa, curled into a ball, shaking all over; the most abject fear had filled me. Moaning, sobbing bitterly, crying out for help, I'd lay there helpless. How long for I have no idea. Eventually, from some far away corner of my mind, a spark of reason emerged, soothing. Calming slightly, I'd stopped fighting against the fear, and let the tears flow freely. The trembling had subsided slowly, leaving a dull thumping in the head. Meditation techniques had been used to gain control of my breathing, helping bring my body to a more relaxed state. Never had I faced such overwhelming panic, never could I have dreamt of losing it so severely; I thought I was always cool, calm and collected. To go so far over the brink was frightening, yet I'd fought my way back, regaining control, it had been reassuring. I could face my demons and survive, I could come safely through to the other side. It had given me confidence, I knew it wasn't over, there would be plenty more from where that came from, but I'd handled it.

My chosen route towards Sequoia National Park meant following the River Kern, a lovely meandering route, on a very quiet Highway 178. It avoided the urban sprawl separating the coastal mountain range and the Sierra Nevadas. Despite being a two-lane highway the route was deserted. It passed through gently sloping hills of green fields. Gone was the environmental harshness from earlier, the temperature was still high but the atmosphere more mellow. The mood encouraged me to ride on, only stopping to decide where to head for, next stop Lake Isabella. There wasn't any hurry, the objective was purely to lose myself in the ride. Allowing road conditions to dictate the pace I set, I made good progress. In the States speed limits are more conservative than in the UK, I largely ignored them, content to judge safe speeds for myself. I wasn't on a race blown bike, my KLR was a fully loaded Enduro bike. It wasn't capable of doing silly speeds, it had a long way to carry me, and I wasn't in the mood for risks. Sitting astride the bike was comforting, like being with a well-known, trusted friend. Why is beyond me, I'd just lost the most important person in my world, due to a fault on an identical machine. Yet it was a sense of familiarity with what I was doing, being more relaxed, more at peace whilst riding.

Unfortunately I had no such distractions camping at Lake Isabella. Choosing a pitch close to others was out of character for me, but for once being close to other people was strangely reassuring, as feelings of panic accompanied thoughts of solitude. Normally I was happier to camp away from others, away from their attention, content with my own company. At that time I would have jumped at the chance to join the other campers, would gladly have shared their space. Too self-conscious to impose though, I made do with camping in close proximity, in plain view and within earshot. This was my first night alone in the big wide world, I felt exposed, vulnerable; I was not familiar with this person. It was a new me, an unrecognisable one, one that couldn't be relied upon; who knew when it might become more than I could handle. The enormity of the task ahead struck me, and frightened me. In all honesty, any thoughts of the future scared me senseless. No wonder Ojai loomed large in my mind, how easy it would have been to simply turn around, run back into the fold of the Coyne family. Was I really up to the challenge ahead?

Setting up camp is a well-established routine for me, honed on previous bike tours. Ironic really, such journeys are undertaken to escape the mundane daily routines. It does make life easier though, it ensures minimum effort for maximum effect, catering to your daily needs without any fuss. Getting food prepared was the first priority, it gave me time to pitch the tent and sort out my gear for the night, while my stew bubbled away nicely. By the time I'd eaten and written my journal darkness prevailed. Perfect timing! I may have only ridden one hundred and seventy miles but I was drained, I hadn't once stopped and gotten off the bike. Sleep was a welcome relief for mind and body. It came without difficulty, leaving me refreshed and confident in the morning. In fact, I was settled enough to feel no rush to leave, no need to instantly lose myself in the riding. It was scorching hot and I was next to a lake, what a perfect setting for lazing in the sun before striking out for the day. By mid-morning my white bits were glowing nicely, and I was ready for the off. Actually I thought I was, but almost as soon as I set off my mood crashed. Plagued by memories of Cai, it was difficult to concentrate on the road, it was still all so fresh, so pain filled me. I rode on nevertheless, determined not to cop out whenever overcome by emotion. It wasn't about to go away, it would be part of my life for some time, I'd better get used to it. And so I did, calming myself down and shifting my focus back onto the road.

Travelling along the lakeside was an inspiration with its natural beauty. There were no flat open fields, very few houses and seemingly no one about. Plenty of trees lined the road, offering frequent pockets of shade, for a more comfortable ride than the day before. Again following the River Kern, the route became gradually narrower, windier and more mountainous. I was headed away from the main areas of habitation in California, through villages dependent on visiting hunters and fishermen for their livelihood. Each of the commercial premises seemed to cater for the needs of the visitors, who like most tourists have only their own interests at heart. But I'm too cynical, any stop I made attracted friendly attention, everyone was interested in a guy on a bike making a road trip. Whether it was just to refuel, a quick smoke break or my late lunch, I was warmly greeted with a barrage of questions. 'Wow, looks like some road trip you're makin'! Where ya headin'? How far you goin'?' I guess it was obvious, saddle bags, tank bag with panniers, camping roll, living the American dream! And it was, I was amazed at how much of a romantic ideal it was, and for so many. What a surprise they got when I spoke; my registration plate was Californian, they didn't expect a foreign accent. Their reactions were always the same, even heartier welcomes, much hand shaking, genuine pleasure at an Australian touring their country. Ouch, that put a sting into the compliment! I'd heard how the Americans love a British accent, shame they didn't seem to recognise it for what it was.

Cai and I had been overwhelmed by people's response when they heard us talk, female shop assistants clamouring for his attention to hear him speak. Was it us being British, or just a taste for the exotic?

Nearing Sequoia National Park the Redwood forests engulfed me. They provided unbelievably twisty roads, with torturous gradients. Sweeping round mountain bends exposed amazing views over tree covered valleys that seemed to go on forever. It was slow going, switch back after switch back dictated a sedate pace but I was having none of it and hustled through, throwing the bike into the bends. The road remained relatively clear, uphill sections were thrilling, ripping open the throttle exiting bends, easing off a touch on the approach to the next. There was no need to use the brakes. Downhill was another matter. It took some effort to slow the beast down. No matter how hard I pulled the brakes it kept going, it showed just how heavily laden it was. This was a different game completely. The angle of lean on the KLR is quite remarkable, and it needed to be! Even leaning far enough to scrape my foot wasn't enough to negotiate some bends, a couple of times I overcooked it. Not slowing enough I ran wide, luckily the absence of oncoming traffic and a wide run off let me get away with it. Jeez, I had to cool my heels, carrying on like this would surely curtail my journey, and I was not ready to join Cai yet. Whatever my rationale told me a deep angst fought for release, probing, prodding, waiting to reign supreme. Care had to be taken, or else I'd succumb to an explosion fury driven lunacy. With a major effort of will I slowed down. The road begged to be ridden hard, I was in the mood for it but the gradient was too severe. The forks felt spongy too, plunging drastically under heavy breaking. I needed to accustom myself to the bike under the more extreme conditions, at least until I could adjust the set-up. Being used to touring on familiar bikes, there was a lot to get used to, a lot of adapting necessary. Mind you, if you stop learning from your experiences there isn't much point in having them, is there?

The giant redwoods themselves are spectacular and riding through them is an uplifting experience. Their size is incredible, and not just their height but their girth too. After being baked by suffocating temperatures entering the forest was sheer bliss, the canopy, though a sparse covering, provided welcome relief. And the smell was gorgeous! An all-pervading aroma of pine resin filled the nostrils; from hot searing air to pine fresh coolness, within two breaths, delightful. All my senses seemed heightened. Without squinting against the sun, vision improved, my skin tingled in delight from the cool fresh air, the density of the forest quelled background noise, and new found moisture unclogged the taste buds of an overly parched tongue. Forests give a sense of stillness, a sense of protection, yet also a feeling of awe, a sense of the unknown. Looking through the tangled dense undergrowth left a feeling of being totally alone, nothing stirred, though anything could be out there sheltered amongst the humongous, thick trees. Stopping and sitting quietly, I envisaged a bear appearing, ambling peacefully through the forest. Wow, wouldn't that have been exciting? Actually, I think I'd have crapped myself! There were occasional warnings about bears, enough to keep them fairly constantly in mind. The National Park campsite entrance was festooned with warning signs, "Recent bear activity, TAKE CARE!" I did. I slept with my camera by my side, hoping I had the balls to take a photo should the chance come. It felt more adventurous, the prospect of bears roaming the campsite, isn't this what I'd come to experience? I'd not imagined it happening in a heaving campsite, not imagined even staying in a sprawling canvas metropolis. What a shame all the bears' summer forage was crowded with holidaymakers, no wonder there are conflicts of interests between the two. They shoot bears for invading people's property, remove them for roaming their own home range. Can't say I saw any tourists being rounded up, tranquilised and removed to another area though. So who's the threat to who?

National parks, a bikers dream, they seemed devoid of straight roads. OK, the speed limits were kept low to allow for sightseeing and to protect the animals. Naughty as it was, I didn't feel the need to comply. I'm the exception not the rule! Making headway was easy, traffic was slow from both directions with plenty of opportunities to nip past. My pleasure was losing myself in the ride which was easier at a reasonable pace. It didn't give me time to wallow in sorrow. I needed my focus on the next stretch of tarmac. Tailbacks were no hindrance, in no time I passed all and sundry. Other vehicles had no chance to weave in and out of the traffic, it brought out the best of two wheeled transport. Isn't that what it's all about? Between Sequoia and Yosemite I'd had to join the peripheries of urban road systems. The natural wonder of Americana was replaced with a taste of urbanity, yet still a far cry from shopping malls and carpet-burgers from McDonald's. A taco stand on a quiet, dusty intersection smacked of by-gone days in Latin America. Mexicans, in cowboy hats and boots, arrived in dusty old Chevy trucks. Men, women and families congregated around the picnic tables, there wasn't a single white American in sight; a scene straight from a spaghetti western, in the middle of suburban America.

As you enter suburban areas the concentration of traffic increases quickly, the network of roads form a grid pattern which becomes more tightly packed towards the heart of each town. Everything is at right angles without any suggestion of a bend, just a profusion of junctions. Constant stop and start, cars coming whichever way, what a relief it was to veer off towards the hills. In the conurbations I was at a disadvantage, I was vulnerable on a bike. Once on the mountain roads I was King. I ruled the roost, only the road ahead mattered, other vehicles were passed with the same ease in which I passed a feature of the landscape. It was far more relaxing than the urban sprawl and there was much less to concern myself about. Until I dropped the damned bike entering Yosemite Valley! Travelling at about 40mph, I took a quick look at the camping permit clutched in my hand to see which campsite I was booked into. As I glanced up, the rear end of a brand new SUV loomed ever closer. I jammed on the brakes, locked the back wheel and slewed sideways. Damned if I didn't control that skid, damn shame I didn't quite get my foot down, and over it toppled. How embarrassing! The poor guy got out his SUV and rushed to help me lift it, he was mortified, so apologetic. Bless, I was the idiot and didn't I feel it.

After Sequoia I felt too much fuss was being made about the risk of bears, so in Yosemite I slept in a hammock with my camera to hand. Every night, shouts would go up and a hell of a commotion would ensue. I never found out what the hell was going on, no-one actually saw a bear, people's overactive imaginations sent panic throughout the whole campsite. Despite many false alarms, no bears chose to frequent my camp, although a coyote did saunter through one morning. But that wasn't my reason for being in that particular National Park. Yosemite's reputation is second to none for climbing. This alone made it worth stopping for a few days, if even only to stand and stare, in awe, at the magnitude of climbs like *El Capitan*. But the whole valley was truly awesome, the climbs breathtaking, and the company much appreciated.

I had only been travelling three days, yet it felt like weeks. Ojai was a lifetime away, friends in another dimension altogether. The scenery and riding had been wonderful but grieving had taken a lot out of me. I felt totally worn out, it will always amaze me how I kept my head in those first few days. Unknown reserves of strength had carried me on, a pig headed refusal to let Cai's death be for nothing. So many times I wanted only to turn back, to seek sanctuary with people I could depend on, who could help sooth away the pain. I was physically wrenching myself away. It hurt to force myself on, but there was no other choice, on I had to go. My decision had been to seek solace in nature, to strengthen my resolve through adventure, to conquer the unknown. Only in this way did I feel I could face life again, only by opening myself to the desperate pain could I hope to come out the other side. Although it often felt I was running away such thoughts were quickly banished. I couldn't outrun the pain. That was with me every minute of every day, my constant companion.

I did feel very vulnerable, lonely, and welcomed the chance to be safely tucked into the family fold, even if it wasn't my own. A large family group took me under their wing, treating me like a long lost, much loved, friend. I shared their pitch, joined them for meals, warmed myself by their fires and made friends with Emma-Louise. I'd recently learnt to more readily accept hospitality and support, to be more open hearted, to lean on people if needed. In Yosemite, I welcomed the chance to surround myself with friendly faces, people who valued me for who I was, there and then, not through pity and sorrow. Besides, Emma- Louise thought I was a real superman for riding my bike so far and sleeping out where the bears could get me, and I love impressing three year olds!

They were a normal family based group, happy to share their time with me. It brought many a smile to my face watching the family antics and brought on many tears at my inability to share such frivolities of life with Cai. My grief was personal though, I wasn't ready to share it with a whole group of strangers which encouraged me to keep it in check. Alone with nature, I could open up completely, allow my feelings free rein. In company it was a relief to tone it down a touch and have a break from the constant emotional strain. But a three day rest was enough, my feet were itching and the way on was forwards. Clean and refreshed, inside and out, the timing felt right. I knew I had covered too few miles and wanted to play catch-up.

With only a brief stop to stare, slack jawed at *El Capitan*, it was nearly mid-day by the time I left Yosemite valley turning east and up to the Tioga Pass. I do so love riding uphill on twisty mountain roads and they were in great condition too. Smooth tarmac, tight and steep, with the camber in my favour every time. What joy, sweeping in and out of sun-dappled bends, casually overtaking whatever other vehicles you meet, how could my spirits not rise? Before the top of the pass there was a cold nip to the air, so different from the intense heat of the valley. I needed to stop to put on more clothes at eight thousand five hundred feet despite the blinding sun. Topping out at nearly ten thousand feet, it was the highest road I could remember riding. It offered magnificent, long-range views of wooded valleys and distant mountain ranges. Once I dropped a couple of thousand feet, I was desperate to remove those layers again, temperatures were in the hundreds and I was melting inside my bike gear. Protection was more important than comfort though. I really could have ridden in shorts and T-shirt, until sunstroke got me. It was good to see I was not the only one of a kind. A group travelling the opposite way were all of the same breed, riding dual sport bikes set up for long distance touring. And they were all suitably attired, so I wasn't the only one who wore slightly more than a sleeveless jacket and fingerless gloves.

Cutting across the Sierra Nevada, the pass led onto Highway 395 heading north through cattle country. The high altitude grasslands spread out across the horizon to the east. I kept the Sierra to my left and rode up to the southern tip of Lake Tahoe. Gorgeous lakeside scenery provided a tempting place to camp but I'd not ridden anywhere near far enough. I was on a mission that day and I wasn't stopping short of Sacramento. To avoid temptation, I didn't bother with the ride around the lake, heading west instead crossing the Sierra again on Highway 50. It was a lovely winding road, skirting along the mountainside, more smooth tarmac and wide sweeping bends. With good open views around the bends, overtaking was simple and safe with plenty of opportunity to see potential hazards well before meeting them. Excellent progress was made because I rarely had to consider easing off the throttle, let alone braking. The country to the south seemed an empty wilderness, no trails, no sign of habitation or logging, just impenetrable forestry. Not an area that seemed accessible, dual-sport bike or not. The thought entered my mind and filled me with fear, I hadn't the confidence to go off-road into the wilds alone. It didn't really matter anyway, I was on a mission, determined to cross the Golden Gate Bridge the following morning.

Deep wooded slopes plunged down to fast flowing rivers, only to rise before dropping again to the next waterway, and then the next. The view had phenomenal depth. The sky was the clearest, brightest blue, in stark contrast to the deep greens and dark browns of the valley but it was the sheer size of the scenery that really got to me. It stretched into every direction, as far as the eye could see, each bend opening a whole new vista. Whooping with joy, I swept through, my consciousness soaring. It invoked a great release, a feeling of communion with the surrounding countryside. The sense of being fully aware of the here and now was awesome. Opening your heart and soul to your surroundings can prove to be a very emotional, spiritual experience. It's raw, hard to control, yet can sweep away thoughts and distractions, completely clearing the mind. Wipe aside the mental clutter, be awed by beauty, wilderness, maybe realise the transient nature of life. The depth and clarity of my feelings were overwhelming. I allowed them free rein, not wishing to intrude, for good or bad their intensity was staggering. From the dizzying heights of such cosmic bliss any fall was inevitably a long way down. All it took was a simple thought of Cai, and from soaring the heights I faltered, and plummeted. My vision blurred, and the world dissolved into tears. I rode on in wracking sobs, struggling to keep a grip on reality, yet determined to let nothing get the better of me. My journal entry that night proved encouraging:

"...really had a problem breathing at one stage. Had to keep focussing on my breath and use that to stay calm. Sort of made myself go through it, without pulling over. I felt it was different though, more cleansing, positive. It wasn't a painful, devastating experience. I'm sure it isn't just my imagination, it felt like a breakthrough. The emotions are still there, ready to surface, to bring on the tears. The big difference was not being afraid of it happening, allowing myself to feel the love I have for Cai, not to hold back."

Yeah, I was buzzing, riding high on a wave of intense emotions, and it actually felt good, (in a perverse sort of way). This may not be the trip originally planned but it was starting to achieve the goals of my solo journey. I rode on autopilot, allowing a deeper consciousness to carry me safely along the way. It was meditation in motion, and it worked well. It was good to find the strength I needed, once again reassuring. Confidence was gained and motivation improved, no way was I tempted to head back to Ojai now. This was therapy; this was what I really needed!

Sacramento came and went, I was spat out onto the freeway as darkness crept in, San Francisco bound. It wasn't to be. I don't enter cities at night. They are best approached during daylight hours, it gives plenty of time to locate accommodation and find secure parking for the bike. Eleven miles from the city was close enough, so I treated myself to a hotel for the night, a first on this trip. Ten hours spent riding makes for a long day. I was completely shattered. A treat was well deserved, the luxury of a long hot bath, a few beers watching TV, then reading a book and drifting off. A double bed all to myself, no need for covers, just spread out and drop into a relaxing sleep.

The day had been great. I felt high as a kite, so positive, so full of myself. This is what the trip had been about, the stuff that dreams are indeed made of. A motorcycle adventure is what we'd hoped for. It is what Cai died for, trying to live his dream. Despite the frequent adrenalin rushes, it also brought a crushing sense of loss. Cai should be here with me. This isn't the way it should be, how could I be here and not him? Life really can prove to be a double edged sword. The range and depth of emotions are vast. It all has to be experienced though. This was one hell of a roller coaster ride that I barely had control over. But it was coming.

The ride into San Francisco was a means to an end only, rejoining the Pacific Coast Highway again, Route 101 and the infamous Route 1. Travelling through the city centre was a non-event, as the traffic was light and I stopped for a bad haircut. Crossing the rusty visage of the Golden Gate Bridge could hardly be described as inspiring; the low lying mist had done a good job of hiding the oxide coated pylons. I felt I should record the event and joined the sightseeing throng. I felt superior to them for some reason, as if my journey was of more significance than theirs, that they were intruding into my space, degrading my experience. Shit, it ain't my bridge. Live and let live! If being around so many people was beginning to bug me, it was time to head away from civilisation. Little had inspired me that day, crowded roads and hordes of tourists, the only solution was to get off the freeway, as soon as possible.

Chapter Four

It was a wise decision, the coast was exposed and craggy, and the first sight of it lifted my spirits. The road wound round each minute bay, climbing over the low cliffs backing them, descending again at the next headland. Vegetation was sparse and nothing obscured the view of the road, blind bends just didn't seem to exist. Switchback heaven! If I wasn't pointed up, I was pointed down, and leant over, one side or the other all the way. The bike proved ideal for it, brilliant ground clearance and not too heavy, so easy to throw around. I wouldn't go as far as to say it was 'hog' heaven, it suited me and mine, even if it proved a bit much for the Harley riders I met. They were knackered by midday and booked into a motel very early. No way was I looking for campsites so early in the afternoon. I happily gobbled up the miles. Riding meant clearing my head, the day had been one of indifference, and this was my release. I may not have soared with the eagles, it may have only relieved me of some tension but it brought me closer to a quiet contentment.

Ending up in an exposed beach campsite, enveloped in a bitterly cold rolling mist, could have been miserable but those were the only facilities available. It had to be endured, I had to eat and sleep, be ready for the next day. So I cooked a really boring meal and ate it without thought or complaint. All I felt was indifference which seemed a positive step up from turmoil, or anguish. I persevered with the cold and huddled round my mug of coffee, using my head torch to read in the failing light. I must have painted a woebegone picture, before long I was invited to share a campfire with the family next door. The only price was my company, a valued commodity, 'From the UK, aah jerst luurv that ack-sent!'. And I was happy to be the novelty guest. I could be who I wanted to be, an anonymous traveller, leading a life of freedom and adventure. Not some poor guy who'd recently lost his son, a figure of pity.

Two days riding along the Pacific Coast Highway had been on single carriageway roads, following the coastline, savouring the scenery. The route was littered with perfect examples of small town America, quiet, dusty places with nary a soul to be seen. I passed through the deserted streets of Westport and Manchester, unimpressed. I didn't dally in those quiet backwaters. More pleasure was to be had on the open road with an uninterrupted view of the coastline. But I was running out of road, Route 1 was coming to an end, my options were limited. There was only one way I could avoid looping back onto the 101, by going off road! Forestry trails featured clearly on my road map, they linked the coastal communities, and all I had to do was locate them. I missed the first one completely, only realising once I'd been spewed back onto the more congested 101. A second wasn't going to elude me so easy. I took the next minor road back towards the coast, it may have led to a dead end but I was fixated on finding those trails. If avoiding the main trunk road meant going cross-country, then that was exactly what I'd do. There had been so much gorgeous countryside with no sign of wildlife, I figured it was about time I put paid to that. I might well have been enticed by the call of the wild but impersonations of Grizzly Adams would have to wait, it was late afternoon and I needed supplies.

The road itself dead-ended at Shelter Cove. It may only have been a ghost town but I prayed there was some semblance of a store. Shit, I didn't even have any idea about closing times, for that matter what time of the day was it, would they even be open? There wasn't really time to mess around, no store meant nothing to eat that night, unless I was prepared to back track an hour or more. I also had to assume there'd be places to camp, official or not didn't really matter, it probably would to some uppity Sherriff though. Oh stuff it. I was pointed in that direction, it was meant to be an adventure. Basically I didn't really care. So I just followed my nose, and stuffed the consequences!

It was a fair ride down, skirting round consecutive hillsides, through leafy canopies. Despite incredibly steep hills and long unprotected drop offs, I enjoyed it. And sure enough, as plain as daylight, the trails were there, clearly signposted. I took the elk grazing at the roadside as a good omen, almost as good as the campsite symbol pointing down the track. Deep gravel disappeared enticingly into the shaded depths of the forest. Temptation and trepidation arose, clashing in their dichotomous nature. I desperately needed fresh food and a place to stay, so despite being eager for my first dirt riding on the KLR, the only logical choice was carrying on to Shelter Cove. I'd ridden for some time and seen no houses at all, please let there be a shop, don't make me turn around and struggle for an alternative so close to dusk! And as if by magic, there it was, more resembling an industrial unit than a general store but a store all the same. It was certainly no well laid out superstore, goods were displayed higgledy piggledy in their wholesale boxes with plenty of variety but little choice. Thoughts of old style trading posts came to mind, the range of goods really was phenomenal. It put my village Spa shop to shame. They had everything a person could have wanted, whether it were to eat, drink, fish, camp, hunt, grow or fix up the range. A veritable treasure indeed. Their service also provided an inexhaustible supply of local information, I'd really hit a gold mine.

I walked out with a spring in my step, towards the free camping at the end of the beach. Les Kay was one happy bunny, until I got down there. "No vehicles allowed on beach." Bollocks! So, do I leave the bike in the car park, a mile or so from where I could camp? Do I risk leaving it out of my protective care, overnight in a public car park, or just ride along to where camping is legal and risk official hassle? Simple solution, neither. Nor do I bother with paying $30 for a dusty, dirty campsite, with foul toilets and stinking attitude. I do have my standards you know, when it suits me!

A dense carpet of mist gently rolled onto the shoreline. The sun was getting low and the temperature was dropping rapidly. It wasn't looking promising. Did I want another cold and miserable night, engulfed in the freezing sea mist? Certainly not, I turned around and went for an early evening ride, dirt trail here I come. I now knew there were a couple of wilderness campsites along the trail. How far I wasn't so sure. I went for it anyway, more taken with a sense of adventure than common sense. Surely a sign of an improving disposition, setting off into the unknown, late in the afternoon, with the thought of marauding bears niggling at the back of my mind.

Well, I was glad of my previous experience off road, although you wouldn't have known it. I was distinctly sheepish at first, crawling along at only 20mph! Tense and wobbly, every slightest shift of the rear tyre led to an ever tighter sphincter. It was obvious pussy footing around wasn't going to work, more traction on the rear wheel was needed. There was little choice, I had to relax and get that damned throttle open. The surface was gravel, mainly loose, and built up around the many bends. It wasn't too bad but it felt it at the time. I've certainly got no grand tales of magnificent riding feats, the object of the game was simply to stay on while I got used to the off-road characteristics of the bike. Luckily there was only five miles to the campsite, during which time nothing but trees were passed, nothing but my bike engine was heard. It seemed to take forever to get there, giving a feeling of total isolation by the time I pulled off the track. I arrived to a deserted campsite, a solitary tent stood forlorn, with no sign of the occupants. It was absolutely silent, eerily so. I pitched within peeping distance of the other tent, still apprehensive of being totally alone. I wasn't about to bottle it, being alone in the wilds was why I was there but for that night I felt happy to share the wild woods with fellow campers. It may have been only five miles into the forest, but shit, it *was* the wilderness. Whilst collecting firewood, I found myself making noise, making my presence known, unwilling to take any bears by surprise. Honestly, there were bears prowling close by, I was convinced of it! Posters and warnings were everywhere. "Don't condemn a bear to death!" "Safely store all food stuff, toiletries and other odorous items!" "Bear proof containers must be used for overnight stays!" Great, on a motorcycle, carrying my very own bear proof box? But they did have large bear proof bins. One was empty, with a clean bin bag! Hmm, brain wave; why don't I use the empty bin? So I half filled it with everything vaguely attractive to a bear's olfactory aptitude, and felt chuffed with myself for being so resourceful. A bear's best friend, that's me. As an afterthought, I put my crash helmet on top of everything else, just in case it was mistaken for a bin. I was deadly serious with all this preparation, as the National Parks scaremongering was having the desired effect. I expected to see a bear, convinced it would happen, whether for my sake or the bears, precautions were absolutely necessary.

Probably the best precaution was putting my crash lid on top of my other stuff in the bin. At least it stopped getting everything covered in fish head and guts. Some locals had turned up, way after dark, and proceeded to cook enough fish for a small army. They got my attention with shouts of dismay at finding my gear in the bin, spotted just in time to save it stinking of fish for the foreseeable future. I felt such a prat, what was I meant to have done? Simple according to them, when you see a bear shoo 'em off, lob a stone towards 'em, treat 'em like stray dogs. And somehow I'd been given the idea they were dangerous, I wonder where I got that impression! Meeting the two guys was great, I gave them a laugh, and they gave me a bit more confidence about bears. They slept with no tent and fish bits laying openly around their camp, what did I have to worry about? Their complacency was strangely reassuring, even when I spotted them getting out their vehicle in the morning; sleeping in the open indeed. No complaints from me though, they were good old Californian hill hippies having arrived with food, booze, friendship and a little local produce for smoking around the campfire. Welcome to the wilderness Les!

Our impromptu party consisted of only five people, two who had travelled down from Oregon, the hillbillies, and me, the alien. It didn't show though, if you weren't from North California you were a foreigner. Any apparent differences vanished with daybreak, we were all bleary eyed. After two rounds of coffee I packed and was raring to go. There was some doubt from the locals as to the condition of the trail. It had been passable with a normal car eight years ago, but there hadn't been any maintenance since and it sounded unused, except by hunters. The general consensus was that my bike could go anywhere, so I should try it. In fact the guys had so much confidence in me, they fed me a couple of pipes of weed to help me on my way. Not the best idea I've ever had, as I rode away I felt tense and filled with dread. There weren't any thoughts of retracing my steps though, I was going to do this, however nervous I felt. It was fifteen miles at most, with only one doubtful section, a river to cross. Gulp, I've never done a proper river crossing!

Overcoming obstacles is rewarding, and the more effort required the greater the reward seems. There was never any question of whether or not to ride off road, that had always been the intention, how well I'd cope was my concern. My limited experience had never taken me beyond a state of forced relaxation, having to deal with the terrain and my own trepidation. That wasn't good enough, it's no fun unless you chill out. I wasn't after cheap thrills, but did intend to enjoy it. And it proved easy to relax. The gravel track wound gently through the forest, creating a sun-dappled corridor through an otherwise dense thicket. Not out to break any records, I kept to a sedate pace and gave myself time to settle down. It was an easy going, loose gravel trail, with cleared tyre tracks to follow. It didn't take long to forget about my fears, and minor slides of the rear end were handled with confidence. Ten miles or so would be a delight, everything was tranquil, the trail included. It was saving the worst for later. Relying on a road atlas for off road trails doesn't help, unmarked junctions posed tricky decisions, nothing but trees could be seen. All I could do was check my compass and take a calculated guess. Thankfully I guessed right each time, avoiding possible dead ends and private property.

I'd heard all about this, the "shoot first and ask questions later," attitude of gun toting Hillbillies. There were a few houses along the way, eclectic constructions, more suited to the hippy generation than country hicks. Beyond these the trees thinned out and the trail worsened. Corners tightened up, and the gradient increased, making for steep switchbacks. Bedrock interspersed with sand, pebbles and cobbles gave a lumpy, often unpredictable surface to ride on. Dipping and rising in and out of creek beds, inevitably meant negotiating rocky, steep, 180° bends. Of course once you're pointing down the switchback there is only one way out, you're pretty much committed, it's much easier to maintain momentum than stopping. This means making snap decisions on the best line to take. There were no chances to go back and try it again. Rising onto the foot pegs, in first gear, I puttered through the first dry creek bed. The temptation to use sheer brute force was resisted, maintaining balance and gentle application of the throttle pulled me gently round the first switchback. It was a slow speed manoeuvre that needed poise, I'd go as far as saying it was elegantly done, leaving me pleased, confident and in control. Each such obstacle I approached in the same way. I wasn't pushing any harder, I was content to get back to basics, slow speed use of rear brake, clutch and throttle. Once again I was getting used to riding the KLR in a different environment and once again I was impressed. We'd made a damned good choice of bike (however ironic that may seem). Little wonder my exit from the trail brought regret with it, I felt chuffed to bits with the ride, such a shame it had to come to an end so soon.

No banners of welcome were out, no-one throwing their arms high in marvel at my heroic deed, in fact there was no-one at all. Honeydew was a dry, dusty hamlet, pierced by a broken tarmac road, with weatherworn clapboard buildings dotted around. The mid-day sun beat down mercilessly, the local store's porch which stood alone just off the road, offering the only respite. I pottered over slowly, heading for shade and refreshment, soaking in the atmosphere on the way. My imagination ran wild, tinder dry clapboard shacks, a hitching post outside the store cum bar, the whole place seemed run down and deserted. It was so Wild West, all it needed was the musical accompaniment and some cowboys. Grinning inanely, I put aside my overactive imagination and parked to consider my options. No plans had been made beyond reaching Honeydew, destinations for the day hadn't generally been decided until later in the afternoon, but T-junctions have a habit of forcing the issue. I could go East or West, onto the 101 or a tiny country road looping further along the coast. The choice should have been easy but they rarely are. From my mileage I knew I had no more than fifty miles before the fuel tank hit reserve, it could easily be a lot less, riding off road guzzles gas. With no chance of fuel, the back road would have been pushing it. Ironically, there was even a village en-route called Petrolia (do they have a Trades Descriptions Act here?). I had to head back to the main highway, despite the temptation of riding through Cape Town as well. All was not lost, rejoining the 101 meant a ride through Humboldt Redwood State Park to be engulfed again with that intoxicating smell of pine resin. C'est la vie!

True to form, the Redwoods lifted my spirits. They really are pretty impressive, even the boring 101 didn't dampen my enthusiasm. Gone was the two-lane highway, miraculously replaced by another pleasantly sedate byway. The way north remained enjoyable, skirting endless beaches and winding through dense patches of giant Redwoods providing many an olfactory delight. I couldn't believe how acute my sense of smell seemed, although obscured from view of the sea, faint traces of a salty tang accompanied the overwhelming scent of resin. Another pungent fragrance, one of flowers, assailed my nostrils, never lingering, there and gone within a hundred yards. It came and went four or five times, and then, on the apex of a bend, I spotted them, growing in someone's garden border. Thick stems held columns of large, drooping, trumpet shaped flowers, orange with yellow fluting. And then they were gone, left behind in shady forest, replaced by the fresh aroma of the seaside, as I rode out into the sunshine between open fields and the sea. An onshore wind carried a profusion of odours, a blend of salt water and seaweed, with a hint of fish and rotting crustaceans, you could almost smell the sand. Such rare moments of awareness are somehow enlightening, when something so simple and apparently common can give you such an intense experience. The more time spent out there, with few people and few distractions, the more I tuned in. The experience really did wash away mundane thought, freeing my mind completely. No need for a prayer mat, nor a place of worship, just give me a bike and glorious places to ride. It can take a lot of effort to ride long and hard every day but if you're in that zone, if you're in an elevated state of consciousness, you can ride relaxed and happy for hours at a time, and it's damn near an out of body experience. It isn't a chore, it's enriching. You don't get this in a car. It isn't you, face into the wind, spitting grit through your teeth. Four-wheeled transport is like sitting in front of a screen, watching magnificent cinematography maybe, but a bike is being out there, part of the scenery, even star of the show. On a bike you are in direct contact with your surrounding environment, the experience made more intense by the consequences if it fucks up. No-one's infallible, but if you allow fear to rule your life you'll never be truly free.

There are some awesome stretches of coast in California, surprisingly very little has seen much in the way of development, the southern extremes being the worst. There the beautiful stretches of endless sand within easy access of LA attracted the hordes, the filthy rich and aspiring wannabes. Travelling north the coastline was more broken, further from the freeway, making access slower. Towards Oregon the land flattened out exposing miles of empty sandy shore. Gone were the tight, twisty bends, the relentless switch backs around jagged cliffs. The roads opened out into long sweeping bends, negotiating them required little more than a brief check of pace, then full throttle again, pulling hard through the bend. They were empty, deserted of people, deserted of life, but littered with huge washed up tree trunks, the only blot on the otherwise featureless sand. Dotted along the road were craft shacks advertising "Burls," chainsaw carvings of North American icons, bears, Native Americans, eagles. In good old American style, they were immense, standing two metres or more. I was initially impressed with the first few examples I saw. The effect was lost on me once swamped by a host of outlets, gaudily painted Burls done 'en masse' with little variety and even less imagination. The taint of tourism was strong, I didn't even bother slowing down through these towns, being happier alone, amongst nature.

Reaching further into the wilderness campsites got more remote, and the isolation suited me fine. A dark and dank, muddy forest trail brought me to a dead end, no vehicular access. I had no choice but to hike in the last mile, needing two trips to lug all my gear to the approved site. There was no evidence of anyone one else that night, no sounds but those of the forest. It was eerily quiet, wonderfully peaceful, with only faint rustling in the undergrowth, yet I had a sad and lonely night. I missed Cai something awful. I felt lost without him, and there seemed little point in anything anymore. Why bother? The only reason I could come up with was to give meaning to Cai's death, not to let it be for nothing. We set out to conquer the Americas, he gave his life for the ideal. Thinking of Cai then brought a smile to my face, he felt closer to me, I could imagine his approval as I steadily traversed the wilderness of America.

Chapter Five

I had imagined camping on the beaches of Oregon, riding for miles across open sand, stopping wherever, whenever, campfires beneath star studded skies. The whole coastline was exposed sand, it should have been delightful, it was appalling. I hadn't imagined immense sand dunes blocking my entrance to the beaches, nor the constant buzz of quads ripping around them. Pay and Play! I didn't feel like playing, or paying, and once it started to rain any notions of sleeping rough on the beach abruptly disappeared too.

Access to the beach didn't improve anywhere, as the barrier of the dunes diminished another took its place, the dreaded "PRIVATE" sign. No physical barriers; between the road and beach lay only sandy scrub, one low lying strand of barbed wire marked the boundary, easily passable. I wasn't tempted. I was in America, the land of gun toting loonies. I may well have faced down gamekeepers with shotguns at home but in the States I wasn't so sure of myself, give me a bear any day. And so it continued, no access, private land, no wonder all the beaches are totally deserted. I never found out if the beach itself was off limits or just the access. What was the point? It pissed down with rain for days anyway. A brief afternoon of clear sky enticed me into stopping to watch Drag Boat racing, a free show at the only available campsite. The distraction tempted me to take a break and stay a few days, but the wet weather finally drove me on once more. After two nights of heavy rain, I'd lost all enthusiasm for camping. A flat field, with bad drainage, is a good test for any groundsheet. I unwittingly put mine to the test, and it failed! I wasn't impressed, and as the rain set in once more, I packed a soggy tent, clambered into my waterproofs and set off again.

Cheap hotels replaced my wet tent. I saw no point sheltering from the weather, getting bored all day in a dreary hotel room. So multiple layers of warm, dry clothing were donned each morning, I straddled my machine, hunkered down and just rode. I'd set off by mid-morning and wouldn't stop till dusk. I ate from my supplies morning and night, taking hot meals in roadhouses mid-afternoon. Oregon passed in a mist of road spray as I followed Route 101 straight through. The clouds followed me into Washington State, relieving themselves at will. Miserable weather through both states failed to slow me down, it was enough to have put off most riders but I stayed warm and dry, content to be making headway. Glad to be on the open road, clocking up the miles, happy to be heading north and greater adventures. Even happier at the prospect of taking a detour to Monroe and the safety of friends, mates from back home in Wales now settled in Washington, who I'd not seen in fifteen years. A temporary safe haven, time to relax, service the bike, repair the tent and prepare for Canada. A few days throwing yourself at a wall of water was easier to suffer knowing a spot of comfort awaited at the end.

North West Washington was the prelude to Canada, nice, smooth tarmac roads through logging country. Whether long sweeping bends or tight twisty ones, the camber was always just right. Traffic was light along the coast, the main route north lay fifty miles or so inland, Interstate 5. The 101 swung in an arc around the coast, weaving in and out of a succession of forests, Quinault Rain Forest, Olympic National Forest, Bert Cole State Forest. It obviously made for the better ride but it was wet and dreary, with little to titillate the senses. Gone was the sweet, resinous fragrance, instead the rather repugnant stench of stagnant water and rotting vegetation assailed the nostrils. To seaward it held a tang of salt and decomposing seaweed, then as the road turned inland a loamy smell, of mulch and mushrooms, signified woodlands not encroached upon by brackish waters. But the north coast boasted fresh sea breezes and clearer skies as I left the wooded depths behind. I only got rained on in the evening there. With a pang of regret I passed through Port Angeles, tempted by the ferry to Vancouver Island. That would be my next port of call, on the hunt for Grizzly Bears and Killer Whales. For now a warm house, hot bath and good company were in order. Time to enjoy the comforts of a real home!

Chapter Six

Indeed, a break from constantly travelling was well earned. Few of the days spent cruising the highways were plain sailing; almost without fail it had been a constant battle against overpowering emotions. The roads were gorgeous to ride, proving a welcome relief from the torment of mind and soul. My head and heart were in agony, thrashing about wildly at times but unbelievably stable when the chips were down. In a nutshell, I'd fooled the world; I'd completely lost it and no one had even noticed. My overall disposition improved rapidly in those early days, which of course it needed to. My emotions couldn't take such a severe battering, not for long anyway. I marvel that I managed to perform even rudimentary tasks in those first couple of weeks, but I had, as a matter of necessity. To me, I had barely been holding on to reality, encounters with other people gave glimpses of alternative realities, of normality. Normality continued in their world and I appreciated sharing it, albeit briefly. It helped me realise that life goes on. I'd been dogged by homesickness, but didn't really feel I had a home anymore. Isn't home where the heart is? Well that was in tatters, ripped asunder.

But it did change, gradually, especially on the ride between San Francisco and Seattle. I began thinking more clearly, my mind focussing more on the journey, not the difficulties. Thoughts became more about the road ahead, not the crap hand life had dealt me. The way was definitely forward. I was no longer tearing myself away from anything, nor tearing myself apart. Non-eventful, boring days were endured, but the good miles far outweighed the dreary. Freeways had to be ridden, which was tedious, but the coast road never failed to enchant me. I relaxed into the mundane aspects and thrived on the thrilling. When thoughts of Cai came grief would engulf me, I stopped fighting it and just let vent the tide of tears. In retrospect it all seems so simple, it wasn't as clear-cut at the time, as my journal entries indicate.

Saturday 19 August

"Spent a long time riding and crying profusely. No mounting panic, just letting the grief overcome me. My vision was so impaired by tears I hung back and followed the blur of traffic in front for a long time. This was the first time I've felt angry too. I shouted constant abuse at God, I really did feel pissed off thinking of a creator who could allow that to happen to Cai. He didn't deserve to die in such pain... The anger was followed by choking tears..."

Sunday 20 August

"This anger business has been getting to me today. Been getting ratty with other drivers and riding more aggressively.... forcing my way through the traffic."

I began to relish the strength of my feeling though, to value the depth of my love for him. I'd lost more than I ever realised I had, and my mind couldn't comprehend it at all. I certainly couldn't control my thoughts or emotions; at best I could influence them. Whenever I tried to think what the future held I was teetering on the brink of an endless void, it was frightening. I didn't want to face it. I could barely deal with the initial loss. I learnt to let those thoughts go, aware of their brief passage through my consciousness but paying them no heed. And this was my way of dealing with it, almost like meditation, you can become more than mere conscious thought and it allows a heightened awareness of all aspects of the immediate environment and your own place within that. There was no kidding myself that life was fine and dandy, but it wasn't escapism. There was no escape from what I was going through. I was lucky enough to open my eyes and my heart, to welcome the complete sensory overload provided by nature, and let the grief flow. It became fortifying, refreshing, and made my bond with Cai feel stronger than ever.

A week amongst the mortals passed so quickly, the feeling of re-entering normality was intense. Immersion in mainstream

Americana was surprisingly welcome, life continued there with no regard to the tragedy that haunted my life. I'm not knocking it; all my needs were well catered for. The library allowed me extra time to hog an Internet connection and satisfy a need to increase contact with the outside world, my own world had diminished in size as the miles passed by. Montrose Kawasaki proved invaluable for the advice and service they were all too happy to provide, even suggesting money saving alternatives to the modifications I'd intended. Without being part of the deal, they gave me a replacement bike whilst attending to mine. Being the same make, model, age, and even colour as mine made it all too familiar. Mr and Mrs Average America accepted me as a welcome visitor into their lives, treating me with warmth and generosity, without any knowledge of who I was or what had befallen me. I could almost forget recent events, I almost became that amazing Brit fulfilling the American dream; almost. Stepping out of my nightmare was not so easy.

Nick and Emma's proved an ideal bolt hole from the hectic life of American suburbia to be found in Montrose, the ideal place to let down my defences. Their Hobbit home, a pair of linked Geodomes seemingly filled to the brim with greyhounds, sat nestled within five acres of trees, hidden from the rest of the world. I fell in love with the place straight away, especially the dogs. Even Bonkers eventually allowed me to approach and stroke her, despite her abject fear of males. It took days with pieces of best quality beef jerky, gradually enticing her closer for the treat, until she managed to pluck up the courage to take it from my hand, only achieved when I looked the other way.

Nick's confidence in me was gratifying, as he dropped an AK47 into my hands he showed no concern for my sanity, neither did he hesitate to take me to a shooting range and blast off a few hundred rounds. Thoughts of going on a berserker rage never even entered my mind, though I acknowledged the ease with which this could happen. Emma played her part by staying up into the early hours plying me with alcohol and giving me the freedom to talk or not, as befitted my mood. I wasn't looking for an escape though, merely a brief respite from the cumulative strain of physical endurance and emotional torture.

With a slightly modified and newly serviced bike further excuses were beyond me, it was time to hit the road again. After a quiet goodbye on their way to work, I was left alone to pack the bike and slip away with no fuss, back into the wild wilderness beyond, back to my own world. Having failed to go Orca hunting in Washington, Vancouver Island was the next destination. Grizzly Bears and Killer Whales awaited.

Chapter Seven

Seals, a Bald Eagle and a whale made the ninety-minute ferry ride pass peaceably. I was happy to watch Port Angeles disappear slowly into the distance, content to be drifting lazily across the watery depths of no-man's land. Next stop Canada.

Boy, had I been looking forward to the open, friendly manner of the Canadians after the officious attitude of the American authorities, but boy was I wrong. Maybe I shouldn't have weaved through the queue to the front, maybe the woman had a problem with motorcyclists, maybe she just had a problem. 'Switch off your engine and take off your sunglasses!' She didn't even bother with cringe-worthy platitudes by addressing me as *Sir*, at least not immediately. 'How long do you intend to stay in Canada, sir?' God, she's a mind reader; though it isn't the words you use really, it's the way you use them. This was one woman with a barb in her tail. She may as well have kicked me in the nuts! 'As long as it takes to ride up to the head of the Rockies then back down to the American border.' Wrong answer! Was it my attitude or hers? An honest explanation of my intentions should have done the job. It hadn't, at this rate she was going to ream me out. I hoped her fingernails weren't too long!

Victoria, Vancouver Island, was only a short hop from the States into Canada and the atmosphere was a far cry from the typical hustle and bustle of American city life. It had a tranquil quality. Its architecture gave a strong feel of colonialism. It may have tempted me to stop and sightsee, had it not been dusk already. Luckily my belligerence hadn't gotten me detained, after reining in my attitude there hadn't been any problem, she'd even given me a six month visa. Being 7 p.m. there was little choice but to head straight into the surrounding countryside in search of a campsite. I don't like setting up camp in the dark, especially not when knackered and starving. A conveniently close alehouse supplied the motivation for a quick, no nonsense pitching of the tent. Cooking for myself wasn't even contemplated, thoughts of an easy plate of pub grub spurred me on. Sitting in the pub nothing looked any different from anywhere in the States, but it certainly felt different. Was it just my imagination, or was the whole vibe more relaxed? A plate of food and a beer was plenty and with a sigh of pleasure I drained the last dregs of beer before wandering, exhausted, back to my tent, where unconsciousness quickly overcame me.

Somehow, my expectations were of a vastly different country from America. On reflection it is: although first impressions did not give that appearance. Out of the island's capital it was little different from Washington; shops and houses were pretty much alike. The natural environment closely resembled that of the States, though seemingly on a grander scale. Wide rivers replaced quiet creeks, choked with timber, all they needed to complete my romantic ideal were the lumberjacks running over rolling logs. Distances were greater, areas more inaccessible. Perfectly clear lakes as flat as a millpond stretched wide, ideal landing strips for waterborne planes, a necessary mode of transport in such a sparsely populated country. For me the big difference lay in the people themselves. For a start there were less of them but they seemed more relaxed and their sense of humour more closely resembled that found in the British Isles. I won't fault the hospitality or friendliness of the Americans. They had done me proud, all I'd met (outside the realms of officialdom) had opened their hearts and homes to me, for which I will be eternally grateful.

Another relieving difference was the quality of roads, the surfaces improved dramatically. Gone were the unevenly chipped surfaces, replaced by super smooth, high quality tarmac. Yep, smooth as silk, I instantly liked the roads. The cambers were perfect, leaving nothing to chance, each affording the ideal angle to sweep round the bend without worrying about due speed. Having gone metric, it conveyed a feeling of quicker progress, distances passed more rapidly whilst I matched my recorded speed (MPH) with that displayed by the road signs (KPH). Regrettably Route 1 was littered with small towns and villages, frequent traffic lights and abundant traffic made the going slow. The plan had been to follow this road directly to Port Hardy, my proposed destination to go whale watching. Whilst impatient to get there my impatience with the traffic was greater, it was an unwelcome intrusion. It wasn't the open road, I couldn't free my heart and open my mind, let myself go. After the freedom I'd found before Montrose this was oppressive and I wasn't willing to forsake my peace of mind.

An alternative route (No. 18) veered off west towards Lake Cowichan as far as Youbou, where the map showed it continuing as an unmaintained trail. No sign of habitation; a couple of campsites, otherwise nothing, what more could I ask for? Youbou contained a tiny shop and a few houses, and at the far end of the village the road abruptly came to an end, as shown. Beyond was logging country, and the logging companies were on strike. Sixty-two miles of isolated trail lay ahead, all dirt, dust, lumps and bumps, once again just me and the elements. It was where I belonged, where I needed to be, and it felt that nowhere else would do. And what a time it was!

Without thought or hesitation an initial cruising speed of 35mph was adopted, with good open bends it was plain sailing. Deep, loose gravel perturbed me not, and the occasional vehicle I caught up with was passed in a flash. There was little choice really, their dust trail brought visibility down to zero. With each overtake my speed increased, as did my confidence, in no time at all 40mph was my minimum speed. At times the back end slewed on bends, the front end got twitchy and slowing down only exacerbated the problem, but opening her up a bit sorted it out. Another 10mph had crept onto the speedo, giving a fairly constant 50mph, for a while at least, until nearly shitting myself when I almost lost it. The back end slid in really deep gravel on an unexpectedly long bend, the bike slewed sideways as I fought to regain control, only on the very edge of the opposite verge did I succeed. That curtailed my enthusiasm, inducing a touch more caution, 40mph felt slow in comparison but so much more in control. My only thoughts were of gratitude that the loggers were on strike, apparently there is normally a virtually continuous line of fully laden wagons plying the route.

When they appeared the views were breath-taking, deserted, crystal clear lakes and murky, serpentine rivers meandering towards the coast with their cargo of timber. From high vantage points log choked waterways were the only break from steep, deeply wooded slopes. Why trucks had become the modern method of transport now is beyond me; the rivers had effortlessly carried lumber for many centuries. Though I realised how so much timber washed up along the North West coast, I'd wondered about the abundance of Burls there. How perfect was my timing, no trucks, no logging camps in operation, nary a soul to be seen. It was all blue skies and sunshine, dense forest, deserted waterways and delightful forest trails.

A possible continuation was to ride up the Campbell river, find a campsite and strike out along an even longer logging track. The perfect way to extend my solitude and enjoyment, if only I'd had the fuel; yet again foiled by the lack of gas. Instead, Port Alberni was sought and reluctantly accepted as an overnight refuge and refuelling point. Common sense won through, I couldn't afford the time for too many detours, it was the end of August and I'd yet to reach the head of the Rockies. Winter seemed far away but so was the Yukon and it was already threateningly close for the cold season up there. I decided to press on. Once the threat of winter was behind me, I'd be better situated for the luxury of side trips which would only be once heading south again. And just to prove me right, that was about the last day I enjoyed hot sunshine and riding in lightweight summer gear until crossing the border again. Leaving Port Alberni under the threat of rain called for the waterproofs again, and from then on multiple, warm and waterproof layers were needed pretty much throughout Canada.

Telegraph Bay had been recommended for whale watching excursions, a remote cove off the beaten track, with professionally undertaken operations catering for small groups of people. It sounded just the place for me, if only my informants had known how difficult I was to please. Bearing in mind the extent of solitude I'd gotten used to nothing less than an individual excursion with orcas aplenty would have satisfied me. It was a fair way off the main highway, only a small cove and the boats were relatively small compared with many of the operations. All in all, it had a lot to offer and certainly delivered the goods I wasn't at my best but managed to make the most of it, after a bad start. Arriving cold and lonely did me no favours, my first impressions left a lot to be desired and took a lot to overcome. There wasn't even anywhere to leave my bike without paying for a parking space. I wasn't impressed and left it where I felt like it, stuff 'em! It wasn't anything but a tourist location, low key or not, offering a host of waterborne adventures; fishing, kayaking, whale watching and Grizzly Bear excursions.

There was a Marina with upmarket accommodation, a string of overpriced waterside cabins, an overbooked restaurant, a basic shop, gift shop/gallery and a campsite along the road. If this was my chance of fraternising with Orcas I had better pull my finger out and get on with it, when would my next chance materialise? With reluctance I booked a place on the morning cruise, being assured it was the less frequented excursion of the day. Seeing Orcas had been one of the greatest inspirations of the trip, no way was I going to miss my biggest opportunity.

Feeling thoroughly dispirited, I made my way to the campsite. Before my tent was even spread upon the ground I was in floods of tears. What the hell was I doing in the place, carrying on with gay abandon? I was kidding myself that life continued regardless, I felt nothing for life, and even less for myself. All I could think about was Cai, the pain he'd endured before finally giving up the ghost and letting go of life. How I wished it had been me and not him, why had I not stuck to my guns and chosen the red bike? All I could think of was his pain as I held him, lying dying in the middle of the freeway. Negativity overwhelmed me, I couldn't shake it off, I cried shamelessly throughout the process of making camp, setting a fire and then walking all the way back to the bay itself. I needed a friendly voice, someone who understood, just a few words of reassurance, was it really too much to ask for? It was. I could rouse no answer from anyone. How often must I prove my ability to deal with this shit? Just as well I could, whether I wanted to or not. I spent a miserably cold night alone, was up and packed before 7.30am, wanting to be done and dusted as soon as possible. It proved a strange experience, long awaited for, much appreciated, but lonely and desperately sad. Orcas were no match for Cai. I'd exterminate the frigging lot to raise him from the dead.

I can only admire the crew and marine scientist for helping me along my way and making it a wonderful experience, it wasn't an easy task to pull me from the depths to which I'd sunk. The other passengers helped not one iota. At the slightest sighting of anything it was a rush for the railings, regardless of anyone else. Each time I had a clear view, camera at the ready, a free for all would ensue, only human forms crowding the rails filled my lens. Not being in the mood I refrained from voicing my displeasure, or elbowing people out the way, and took a step back. I retreated to the galley, disgruntled and extremely frustrated. Which is where the marine specialist came across me, concerned at my obvious displeasure. 'What's wrong, is there anything I can do?' she asked. My answer was short and to the point; 'Throw the other passengers overboard!' She understood all too well, she also had a solution. Once the engines were cut, I was allowed to stand on the engine cowling forward of the wheelhouse, a metre above the level of the other passengers. So pleased was I, I made room for one or two others as well, youngsters also squeezed out from the railings by inconsiderate adults. How could I do otherwise? I believe in setting a good example. With Orcas to one side and a trio of Humpback Whales on the other, with a viewpoint second to none, it proved more than I'd hoped for and gave me a multitude of brilliant pictures. To top the lot, it was rounded off with a large school of Pacific White Sided Dolphin, literally hundreds of them. They're not as athletic as some dolphin species but riding the bow wave must be like a fairground ride for them, enticing them right into the side of the boat, lots of them, time and time again. Even at my worst I could not maintain a sour disposition in those circumstances. Gone was the grumpiness but not the depth of emotions; it brought on the most profound sadness not to be sharing it with Cai. I had to go below deck in search of privacy, just for a short while to get a grip of myself. What an overflowing mess of emotional turmoil. I couldn't quite shake the grief, writing my blog in the Port Hardy tourist office with tears streaming down my face should have been an embarrassment. It wasn't in the slightest, I didn't give a damn! Being filled with the purest and cleanest of emotions wasn't to be denied, I actually felt good about it, not proud of my exhibition but good to be in touch with the deepest aspects of my soul. What I find difficult to accept is how people shut away these feelings when they lose their loved ones. To me it is either denial or a lack of true love and affection for them. I will never be ashamed of my love for Cai, will never deny how grievously I'm mortified over my loss, though I hope it won't drown my enthusiasm for life forever.

Life is for living, don't throw it away and don't shut it out. With such a philosophy I appreciated my one and only night in Port Hardy. It was deserted, lashing rain meant few ventured out, and it brought to mind a night spent in Aberdeen. Not many people came for pleasure, it was a boring fishing port, offering little and providing less. Dismally wet with a dour populace it hardly offered a warm welcome but the place humoured me. My guesthouse was on the outskirts of town, though not wanting to traipse back into town I'd no choice. Food had to be found and I cared not where, the bike was safely tucked away for the night and I was on foot. I wasn't about to be fussy, a few beers over a plate of pub grub would be fine. A large unattractive bar provided the venue which actually afforded more than promised from outside, I was treated to a dining room with waitress service. The menu was half decent and the waitress very obliging, in fact so obliging I wistfully dwelt on thoughts of forgetting the 5 a.m. sailing I'd booked for the following morning. Almost, being only half my age her advances were regrettably ignored. Making do with the lift it gave to my spirits I sauntered back to my lodgings with a definite spring in my step.

Chapter Eight

Fifteen hours along the Inland Passage meant arriving in Port Rupert quite late at night. All I managed before turning in for the night was registering at the Youth Hostel. Dorm accommodation was all that was available, true to form I'd not bothered pre-booking and was beyond caring. Sailing along the Inland Passage had been enough to satisfy me for one day. Apparently it was a sought after journey, detours through Vancouver Island were made specifically for it. The whole experience was quite surreal, sinister almost, only the deep throbbing of the engines broke the unnatural silence. Without the slightest breath of wind the only movement was our passage. Thin ribbons of mist hung between tree covered islets, motionless, foreboding. It wasn't all weird and ghostly, a couple of fish eagles welcomed me onto the ferry. There were also sightings of sea lions, dolphins and Humpback Whales. One breached high out of the water, amazing, all I caught on camera was the splash, so much for autofocus. Taking on the effect of a sightseeing tour, announcements came over the Tannoy forewarning us of approaching marine life. If only my eyes were as sharp as the crew's, hours were spent scouring the waters in the vain hope of seeing more. It was cold as well. I couldn't endure it for too long and sat inside, my mind on the journey up to Watson Lake. That was my turning point, where my map showed the northern-most point of the Rockies. Being six hundred miles further north than Prince Rupert it would be damned cold, snow streaked mountains already lined the way. There was virtually nothing between Port Rupert and Watson Lake, and I planned to camp in the wild? Let it not be said I'm not game for adventure, let not my determination be in question, my sanity maybe but not my fortitude!

Stocking up with a supply of fresh veg, supplemented with packets of soup, a hot meal at the end of each day could be looked forward to whatever the weather. Two days should be long enough for the journey, three to four days' worth of food would suffice. I had no intention of following the main highway, Route 37, there were more interesting alternatives. Off-road shortcuts through remote areas would invariably take longer to circumvent, but they'd also be more challenging, and I wasn't about to take the easy way through. With enough food I was packed and ready to roll, first stop Terrace. Actually, a roadside hazard brought me to an abrupt halt just miles out of town. Cars came to a stand still, people jumping out of their cars, running up and down the carriageway. What the hell was going on?

WOW, a bear! Walking nonchalantly along a railway track, grazing, seemingly oblivious to the commotion across the road. As it sauntered along the side of the track vehicles would move slowly forward, take more photos, then creep forward again. Half a dozen cars had pulled over, cameras clicked rapidly, people's hushed tones of awe did nothing to disturb it. Until one pillock had to go and spoil it. Of course it was the one with a really expensive camera, sporting a gigantic lens. Regardless of the fact he could have taken better photos than the rest of us from one hundred yards away he had to be the one, had to get as close as possible, push it to the limit. And the bear was off, vanishing into the undergrowth, its meal brought to a premature end. I bet the guy never questioned the reasons for the rapid departure, never thought he was in any way responsible. Never mind, for me it was a wonderful initiation to the Canadian mainland, it was right up there with the Orcas for most wanted experiences. I'd expected, deeply hoped, to see bears in the wilderness. Having only just cleared the city it came as a surprise, regardless of hearing reports of urban problems with bears. It felt a privilege, an honour to share those brief moments with my first bear, I felt elated. If only my emotions were so simple though.

Whilst opening my heart, my soul, to the wonders of nature it also brought on sadness again because I was not sharing it with Cai. As with the Orcas, my awareness of the beauty, the wonder I faced, soared. My heart and mind opened to the marvels I witnessed. Unfortunately my heart was so full of pain I couldn't contain it, and I didn't want to. Using meditative techniques I reached in and released the pressure valve allowing the love and pain free rein, lessening my burden, easing the pain. In an arse about face sort of way it was good for me, it was a dichotomy of emotions, confusing, hurtful but welcome. So with my head in the clouds and a bleeding heart, away I went, both jubilant and saddened at the same time.

With only a few miles under my belt there was little time for further reflection. Distant mountains beckoned, ahead and to the side ribboned with snow they brought to mind the task ahead. Heading north for another one thousand kilometres with winter already showing its presence, the days of glorious sunshine were gone. It really was about time I got cracking. Terrace lay directly inland, along a one hundred and thirty kilometre long salt-water inlet, there were no alternative routes. A fairly straight and boring road in itself, the surrounding environment was terrific, a broad, flat glacial plain edged by hills. Each mile brought an increase to the amount of snow present on the hillsides, intensifying the sense of true adventure. Creeping cold found its way through my bike gear in no time and thermal underclothes were essential, yet lay unused at the bottom of my saddlebags. Convenient stops for warmth and refreshment were few and far between, and I wasn't about to strip off at the roadside to redress the problem. Likewise, fuel was a major concern in such sparsely populated areas every opportunity to refuel had to be taken. Consumption had to be watched carefully, no more blasting along at fuel guzzling speeds. With care there shouldn't be any problems.

Bugger, where had I miscalculated? Only twenty miles from the coast I went onto reserve, the bloody tachometer only read one hundred and seventy miles since the last refuelling stop; SHIT, SHIT, SHIT! Another eighty miles before Terrace, no chance, back I go. Now then, this art of refuelling, what was that about conserving fuel and topping up whenever possible? Maybe the thrash from Telegraph Bay to Port Hardy at 80-90mph hadn't been the most fuel-efficient ride, refuelling before leaving Prince Rupert would have made that irrelevant. It didn't matter though, what's done is done, there was no point beating myself up about it. It wasn't the best of starts, but at least it was only a five mile ride back to Prince Edward, the nearest gas station. Nothing but time lost, and a lesson learnt. Another two tanks of fuel should see me through to Watson Lake, during which I would wise up and conserve fuel. It was going to be hit or miss on the second leg anyway, my map made it almost four hundred miles without a fuel stop. Including reserve my range was a little over three hundred miles. I had no extra capacity for carrying fuel, only a length of rubber tubing to siphon fuel into my camping stove. No worries then, off I go.

I filled up again in Terrace, managing to squeeze in another five litres, it could after all make a difference of sixty miles or so. Sporting a smug smile I veered away from Route 37, it would be rejoined later after an excursion through the traditional lands of the First Nations people. The chance to see how they're coping with modern life was the hope, although after my experience in Port Alberni my hopes weren't high. The original inhabitants seen there had consisted of crack-heads stumbling around the streets and dealers calling across the street to me, touting openly for business.

After Terrace my smile increased in proportion to the number of bends per mile, not even the bitter cold and freezing rain could curtail my elation. A profound sense of isolation brought contentment, the further from the trappings of civilisation the better I felt. New Aiyansh, home of the Naga'a last bastion of a forgotten world, as a First Nations settlement little of their traditional life was in evidence, barring the spanking new Totem poles guarding the entrance to the community centre. Well-spaced, well-tended houses and their accompanying, shiny new pickups suggested reasonable wealth, yet it appeared bleak and inhospitable. Where were the people? No-one even came out to attend to the gas pump, was it actually populated, had my presence even been noted? Neither the town nor the people showed any signs of welcome. Mind you, forced into a tiny portion of their former territories is it any wonder they show indifference to white interlopers? I was merely another intruder poking his nose somewhere it wasn't wanted, marvelling at the surrounding beauty, happy snapping twenty to the dozen. Cardboard-coated chicken passed as KFC in the service station cafe, whether in nugget form or drumsticks it barely resembled food, but being all that was on offer it had to suffice. With a distinct lack of enthusiasm I forced it down my throat, filled the bike again and got the hell out the place.

Native American reservations in the States were so different, most hosted casinos or other communally-owned businesses, and generated a lot of wealth. Their business acumen was superb making the most of their privileged position outside the state legislative restrictions, they fleeced the white man. They ran their own affairs and generally wouldn't tolerate their own tribes´ people in the casinos. One in Washington had the only gas station for many miles.

It was extremely busy and very well run. For Native Americans prices were heavily discounted, I'd been impressed. It was a far cry from what I witnessed at New Aiyansh! With a beautiful set of totem poles standing proud outside a large pristine community centre I would have expected a people swollen with pride, a vibrant community. In spite of the new houses and pickups it was lifeless, suggesting a run down, exhausted community. Without these trappings of modern suburbia the picture was one of rotting metal hulks, a shabby gas station, a badly maintained shop cum bar, a near derelict frontier town on the verge of desertion. It portrayed a people at odds with the material world, a people without hope, stuck in a nether world between a lost past and bleak future.

At Nass Camp the fun really began, an unmaintained gravel track cut through thirty miles of logging country. It was wet, muddy and very lumpy, the potholes were hard to see and impossible to avoid. What a fabulous ride! My mind was focussed, my body relaxed and my enthusiasm intense. Not caring about what the conditions were, what it threw at me, I relished every minute of it. The bike tackled every aspect of the ride with ease, as did I. Corrugations, potholes and deep muddy puddles couldn't make me reduce pace, noting a speed of 60mph nearly did but it was so exhilarating there was no chance I was slowing down. Each set of potholes were taken standing up on the pegs, winding the throttle on even more. A stretch of deep gravel got the same treatment and the bike hurtled straight through with not even the slightest twitch. Twice I spotted bears ahead, none too keen on the fast approaching noise they hightailed it out of there before I got close. For sure I wanted a close encounter, and it wasn't about to happen blatting along at such reckless speeds, but it was so much fun I couldn't help myself. Oh joy, oh joy, I was as happy as a pig in shit! With mud flying thick and fast it was over much too quick, Cranberry junction jumped out of nowhere and I was back on Route 37; bummer! Smothered from head to foot in mud, both the bike and me, you only get that dirty when having fun. But it was fast approaching nightfall, I was miles from anywhere, the rain showed no sign of abating and there were bears in them there woods. The prospect of camping didn't enthral me in the slightest. Grateful then for persevering with the cardboard chicken, sleep was the main objective, anywhere would do as long as it was dry. And so I found a deserted logging office, rat infested maybe, but dry with shelter for the bike too. I truly appreciated the logger's fight for more money and better work conditions. Right on, and how about soft comfy beds in their deserted site offices?

Lacking precise information about gas stations I had no choice but to keep a sensible 60mph cruising speed. My American Automobile Association map showed occasional fuel stops but I couldn't rely on them, office staff couldn't confirm how up to date their non-USA roadmaps were. No joke, reaching Meziadin Lake found no sign of the gas pumps having worked this side of the attack on Pearl Harbour. Maybe the AAA missed its closure during the invasion. Oh well. It was raining hard, low-lying cloud drastically reduced visibility and with limited fuel and an unknown distance to cover the outlook was bleak.

Water seeped through my waterproof gloves, my boots were soaked and I was bitterly cold. By constantly moving my fingers and toes I attempted to maintain circulation, some semblance of warmth in my extremities. I still hadn't put my thermals on. They sat unused in the bottom of my bag still. Each stop had either been too wet or too cold to entice me to strip off completely and put them on, I'd started to regret it. Too late for regrets, yet too early for concern, the only option was to grin and bear it, trust in fate, not tempt failure. Deese Lake, the next source of fuel marked on the map looked an unobtainable goal. So do many things in life, and rarely will fear or paranoia improve the situation; something would come along, sooner or later. And out of the gloom appeared a truck stop, big rigs stood in orderly lines, engines kept running, truckers sat in their cabs cosy and warm. Stiff limbed, frozen and wet, I wasted no time contemplating such luxurious modes of transport. Hot coffee and a warm meal were number one priority. A slightly warmer cafe would have been better appreciated but beggars can't be choosers, it was a definite improvement and heard no complaints from me. Bell 2 Service Station, my saviour, a shoddy, shabby roadhouse, a veritable palace in the heart of nowhere. You can bet I rode away snuggled into full thermals and a warm, dry scarf. Sealskin socks completed the transformation, I felt like a new man.

Swinging still further inland the altitude increased and the top of the tree line was soon reached. The hills bore only stunted growth, straggly, multi-hued scrub dotted the roadside barely below the snowline. Boy was it beautiful, patches of red, pale yellow, lime green, crispy brown and russet gold. Autumn colours in their full glory, a magnificent sight but a cold one. Without the natural shelter of surrounding trees providing a windbreak, the temperature dropped drastically. I was frozen solid and it didn't matter, such were the wonderfully intricate details of nature. Faced with such extremes the whole landscape appeared scoured, scraped clean of detritus. Subject to such a harsh environment the tarmac had also taken a battering. With subsidence encroaching into my path and potholes spread along its edge, it regularly lost any semblance to a highway.

Bands of loose gravel stretched across the entire road without warning. Such changes in road surface aren't nice on a bike but need a gutsy approach; no hesitation, drive hard across. Bridge crossings couldn't be tackled the same way, iron grid work makes an awful surface for traction especially in the wet. Back wheel snaking, the first two were attempted disregarding the inherent problems. Woah, never again! Caution was definitely the order of the day, the bike may have stayed upright but that was pure chance, I didn't feel in control at all. Driving rain continued, prompting thoughts of thrashing 200 miles straight to Watson Lake, the temptation was proving a distraction. A hot bath and comfortable bed was very appealing, a hotel with hot and cold running generosity. No longer was fuel a worry, I could thrash it all the way there and spend a night of unreserved luxury. Surely I could make it by 7pm, 8 p.m. at the latest? It wasn't out of desperation; regardless of the relative discomfort I was quite content. Notwithstanding the sodden gloves (my hands felt encased in bags of Slush Puppy), I was dry and comparatively warm, considering the abysmal weather, and chuffed with myself. So chuffed a reward would be so well deserved But then....

Oh, glory be! Mud, sweat and gears! The bands of gravel got muddier, then longer, until finally at Deese Lake they replaced the tarmac altogether, presenting a packed earth surface awash with mud. A thin watery mud coating lay over a solid even surface. Hog heaven (and I don't mean Harleys), I fair flew along, happy as a pig in shit. In my mirrors the world vanished in a flying spray of crud, my legs were thickly coated and the bike completely covered. It was dirty: it was filthy: it was tremendous fun. When the rain threw itself at me in buckets it mattered not, merely reduced the amount of muck clinging to us. We were so filthy it was immoral! Watson Lake, a hotel? Stuff it, I wanted life the hard way! I may have reached clean smooth tarmac again but raining or not I wasn't ready for civilisation. Sidetracks boasted "PRIVATE PROPERTY" signs which was frustrating, all I needed was a clearing big enough for me and the tent. Starting to consider once again a fast blast into Watson Lake, I spied a tiny lake hidden amongst the trees and an almost completely obscured track. Overgrown with overhanging trees the going was slow, I had to force my way through, breaking branches as they snagged. It got to the point where turning round would prove nigh on impossible; I'd better keep on then, eh?

Reward indeed, thinning into a clearing the trees released their grasp and the struggle was over. Behold, a crystal clear lake with not a ripple disturbing the wondrous mountain scene reflected upon its surface. The only sound, that of the bubbling brook carrying away the overflow from the lake. What a find. Plenty of room to manoeuvre the bike, more than enough room to pitch the tent, how cool was that? But the real gem, the icing on the cake, facing me stood a derelict log cabin. Broken and cracked windows showed clearly it wasn't inhabited or even habitable! Both the floor and roof of the porch were collapsed needing a minor excavation before gaining entry. Unbelievable, the place was dry except for one wall where water had dripped through a broken roof timber. A tatty fold down sofa bed dominated the single room, it was bone dry and devoid of unpleasant smells, so I had a ready-made bed. The floor liberally covered in rat shit, needed sweeping. It had been ransacked at some point, not hopelessly so, drawers still held cards and a candle stub. An hour of cleaning turned it into my home, what a pity no stove had been left, that would have been too much to expect though. I made a fire in a pit outside using all the dry timber I could find, a great shame as a second night there would have been appreciated. A day of relaxing and reading wouldn't have gone amiss but without a fire it was out of the question, I saw no sense spending a day cowering in my sleeping bag for warmth. But for that night it was my own isolated, luxury retreat.

I left the following day, marvelling at the picturesque waterways littering my course through the landscape. Countless lakes and rivers lined the route into the Yukon, a host of finely sculpted mountains giving glorious depth to the artistic display. A fast ride cut short the natural delights surrounding me, arriving in Watson Lake much too quickly. Bringing an abrupt end to my day wasn't the plan. It was just such great fun throwing the bike round the bends with gay abandon, reaching the town was bound to be an anti-climax.

Watson Lake was my turning point, the northern most point of the Rockies, as close as my road maps could discern anyway. I was confident I'd outrun the approaching winter; from now on it was all downhill, into the warm and welcome arms of sunshine. Both the bike and my riding had been put through their paces, and neither had been found wanting. I had felt an overwhelming abundance of elation and endured extreme hardship in a matter of days. Grief and gratification had been my constant companions, an unfathomable mix I felt no need to decipher. The intense feeling of loss had not diminished in the slightest, my thoughts of Cai grew more positive though, my determination not to give up on life drove me on. Life was precious and my world a wonderful place, I held onto those thoughts, they maintained my fragile grasp on reality. What awaited south was a mystery, the extent of pleasure or pain remained unknown. Only time would tell, and I had plenty of that. For now, I at least felt satisfied with myself

As a mark of appreciation I actually cleaned my machine thoroughly, and treated it to a slap up meal, one full tank of premium please. Practicalities came second, a hotel with endless hot water to scrub my body and clothes clean, dry my gloves and waterproof my boots. Last came the luxuries, food that didn't come in the form of a stew, to laze around warm and naked, bury my nose in a book and drift off to sleep feeling deeply satisfied. Such simple pleasures, taken for granted so often, truly appreciated so seldom, though I did miss my little log cabin.

Chapter Nine

Initially the way south was yet more Lakeland. Maybe my expectations had been too high but I wasn't instantly materialised into the heart of soaring mountains. Instead a gentle ride between lakes and connecting rivers instilled a relaxed feel, encouraging me to sustain a speed dictated by economy rather than a rush of adrenalin. It had a sobering effect, not for another hundred miles was I rewarded with my first decent view of mountains, The Rockies. Initially not exactly stunning in size or abundance, I was however presented with an amazing diversity of carefully sculpted rock. Each outcrop, every peak was distinctive, there was an immense difference in the formation of the rock around me. Gently sloping shelves of smooth, bare rock would plunge suddenly into the next valley, the steep leeward slopes bristling with dense conifers. Pockets of stunted trees sprouted from the smallest pockets of soil in the slightest fold in the rock. An upturned cone of rock stood like crumpled and scrunched paper, a multitude of ridges running down the sides. Jagged peaks with snow-filled craters stood in line, like cracked and broken molars exposed to the cold. A nicely rounded breast nestled amongst the erratic jumble of rock, its pert nipple, cold from the overlaying snow, pointing skyward. Entering the rocky chaos changed the character of the highway too. From the boring uniformity experienced since Watson Lake, it blended in with the nature of the surrounding environment, snaking around the mountains, following the lay of the land.

Regardless of the twisting, undulating road I merely pottered along not wanting to miss the views as they appeared, not wishing to miss the smallest detail. Every yard of progress offered something different, changes in the colours, the layering, the shapes found in the rock. Veins of sedimentary layers showed the ancient origins of much of the rock, eons before it was scoured by glaciation. Most impressive though was the scenery taken as a whole. It was a sin to lose the bigger picture by concentrating too hard on the finer detail. The scenery was breath-taking, and seemingly endless! Cresting one hill, Mordor stood to the side, a dark, bleak and inhospitable valley, challenging me to venture forth. Although leading towards the central plains of Canada, little access was afforded the bike and me, unless I sprouted some wings. Even looking behind I was taken aback, by immense undulating plain of bright green conifers, the occasional thin thread of a river and barely discernable, so far away, other, distant mountain ranges.

An end to the summer holidays meant fewer tourists, the roads were almost empty, encouraging more wildlife into the open. A trio of Daal sheep complete with tracking tags, grazed nonchalantly oblivious to my passage (apparently a rare treat as they seldom come so low). A skittish Caribou, unwilling to tolerate my presence, allowed only a distant camera shot before taking flight. I thought they remained in vast herds, safety in numbers, maybe he'd lost his way. Bison care not one iota, whether solitary or in groups their sheer size supplies ample protection. A lone bull barely bothered to glance up as I passed merely feet from it. Bison gore more people each year than are attacked by bears, with so few wolves in the wild now they have no natural predators. A group sauntered along the road not giving a damn about the traffic. And who can blame them? Beside a caravan they made it look like a dinky toy. I wouldn't like to collide with one of them, even in a truck!

But the bears, oh yes, the bears. Once realising my exhaust note frightened them off, I'd kill the engine if I saw one, cruising silently along so I could approach without scaring them away. I finally managed to get within six metres and get some really good pictures. My finest achievement was to take a thirty second video as one munched on the roadside vegetation. I'd freewheeled past it, dismounted and slowly, cautiously moved closer, making sure I was downwind. A passing car caused it to look up, checking there was no threat. It looked straight in my direction, as I stood perfectly still, and it seemed not to notice. Their eyesight is appalling, smell being their most acute sense. So clear was the detail I could see bloody gouges in its flanks, it must have been fighting with another bear, nothing else could inflict such damage. It was amazing, on reflection it was stupid. I was nearer the bear than my bike, much nearer. At the time I didn't care, the excitement took over and fear didn't get a look in. A bit like my first encounter with a shark, my first reaction was to go to try and shake his hand (figuratively speaking of course).

After barely two hundred miles of delightful mountain wilderness the road swung away from the mountains and the snow taking me into Fort Nelson. What a dive, a most dreary, uninspiring town if ever there was one. What had brought me here, why hadn't I braved the cold and camped out again? I was clean, I had food, I was living the life but of course the bike needed fuel, I'd covered three hundred miles that day. Fact is, I was so enthralled by the abundance of nature I neglected to plan my overnight stop, so ended up in a ropey Motel, too knackered to look any further. The supermarket sold no beer. There were no convenient bars and less in the way of cafes, at least there was a Chinese restaurant close by. But hey, it was Fort Nelson, did I really expect it to be a good Chinese restaurant? If I had I was sorely mistaken. I hurriedly shovelled as much down my throat as possible, washed it down with a beer and got the hell out of there. I was more than ready to hit the sack, certain in the knowledge that Fort Nelson wouldn't miss me too much.

Buddhist philosophy praises the state of equanimity, a balance between the highs and the lows, neither succumbing to extreme pleasure nor intense displeasure. Life should be one harmonious continuation. The calm and peace of equanimity is indeed a state of beauty, life becomes more profoundly tranquil, allowing a deeper appreciation of the world around you. In theory I can't fault this, there again I don't make for a very good Buddhist. I crave excitement, loath immobility, for me intense pleasure is the ultimate. Light up your sky with explosive fireworks, burst forth with uncontained passion. Don't hold back, live life like each day is your last. Of course, I believe life tends to balance itself out. Alongside the heights of pleasure lay the depths of gloom, we have adrenalin to drive us on and endorphins to aid the pain. With adrenalin we can achieve the impossible, push ourselves to new limits. When we push too far, if it goes wrong, endorphins step in. They also give us a feeling of contentment, like after a heavy session working out. I find endorphins useful to help overcome the negative aspects of myself, a precious tool to tackle anger, fear, lust and pain. Isn't that why regular physical exertion is so beneficial for depression? We can induce the production of both these natural chemicals, so we have the means to combat all aspects of our lives. With the highs come the lows, accept it, deal with it, and move on. It isn't always easy, but the greater the effort, the greater the reward. What is it the Buddhists claim? Life is suffering? They've certainly got that one right.

For such a brief visit to Fort Nelson the effect was abnormally profound. It sucked me dry, left me an empty, shrunken shell. Awareness of this spiritual depletion didn't tempt me to hang around, or work out why. Wasting no time I refuelled and set off, breakfast would be taken on the move, there was bound to be a roadhouse with coffee and grits. The drab, dreary feeling hung over my shoulders all day, there was no shaking it. The highway was less than impressive, being flat, straight and totally uninspiring. The surrounding country was also flat and boring, I was meant to be following the Rockies, where were the bloody mountains? And without a single sign of wildlife nothing occurred to bolster my diminishing emotional fortitude. Autopilot was engaged, a steady 70mph maintained, adopting economy-mode bike and brain settled down to a lacklustre day. It wasn't a lack of determination, purely a complete lack of enthusiasm. I was bored stiff but resigned myself to a long, boring ride, resisting the temptation to hurtle along at top speed and get it over with.

I resorted to cloud watching. Not the best of pastimes whilst riding, yet the road was so straight and so deserted there were no hazards to avoid. The sky, a deep azure blue, was liberally festooned with light fluffy clouds. A slight breeze encouraged them to drift along, forming continuously shifting shapes overhead. Neptune resplendent with bushy beard, then a snorting bull, a passing kaleidoscope of human and animal caricatures, constantly morphing between realism and fantasy. My main concern was staying awake, the infrequent coffee houses were utilised to maximum effect, yet it was still a chore to stop the inevitable drooping of my eyelids. Through hooded lids I would catch tantalising glimpses of mountain peaks, jerking me to full wakefulness. My hopes would soar but then the road would swing away again, leaving me a touch more dispirited each time.

Fort St John came and went. It held as much appeal as Fort Nelson so I decided not to grace it with my presence. At this point my morale was low, it had been such a long, tedious day it was a struggle to maintain a positive frame of mind. The last straw had been entering Fort St John; it felt really oppressive, even worse than

Fort Nelson. Boring, utilitarian buildings lined the road; it was a place to work rather than to live. Nothing to encourage joy, nothing to arouse playfulness. I slowed while passing a group of First Nations youths, stoned, full of hostile attitude. I could understand why, unlike me their choice to leave wasn't so easy!

I turned off Route 97 and took a detour through Peace Valley, hoping it would live up to its name. My thoughts and emotions were collapsing in on themselves, a dark gloom persisted, and it was about time to do something about it. The valley did portray an aura of peace, a tranquil setting with lush farmland and a gentle river meandering gracefully through. It was open countryside and good road, once again the belt of tarmac wound along following the natural curves and undulations of the land. Though purely agricultural it instilled a more relaxed, content demeanour; more conducive to the nature of the land. It was a huge relief negotiating bends, reading the road ahead and not having my head in the clouds. Sitting on a bike merely holding open the throttle does nothing for me, more involvement is a must, the more the merrier. Disregarding the occasional pickup the scene probably hadn't changed for decades, I soaked it up, once more feeling in touch with my surroundings. Notice boards of a forthcoming hydro-electric dam tainted my perception of peaceful perfection; my mood remained a bit subdued, what a shame to spoil such a beautiful valley. Frequent measuring posts indicated the height at which the water level would reach, such a waste. All I could do was to enjoy it while I could.

The afternoon drew to a close, dusk was on its way, and preparations for the night were overdue. As if on cue, a campsite signpost pointed up a gravel track enticing me towards a copse of trees well off the road. Everything was falling into place, or so it seemed. "NO MOTORCYCLES," declared the most prominent of the notice boards at the entrance, I was gutted. In fact I was livid, taking it as a personal affront. So much so I had to quell a desire to rip the offending sign off the fence and stomp it into the dust! As a quiet, solo motorcyclist I couldn't understand the problem. I'd come across such bias too many times before; I dare say there'd been an incident at some stage, maybe bikers being loud and rowdy. But are all car drivers banned when one carload arrive and cause trouble? Having never seen a notice banning car drivers, I don't think so. And off went Mr Grumpy, once more dissatisfied with life, unable to see where fairness ever came into it.

With little time left before darkness fell my choices were limited, in the last glimmer of sun I left the road and pottered down to a semi-clear patch by the river. Imperfect by any stretch of the imagination, it would have to do. It could easily prove an obstruction to any fisherman wishing to launch his boat, it could also be blocking animal trails along the waterway, and by that I mean bears. But I was at the end of my tether, I was camping in that spot, come what may. By torchlight I proceeded to set camp, fighting off hordes of mosquitoes, only once food was cooking did I soil my hands with insect repellent. Peeling and chopping the vegetables was purgatory, the little bleeders made my life miserable, not that I needed their help. At last the tent was pitched, the food was ready, both bike and I were out of sight and the bear spray was hanging from my belt. I pitied any bear that chose that night to disturb me. Without enthusiasm I again shovelled a hasty meal down my throat, satiated but not satisfied sleep dominated my thoughts, until looking up and noticing the sky. Was it a hallucination? I literally stepped back for a better view, no, not my imagination. The Northern Lights! A shimmering veil across the whole sky, like a luminous net curtain wafting gently in the breeze. Now that was something to take the breath away, so spectacular, so unexpected, so beautiful! Standing, mesmerised by the display, every gram of stress drained away. The effect was uplifting, all the negative thoughts left me and I just stood, mouth agape, in awe. I never thought to get the camera, just never thought anything at all. After some time it gradually faded, how long I have no idea, it didn't matter. A simple quirk of nature opened my eyes, cleared my mind, draining away the manmade problems of the last couple of days. The timing couldn't have been better, at a crucial moment nature had come to my rescue, opening my eyes and lifting my spirits. If I gave any credence to religion I would have prostrated myself in gratitude.

Waking at peace with the world makes for a perfect start to the day. Surrounded by gently rolling hills in a sparsely populated valley the setting was wonderful, Peace Valley indeed! Tranquillity pervaded my soul, no high, no low, a sense of equanimity obtained with no effort on my behalf. Hudson's Hope stood at the end of the valley, an example of rural Canada in all its glory; log cabins and laid back lifestyle. A serene backwater with friendly inhabitants pleased to assist, a pleasure to delay departure, to meet and share a few, brief moments with them. An area destined for destruction, the homesteaders refused to give up the fight, though with the Hydro Company already owning most of the land the future was bleak. The opportunity to share a small part of their world, while it lasted, was truly appreciated. Almost with regret, the bike was once again cranked into life. It was hard departing with the knowledge that a second visit would be met by a huge concrete monstrosity and an immense body of water. So much for progress.

At Chetwynd,I rejoined Highway 97, finding myself back in the main tourist belt, destination Jasper, the head of the glacier fields. Gone were the boring straight roads prior to St John devoid of interesting views, in front lay lofty mountain peaks, winding roads and promising scenery. The way ahead lay before me, twisting and turning tarmac spurred me on, its black ribbon vanishing into tree filled gullies, reappearing God knows where. Invigorated by the promise of excitement, I wound on the throttle, delighted with the chance to once again test the grip at the outer edge of my tyres. Another river led the way, followed closely by the road and flanked by immense mountains. Between the rocky promontories lay a broad belt of farmland, hay ricks and horses completing the perfect picture of agrarian paradise. A speeding pickup broke my reverie, filled with hollering hicks hurling insults. Even thick country hicks couldn't detract from my elation though, I was back on track, my world once more an adventure playground. Like a little kid I whooped with excitement while cranking it round the bends. Breath-taking views filled the horizon but I couldn't be bothered stopping for photos. The experience is so much more than the view, much more than a photo can portray. Sometimes you have to live for the moment, keepsakes come and go but memories live forever.

For days economic speeds had been adhered to, common sense dictating my pace. Both route and landscape had proved uninspiring, now it was thrilling and I wanted to make the most of it while it lasted. And of course it didn't last too long before I unexpectedly ran out of fuel. Onto reserve in two hundred miles, that was going some; damned bike should get two hundred and fifty miles out of a tank before reserve, minimum. Not that it mattered, gas stations were frequent enough, if you remember to stop and fill up that is. It's generally best not to take your mind off the job in hand, distractions can prove very inconvenient. My crash helmet had gotten loose, flopping around on my head and letting in a lot of wind noise, and way too much cold air. Having stopped to treat myself to a new helmet in Prince George, my thoughts were on how cool I looked. I nearly blew the chance to fill up as I left town. A dodgy U-turn had to be made at a sign declaring no more fuel for one hundred miles, if only they'd situated it before the gas station, rather than half a mile after. I wasn't the only one either, another guy at the gas station was shaking his head in bemusement. We laughed about it, breaking the ice. He proved a fountain of knowledge on my proposed route so it was actually a fortuitous cock up. Especially for him, I left my shades on his car. How the hell was I meant to look cool without shades?

All in all the day was stupendous, everything fell into place nicely, despite the slight glitch. As is so often the case, if your demeanour is negative that's what you attract. Fill your head and heart with joy and positive thoughts and so much more comes your way. To quote an old adage, "*You reap what you sow*". There are no guarantees in life but this philosophy rings true for me, the best experiences happen when you're open to the possibility. So, content with a mere two hundred miles for the day I chugged into an inexpensive campsite, happy to chill out and rest. As was a Canadian biker, a guy called Rob, who happened to camp in the pitch next to mine. It only took a brief introduction before his bottle of bourbon came out and we proceeded to demolish it, in spite of hangover warnings ringing at the back of my mind. Live for today I countered, and down it went with no further resistance. We struck an instant accord, our conversation was deep and meaningful, our philosophical views striking in their similarity. The level of drunkenness didn't diminish the effect it had on me, Rob's appreciation of meeting a kindred spirit was transparent. And no, it wasn't drunken bullshit, the alcohol merely loosened our tongues, lubricated our vocal cords. We talked of life, love and loss. We covered aspirations and dreams, past and future. We discussed my journey, my son. Without pity or awkwardness he listened, empathised and encouraged. Miraculously I coped without getting upset, with relief I divulged every aspect of my life with Cai, the depth of my loss, the emptiness of a future without him. Fair play to the guy, he was a rock. It did me the world of good, bolstered my spirits no end, and that was the last I saw or heard of him. I only hope he might, someday, appreciate how exceptional our meeting was for me. I also hope his hangover the following morning was as drastic as mine, it was a real humdinger.

Mountains lined the way without a break, in every direction. A continuous ridge ran to one side of the road, behind stood rugged peaks laced with snow. Opposite a broad, slow moving river slid over glacial silt, seemingly disappearing into a distant wall of rock. It didn't matter which way I turned another scene rocked my boots. Though riding hard and fast I took in every sight as it came into view, each change had me gasping in delighted wonder. With no apparent end in sight I could afford to squander the experience. The road was exhilarating, not for its curvature but for the fresh panorama that unfolded round every bend, my pleasure increasing exponentially. Bright sunlight shone forth and the skyline showed startling white mountains but there was a distinct nip in the air. As long as I could maintain core temperature I wasn't about to hang around. Stopping at McBride to down some painkillers, in a vain attempt to purge my God-awful hangover, I had to admire the passing graffiti. Rumbling rail carriages acted as a mobile canvas for youthful creativity. Artistic, rather than autistic, the quality artwork brought a smile of appreciation, it may not have been fine art but it was fine by me. A defunct railway station restored as a coffee shop/ Internet cafe supplied sustenance and set me on my way. I was more than ready for the next instalment, wasting no time I hammered through the gears hitting 80mph as I notched it into top. Nothing was going to slow my progress, approaching another pickup I pulled out for the overtake. Drawing alongside I glanced over, to be met with a beaming smile and thumbs up. The guy sure knew where I was at, he was with me all the way. With a nod of the head and the wink of an eye I flew past, spurred on by his inane grin.

It just got better and better, the trees thinned revealing more bare rock, the mountains closed in and became heavier with snow. The features became more defined without trees blurring their outlines. Where the snow lay thinnest it further accentuated these features, again showing numerous stratified layers, now clearly seen as multiple thin horizontal lines, almost like veins of quartz. Here, I did have to stop and capture the details for prosperity. It was little more than a hop off, hop back on the bike, allowing barely enough time to agree with a truck driver how awesome it was. I left him to enjoy his coffee while setting off again in search of cheap thrills. And then ahead, an immense solitary mountain stood, seemingly blocking all ways south, dwarfing the whole landscape. The enormity of the rock was incomprehensible, snow bound peaks of ominous dark grey, on a foundation of lighter, layered composition. Various rock sandwiched between each other, bonded by subterranean forces, shaped by erosion, a magnificent example of nature's extraordinary power. Faced with a single lump of rock of such proportion, sculpted to such perfection, how could we doubt that forces greater than ours were responsible for its creation? Is it any wonder humanity has sought mountain heights to commune with God, that the ancients believed mountain tops the abode of gods? It didn't reach the sky, it consumed it, blotting out the rest of the world. It even made me forget my hangover!

That was only for starters though, the main course was yet to follow. From Prince George, Route 16 had paved the way providing glorious views of enchanting mountain vistas. By comparison the road itself was tedious, with few bends and little to demand my attention which was just as well as I gave it scant regard. Between Jasper and Banff, Route 93 carved its way through the heart of the Glacier fields reputed to be second to none for scenery. Jasper marked the official start of the Glacier Fields Highway, it was heaving with tourists. Every shop and building's sole purpose was to relieve the tourists of their money, and each was packed to the gunwhales. I had no intention of fraternising with the plebs, so I went in search of a campsite instead.

Being barely below the snow line it was damned cold, yet still the crowds flocked onto site, squabbling over the limited bundles of wood at extortionate prices, interested only in comfort. Again I left them to it, found my allotted spot, and gathered the remaining wood of previous fires around; plenty for a small fire before an early night. Even better, my scavenged firewood had dried out, unlike the fresh, hard to burn bundles supplied by the site office. Winter wasn't letting me get too far ahead of it, my thermals had stayed on since donning them at Bell 2, twenty four hours a day. I wasn't cold thanks to the correct combination of layers, even when riding long hours I kept warm. It only took six layers on my upper body and three below, underwear was essential due to the airflow crotch of my desert trousers, it's just as well I'm not a brass monkey.

Our minds can be our best friends or our greatest enemies, our salvation or our destruction. When events in our lives become beyond acceptance, beyond endurance, our minds can be in mortal danger. Sanity is a fickle thing, once lost it is hard to find. Cut off from the outside world it swirls around, adrift, folding in on itself, reaching out in desperation. Adverse circumstances can repel us from the familiar, the source of anguish, thrust us into another world or to retreat into our darkest recesses. With luck events will bring secure mooring points, safe havens, resources to effect repairs. And so my journey continued, a recurrence of safety stops, of people who paved the way providing temporary safe havens. Casual acquaintances come and go, maybe. Sometimes a fleeting moment in your life by the right person can prove to be so much more. Generally as I travelled I maintained the image of the great white explorer, hiding behind my achievements, relishing the anonymity. Occasionally I'd open up, let it all out, allow someone to see the real task at hand. Maybe subconsciously I became adept at choosing those I could trust, to me it happened seldom and randomly. However it came about, rarely was it a mistake. Of the few I opened up to they all turned out to be gems, and at Jasper I met another.

Another biker, a long term traveller, with nearly one hundred thousand miles under his belt. We talked bikes, made comparisons of equipment and clothing, listened and learnt from each other. He was another Horizons Unlimited subscriber, yet with disdain for the *Touratech*-equipped monstrosities favoured by many. His contempt for the over wieldy beasts produced by BMW matched mine, he favoured lighter machines with off-road capabilities. He wasn't afraid to admire my choice of bike gear, and admit the failings of his own. He was also aware of the guy who lost his son; it took a while before he made the connection. Respect and encouragement was his response, not pity, not sympathy; it came straight from the heart. He'd lost his brother some years before, it had haunted him much of his life. He could only imagine what I was experiencing. He could not imagine a better way to deal with it. Another kindred spirit, a delight to meet and a person I quickly admired. We shared his meagre supply of beers that night, and my plentiful supply of coffee the following morning, then went our own separate ways.

The morning crept in hidden by low-lying mist, a dense carpet swallowing scrub and tents alike. Though thinning above the waist, everything beyond the immediate trees was still obscured by a wispy, greyish blur. Neither sight nor sound permeates its depths, a quiet, still fairy tale land. A harem of elk appears from the gloom, *blasé* to say the least, not so much as a flicker of an eyebrow as they pass close by. It was the stag that warranted attention, and he made sure we all knew it, standing tall and proud, casting his watchful eye over anything that moved: a wary creature in an ethereal world, a world of magical creatures, and enchanted woods. Are those wood elves winding their way merrily through the misty depths of the forest? No, it's the German family coming back from the toilet block. Time to depart methinks!

Chapter Ten

The Colombian Icefields (nothing to do with its South American namesake) claimed as one of the largest glacial troughs in existence, is reputed as a "not to be missed" destination in North America. I can't argue with that, it lived up to all expectations, and then some. Main highways in Canada have a tendency to be long, straight and boring, Highway 93 was no exception but for once it proved beneficial. Staying within the National Park's 60mph limit was a breeze, it meant little attention had to be paid to the road. Almost my full attention could be paid to the outstanding geological wonder all around. Other vehicles were actually overtaking me. It was more stop than start anyway, barely a mile went past without jumping off the bike and taking pictures of yet another unbelievable scene. After an hour and a half, I'd only covered fifty miles, would I ever reach Banff at such a pace? With considerable will power the decision was made to lessen the time spent viewing life through a lens and just appreciate the magnificence. No matter how hard I tried I knew pictures would never do the route justice, it's truly a place to experience up close, a place to feel as much as to see. It was almost a shame each time I mounted the bike again. Standing, slack jawed, in appreciation of the display was like paying homage. Only passing vehicles intruded on the feeling, bringing me back to reality and the pressing need to keep on the move. Despite being a bright sunny day occasional flurries of snow brought back to mind the close onset of winter, try as I might there seemed no escape but try I must. If only the scenery were not so awesome!

Which way to look? Mesmerised by the rock formations to one side all else was forgotten, then a glance round would reveal a completely different picture, a whole new vista. It was too much to take in, each peak stamping its individual character, easily distinguishable from the others. To my untrained eye the abundant layering suggested the majority was rock of a sedimentary nature but all similarity stopped there. A sandy coloured ridge, long and jagged, evoked memories of Roman or Greek architecture, ancient fortifications, weather worn over the ages, now battered and dishevelled, merely a suggestion of their past glory. Darker rock dominated towards the west, still clearly stratified, weighed down by deep pockets of snow, once again giving definition to the stratification. Huge plates thrust up from the earth's crust as if on hinges, like a giant trap door. The ancient seabed, smooth rock sloping at 45° with sedimentary layers exposed on the ragged vertical side, showing the direction of force, the line of fracture; numerous angles on numerous facets of rock, show unimaginable destructive forces creating tectonic havoc in days gone by. They looked like parts of a giant jigsaw puzzle, pushed out of place and exposed, then weathered over millenia. Softer layers, more susceptible to erosion, scoured from between their rocky sandwich created channels for deeper deposits of snow. Above, serrated-edged ridges cut through the sky. It was so jumbled and chaotic, yet gave the impression you could almost push mountains back into position like re-engaging displaced gearwheels. All too apparent was the upheaval of a fragile planetary crust, simple geological theories brought to life. Now I truly understood the might of nature, how punitive are our attempts to interfere with such power.

Once subjected to tectonic transformation newly exposed features are at the mercy of atmospheric mayhem. For thousands of years scoured and scraped, gouged and ground, pounded and pummelled, left to stand abused and battered, as evidence of a merciless assault. Apparently random devastation could as easily be the arduous task of a skilled sculptor. Impossible to replicate yet simple to appreciate, the glacial trough took me away into a dream world of fantasy. Preconceptions bore no relation to reality, glaciers are so much more than large flows of ice gouging through valleys, a host of icy tributaries cascading down the mountainsides. Like double cream poured from a jug, a rivulet overflowing to gather on a lower ledge, spreading out thickly until again overflowing, onto each successive ledge laying thicker on its descent. Gleaming purest white in the sun, each branch of the glacier gathered to become a vast field of imperceptibly slow creeping ice, a dirty mottled grey in the shade.

The freedom on a bike allows brief stops at any point, without causing an obstruction; it was these stops I favoured. At viewpoints the tourists gathered, by the busload. People of every nation crowded the lay-bys, queuing to be the next in line for a photo of themselves obscuring the wonderful scenery behind. 'Please, you can take a photo of us?' If that is what they wanted I was only too happy to oblige, eager to see them on their way, keen for more solitude, a chance for undisturbed amazement. I could only imagine them showing family and friends the holiday snaps, Here's a picture of me and Wong si Toa, here's another with Wei Ling. Look here, Mai Li is poking out her tongue!' Incomprehension darkened their features when I insisted I didn't want my photo taken with my own camera. Relentless insistence by a Japanese family got the best of m, so I posed and it made them happy. It was no skin off my nose really. I'm sure the folks back home appreciated it when I put it on my blog, although I'm equally sure they know what I look like!

Lay-bys and photo opportunities increased as the main glacier approached, temptation for further stops decreased as the hordes swarmed around every vantage point. Behold, the main feature, I couldn't believe my eyes. Not only were the vehicles parked nose to tail, the glacier itself was awash with activity. Specially designed coaches ran excursions across the ice field, carrying the lazy rich onto one of Canada's pride and joys. Unable to hold contempt for individual tourists it still saddened me to see nature cheapened in such a way. Holding a strong 'look but don't touch' attitude made it difficult witnessing the commercial exploitation of the natural heritage. How many years will it be until, with hindsight, such activities are looked at with scorn and regret, when the wearing away of the glacier field becomes measurable to the eye? After a phenomenally exhilarating experience leading up to the main attraction, it was almost a relief to turn my back on it, I'm surprised they haven't renamed it 'Winter Wonderland'. I'd been heading for Banff but forewarned of the commercialism there, it was no longer on the agenda, I'd had enough. Route 93 would have carried me through Banff and on into Montana, instead I could hang a right onto Route 95 at Radium Hot Springs. A forestry trail from Canal Flats would take me many miles away from any highway. It wasn't a difficult decision and there were no second thoughts.

Looping through the wilderness and spitting me out just before the American border it offered everything I'd learnt to relish, another day of isolation, another sojourn into the heart of nature, another challenge. I even had enough time left that day to ride twenty miles to White Swan Lake, and camp for the night. With a nice early start I'd be finished and in the states by mid-day. I'd only have a one hundred kilometre ride in the morning, how long could that take?

With a promising start I reached the campsite as dusk approached. The trail had proved reliable with a flat gravelled track for most the way. Potholes and corrugations posed no problems, they were negotiated at full speed without the slightest twitch. Uphill most of the way, the views had begun to improve; it was only the drop-offs that made the mind boggle. Plunging down almost vertical slopes of loose screed for more than one hundred feet; it certainly added a degree of danger. With loose gravel to the very edge, no side barriers and nothing to slow the descent, going over the edge wasn't an option. Going wide on left-handers was to be avoided, at all costs. The going was easy enough though, straight past the Hot Springs and up to White Swan Lake, once more into the heart of the mountains. A virtually deserted campsite suggested an uninterrupted ride the following day, folk just didn't frequent these parts. Crystal clear skies promised a bright sunny day, for that night though it meant freezing temperatures, without a fire. Needless to say it was an early night, huddled in my sleeping bag wearing full thermals, including my Sealskin socks; my own stench was preferable to exposure.

An early start should have been made but being curled up 'snug as a bug' in my sleeping bag was just too cosy. Despite waking at 6 a.m., I buried myself deeper and stayed put until 9 a.m. Mmm, cream cheese and Ritz crackers, so much for forward planning, the hot coffee more than made up for the lack of sustenance though. And at last, a chance to dump my old crash helmet. An eager Park Warden had posted a warning notice on my tent, without change, I hadn't put my camping fee into the payment box on arrival, and I wasn't about to pay $20 for an $8 fee. I left my change, about $5, a note and the crash helmet. The note gave my home details and offered the crash helmet as part payment. Stating clearly my nationality, and how long I proposed to travel, I suggested the Park authority notify me at home if this wasn't acceptable, at which time the outstanding amount would be forwarded. It appealed to my sense of humour and rid me of excess baggage. I never did hear from them!

As the sun crept into view the temperature rose, with the warmth came some form of enthusiasm, and so began my last leg through Canadian territory. It was a simple matter of following White River and then Bull River. With no signs of habitation on the map it was set to be a peaceful ride without interruption. Continuing from White Swan Lake was a rougher track, sporting more variety of surfaces, gravel gave way to stonier ground interspersed with sand and occasional muddy hollows. There was virtually no ground water, the only intimidating aspect was the constant drop-off plummeting into the depths. Not being in a hurry, a reasonable speed of 40-50mph was plenty to maximise the grin factor. Behaving itself perfectly the bike responded to my every wish, twitches and minor slides were expected and taken in my stride. An unexpected patch of deep crud saw the bike slew sideways, carrying us to the very edge of the precipitous drop. I slowed down a touch then but not for long, only until my heart rate returned to normal. It gave more confidence again, allowing me to relax, not be daunted by the drop off. Twenty miles in, rounding a tight bend on well compacted earth, keeping the throttle open, I damned near shat myself. The trail had turned into a badly rutted, mud splattered, slippery nightmare. With no time to stop, I had to go for it, pick my line, keep out the ruts on the thin band of solid(ish) dirt and keep on the power. Wey hey, it worked, emerging victorious I felt as pleased as punch for not panicking, wet slippery surfaces scare me, I'm not used to them. Maybe that should have been the time to reassess speed versus surface conditions, but no, it spurred me on. I was loving it. Further from civilisation than before and unperturbed by either the isolation or conditions, everything was under control.

Getting progressively rougher with every mile, the trail became a riverbed. Gone were the compacted gravel surfaces, even the sand had been scoured clear by seasonal torrents of water. Solid rock, pebbles and cobbles dominated. Luckily the plummeting drop had been left behind, now it was only the instability and unevenness of loose rocks to contend with. Smaller substrate tended to form a ridge along the edge of the main track. These dictated my line of travel. They made a narrow trail and weren't subjected to the unpredictable movement of the cobbles. The only safe solution to tackling such terrain was painstakingly slow and I wasn't in the mood. By picking my lines with care, good headway was made. The bends and deposits of rivers are fairly predictable, lines of silt and sand would form an arc round the bend, held together by the matted roots of riverside vegetation. Alternating, left then right, I sometimes took the inside line, sometimes the outside, it depended which offered the best road surface. Swapping sides would be achieved upright, in a straight line, carefully choosing areas of smaller pebbles or solid rock. The cobbles posed a hazard, moving haphazardly and sliding from under the wheels, completely unpredictable.

And so it happened, I was over confident, sweeping round on the outside of a bend, following a good line of stable sand, only to run out of tractable surface smack bang into a virtual field of boulders. Caught unawares the bike started bucking and bouncing amongst the cobbles before any action could be taken. I fought with it to get it upright, hanging on for dear life trying not to get thrown off. Smoother ground lay over the far side and the bike was wrestled in that direction. Momentum had been lost and I was in too high a gear, having to think my way through all the variables took too long. Before usable power could be transferred back to the rear wheel we came to a standstill. Off balance, with cobbles rolling beneath my feet, we went down, the bike pinning me beneath it. BOLLOCKS!

Miraculously the unevenness of the terrain meant I wasn't hopelessly trapped, my luggage provided a cushion, a protective pocket between the front and back of the bike, saving my leg from being crushed. Managing to squirm from beneath it my instant reaction was to heave my precious machine back onto its feet but it wouldn't budge. Stepping back I surveyed the scene, there it laid, wheels in mid-air, handlebars laying downwards into a slight ditch. Try again, no chance! It was not to be a simple matter of lifting it up, nor could I expect any help from the odd passerby, I was at least forty miles from the nearest highway. A few attempts were made to manoeuvre it into a better position, I tried dragging it further into the ditch, pulling either end up out of the ditch, nothing, it was reluctant to cooperate in any way. Time to use my brain, having more of that than brawn. In full gear, with thermals beneath, the blazing sun boiled me dry in seconds, stripping to the waist I downed the last of my water and set to work. Using a tree branch as a lever, it snapped. A stouter one was tried, it held out but the bike merely slid along it, and settled back into the same position once the pressure was off. A pile of boulders were used to rest the lever on, the bike was halfway up but beyond my ability to raise it further. Resting the fuel tank on my knee, I struggled to get a decent hold, straining to lift it that bit more. It was a long way from upright and my strength was fading fast, no matter how hard I strained it was going no further. My mind was racing, my thoughts jumbled, I needed to clear them. *Step back again, re-assess the situation, think.* With fuel leaking from the overflow time was at a premium, there wasn't long enough to come up with any fanciful methods. Lightening the load was the only way I could see round the problem, get the luggage off and try again. With us both stripped our last hope lay before us, putting every ounce of remaining strength into it, I heaved, swore, shouted and screamed as it slowly neared a vertical stance. Painfully slow I struggled, until, with one last gut-wrenching heave, it stood upright. The relief was so overwhelming I nearly dropped it over the opposite side, not having put the kickstand down for that eventuality. I also neglected to push it out the boulder field before loading up again, what was that about using my brain? The bike and fuel were checked, only slight damage and seemingly plenty of fuel left, it would have to do. Exhausted and dehydrated I may have been, beaten I wasn't. I would persevere, come what may! Ten minutes later I came across a couple of hunters in their pickup, heading the way I'd just come. Typical, just bloody typical.

The distance of that trail remains a mystery, in the process of trying to lever up the bike the speedometer trip counter got broken. Thirty minutes after the fall a sign declared another one hundred kilometres to the highway, one of us was definitely confused. My calculations, by average speed and time, made it over sixty miles, that morning alone, with another twenty the evening before. There again who was counting? An unknown amount of fuel remained in the tank, an unknown mileage had been ridden, there really was little point. It would be nice to put it down to blind faith, but no, it was sheer pig-headed determination. The only way was forward and nothing was going to deter me, which seems to work once in a while. Whatever the distance remaining, it proved a delightful ride. A short way ahead the track levelled out and the surface improved. Not quite flat, compacted gravel led the way, only a little mud and short, washed out sections were encountered, where good sense won over bravado for a change. My speed rarely crept above forty, for economy reasons, recklessness only goes so far, I had no desire to run out of fuel if it could be avoided.

Bull River hosts lovely venues for eager rock climbers, nothing of the magnitude of the days immediately before but gorgeously exposed, clean rock, with untold new routes to discover. My only concern was in the pleasure of gently winding through shaded avenues, thankful for the peace and tranquillity, the total absence of another living soul. In fact there was a distinct lack of life, the gentle swaying of the trees the only sign of movement, the only noise that of my own engine which never fails to satisfy me, even if it is only softly burbling along. Finally I emerged onto the highway again, without even reaching my fuel reserve. I'd not worried unduly, it would have been pointless, apart from conserving fuel the matter was out of my hands. Without relief or exuberance Canada lay behind me, my endeavours had won through. Resilience had seen me through the hard times, awestruck enthusiasm gained from the good times. Both had played their part. It had been a journey largely of self-gratification, it had needed to be. And now I was ready to continue, ready to face the long road ahead. It was with that feeling of contentment the American border was approached.

Press shoot of the intrepid pair

If you go down to the woods today!

Initial view of the Rockies ahead – Watson Lake to Fort Nelson

Valley overview from 11,500ft - Montrose to Durango, Colorado

Natural skyscraper - Arizona desert

The Grand Canyon - Arizona

Chapter Eleven

By the time I'd been granted entry back into the States any sense of contentment and tranquillity had been ripped asunder, all by one hard arsed border official. Where else in the world are youthful exuberances held against you for the rest of your life? Long forgotten misdemeanours must be declared, even after twenty five to thirty years, making me a marked man for life. For joy riding at the age of seventeen and smoking a bit of pot in college, I have a whole rigmarole of extra hassle every single time I enter the States. Each time alarm bells ring in Homeland Security's computer system, and I have to go through "secondary evaluation," further questioning. In some dark recess of my mind I could appreciate this, but there are ways and means. So it was no surprise when I was asked to park the bike and step inside, only to be meet by Jarhead in the reception area. Probing questions I expected, the purpose of my visit needed explaining, intended duration stated, previously it had all been a formality. Not this time, Jarhead wanted his pound of flesh! The nature and dates of my convictions were requested. They were all in front of him on the computer screen, he just wanted to make me squirm. Demanding explanations for every aspect of my journey started getting personal, too personal for a public reception room. I requested more privacy and was taken into an adjoining office, where he got even worse. The basic story of my journey was explained, surely anyone would understand where I was at. I wasn't expecting sympathy, there again nor was I expecting his ire to rise. What was his problem, had the lack of an appropriate, "Yes Sir," pissed him off? He really started getting on my case, accusing me of expecting special treatment because I'd lost my son. The bloke really had some problem. He was the worst sort of corrupt official you can find, one who gets off on the power trip, who bullies and intimidates because it makes him feel good. A person who uses his position to the detriment of anyone he can wield his power against, this was what I'd expected in the States, why it came as a shock I don't know. No-one had been like that so far, a blessed relief at the time. There was no way of placating him, my only thoughts were to leave and find another option, another border crossing. Half rising off the seat I told him to forget it, I'd head back into Canada. If there was a right thing to say that was not it. He erupted, 'I could bust your arse boy, I could make sure you never step foot in the United States again. I could...' Unable to do anything else I stayed put and clamped my jaw firmly shut, looking at the wall, not even trusting myself to look at him. For the first time it was the right response, it allowed him to feel I was powerless, he was the one in control, and I was at his mercy. And that was all there was to it, after that outburst he acted as if he was my best friend. What a jerk!

It wasn't the welcome I wanted back into the States. It left a sour taste in the mouth, a bitter tang at the back of my throat that no amount of spitting would clear. Being scorching hot didn't improve my demeanour, I rode into the first town, Eureka, outraged. It failed to provide any revelations, merely a useful gas station, a place to strip naked and shed my thermals (in their toilet of course). Once rid of my winter warmers I could spare the energy to mingle, to listen to the locals' views on the presidential prelims, if that town was anything to go by Hilary Clinton had no chance. Montana was a land of mere mortals, of simple folk with simple needs. It was a land inhabited by staunch supporters of freedom, the freedom to bear guns, the freedom to ride without crash helmets. With a seeming disregard for either wildlife or their own lives you could say it was the freedom to kill and be killed at stake. I mustn't let the views of a few tarnish the good name of them all, that would be so unfair. All the Montanans I met were a fun-loving people with a warm and hearty welcome for a lone Brit on his "modersickle". They weren't toting guns or blowing away anything that moved, not on the streets anyway. Hogs and hot rods were paraded around the towns, big brazen machines dressed to impress, hot metal with a thunderous roar. It made me come over all American, "*Goddamn if I don't jest lurv them mussle mersheens, if it don't have a beefy V8 packin' the power, slurping the juice, it ain't worth havin'.*" Yep, they surely loved their heavy metal, I bet they dig shit-kicking music too.

One of the handful of States without crash helmet laws, it had to be taken advantage of. Of course it did! Fifty miles spent cruising, the wind in my hair, total freedom. The only trouble was it made the eyes water something wicked, every head check threatened to wrench the shades off my face and the wind noise was horrific, it did my hair no favours whatsoever. This isn't how I remembered it. Unlike my days as a reprobate youth, riding helmetless through the back roads of Wiltshire, this wasn't exactly exciting. For some reason being legal made it somewhat boring, I guess forbidden fruit tastes so much sweeter. So back on went the lid and up went my comfort levels. Bugger the freedom to splat my brain, if I couldn't do it in comfort I didn't want to know.

Winding through the upper reaches of Montana and Idaho a serene rural landscape unrolled before my wheels, bountiful and beautiful, in a purely agricultural way. Gone were the monumental peaks, the blinding snow, mind-blowing vistas, and freezing winds. Those days of intense joy and extreme wonder seemed a million miles away. Lazy days and sleepy byways seemed the norm in rural Montana. The change was nice, not wonderful but nice. It's difficult to get excited over cows chewing the cud and a landscape empty of anything but cattle, water and grass. Being woken by blazing sunshine was delightful though. No wet tent to pack away, no huddling over the camping stove to fend off the encroaching cold, no need to treasure the precious warmth of my morning coffee. How could anyone begrudge a leisurely start with the sun beating down on his back? Gorgeous sunshine has a knack of improving one's disposition. Pottering along through a mix of pasture and wetlands, waving trucks past at the sedate pace of 50mph was as relaxed as it gets. The world was on a go-slow and for once I wasn't about to upset the applecart, with time to kill I was in no hurry. And so with a sense of tranquil acceptance I passed swathes of open grassland, crystal clear lakes, and lazy rivers meandering through steep escarpments of crumbling sandstone.

Heading through Troy, taking Route 56 south past Bull Lake, west along Route 200 and finally the 90 to Post Falls. I had a pre-arranged rest stop at Coeur d'Alene and was more than happy to be met at a convenient fast food joint and be escorted back to Iona's. Actually, it was meant to be a prearranged stop! Somewhere between leaving home and Cai's demise, my caring friend and former employer had neglected to pre-warn their sprightly great Aunt that I was due. I'd phoned the day before expecting recognition, a hearty welcome, maybe relief to hear from me. But no, there was no knowledge or prior warning of my possible arrival, no knowledge of who I was or what I was doing. But what a sweet lady, I faltered in mid-speech, lost for words, only to be asked if a place to stay was needed. What could I do but accept? So hats off to kind, sweet Aunties, Iona proved much more than just kind and sweet, few could have understood my grieving heart as completely as her, nor provide a safety net to cushion my ragged emotions.

Chapter Twelve

Again a break in the journey was well timed. With six thousand six hundred miles on the clock a third service was overdue, and replacement parts were needed. The boulder field bungle in Canada had taken its toll, the damaged trip counter needed sorting. At a glance the odometer had allowed immediate knowledge of how many miles I had left in the tank. Relying so heavily on it to calculate fuel consumption meant I wanted it repaired, or replaced if need be. And that wasn't the only fault since my moment of moto misfortune, whilst stuck in congested traffic problems with overheating had occurred. The fan refused to switch on, the bike had to be turned off whenever caught in a traffic jam. I can't claim to be impressed, either with the cooling switch failure or the rapid wear of the Dunlop tyres which had come as standard. The rear needed replacing again, three thousand miles for a rear tyre is not acceptable. It was about time for an upgrade. Despite the front having a reasonable amount of tread left they were being replaced as a matching pair, the dealers recommended Avon's. I'd have preferred Bridgestone's, I knew the quality and longevity of their Trail Wing range. The deciding factor proved to be delivery time, one day for the Avon's as opposed to a week for the Bridgestone's.

Large dealers with multiple franchises are not who I would have chosen if given a choice but I wasn't given that choice. They were the only Kawasaki dealer around, and their services were what I would have expected of a large franchise rather than what I'd have wanted. I was just another customer, I could take it or leave it. It mattered little to them. They were certainly not going to go out their way to help, they didn't even bother to sort the cooling switch on warranty.

'Here sir, send this bill to Kawasaki and they'll reimburse you'. As that seemed my only choice, I did, and never heard a damned word from Kawasaki. The work was of a good standard though, there were certainly no grumbles with what was done, purely their lack of effort. I knew the tappets had become a touch noisy and had asked for them to be checked, 'That's perfectly acceptable sir, we decided there was no need to check them.' Whatever happened to the premise that the customer was always right? I knew it was a bugger of a job, it required a top-end strip down, which was why I asked them to do it.

Whilst the dealer failed to impress, my host more than made up for it, in ways that could never have been foreseen. Before leaving the UK, I'd known that Iona had lost her husband unexpectedly, I'd been assured she'd appreciate the company. I certainly did. And how much more poignant my visit was by then? Of course, by the time I actually met Iona she'd confirmed who I was, and been appraised of recent events. I was so glad, it wasn't a story I'd want to dump on a stranger whose house I'd just arrived at to stay. But common ground gives a common understanding between people, Iona welcomed me into her home with open arms, and an equally open heart.

Another home, another hound. Joe, the Coonhound who posed no problems with friendship or trust. What he gained in nasal supremacy he lacked in mental agility. A true pleasure to be around, just don't let him loose, once his nose is to the ground nothing else exists. Apart from following whatever scent he can find, his favourite occupation was being as close to me as possible, preferably making physical contact and receiving all of my attention.

Coeur d'Alene (Heart of an Awl), so named to describe how sharp the local Indians were when trading with early French settlers is now a quaint old colonial town. A very quiet town in itself, centred around the Lake, with tree lined paths around it and continuing along the river. Seaplanes bobbed at the end of jetties, locals played beach volleyball on imported sand, and cafés lined the sunny sidewalks. Art and culture feature high on the agenda, with open-air concerts organised by local celebrities. My brief visit took in only the places that kept me fed and watered, cafes, restaurants and the local sport bar (which is, after all, essential American culture).

Most of all I appreciated the companionship, another kindred spirit, someone who knew all too well where I was at. A simple coffee in the sunshine proved so much more than the chance to soak up the local vibes. Our openness centred on our shared grief, it had me in tears, closely followed by Iona. First she had to comfort me, and then I needed to return the favour. We must have painted a terrible picture, but it gave us both a chance to unload and move on, if only a little at a time. Support and understanding always bring relief, many people are touched by another's tragedy, the special ones actually make it easier to bear. Only fellow sufferers truly know just how deep the barb bites! Once again my heart was lightened by a perfect stranger, as with all who helped, I left owing my eternal gratitude. Transactions of any kind, and I do mean emotional too, are so much more meaningful when both sides benefit. It was a pleasure to assist in someone else's grieving process, rather than concentrating solely on my own!

Chapter Thirteen

A jumble of routes and directions followed my departure from Coeur d'Alene, unable to avoid the Interstate entirely I belted along for fifteen miles, before exiting onto a smaller state route. The detour had taken me over one hundred miles west of the Continental Divide, my primary goal was to head east, back on course to follow the backbone of the Rockies. Forward planning didn't come into it, as each hour followed the last, snap decisions were made, mostly to avoid busier roads and larger towns. More and more time was spent on county routes and unmaintained gravel roads.

State Route 97 rose sharply above Coeur d'Alene Lake cutting through dense white pine forests. The road alternated between deep shade and bright sunshine, affording excellent views when the opportunities arose. Undulating twists and turns rising high above the lake, before plunging back down again, to cross ancient bridges over muddy creeks. Constantly doubling back on itself, the road's severe switchbacks required respect and were negotiated with a degree of care. There was no point holding back though, maintaining momentum makes for more economic riding, and a certain degree more fun as well. The hillside, falling sharply to the lake below, was devoid of protective barriers; it was a long way down which didn't perturb me in the least. After plying my way over passes of loose slippery substrate, with deadly drops into the unknown, I didn't give it a second thought. Other traffic wasn't a hindrance either, there was very little of it and what I encountered was slow moving. Despite keeping to a casual speed of about 60mph, I overtook everything without delay, watching them vanish from my rear view mirror as I cranked the bike over into the next steep bend.

Both land and road opened up after Harrison, being flatter with more forgiving bends, though still continuously switching first left then right. Pasture lay to one side whilst from the other side slow moving, swampy creeks gave off a smell of rot and decay. Heading east from St Marie's, I followed St Joe's Creek, a quiet meandering river reminiscent of Scotland. A wide yet shallow, fast flowing stretch of water, with infrequent homesteads yet littered with fly-fishers. Barely anything stirred, it was hot but fresh and I delighted in the ride, savouring the experience, rather than ruining it in an orgy of speed and adrenalin. Scenic byways dictated my choice of route, along with off-road rides and high altitude passes. True, my intention was to close the gap with the Continental Divide, but travelling shouldn't only be about your destination, the journey itself makes all the difference. Idaho and Montana both hosted a multitude of unpaved forestry routes, I could have spent weeks winding my way through them and gotten little further. A compromise was made, progress mixed with pleasure, the best of both worlds.

While St Joe's Creek took an abrupt turn south I swung northeast, using a forest trail to cross the Stateline, back into Montana. It could easily have been an old moonshine run. I imagined Hillbillies in Model T Fords, broad siding round the dusty bends, Sheriff Justice on their tail. My passage attracted no such attention, and I slipped quietly by, nursing a bottle of Bushmills in my tank bag. At exactly what point I crossed the Stateline I have no idea, somewhere amongst the trees. There was certainly nothing to signify a border. All I know is that I veered away from one river, entered the forest on a gravel track, exited onto tarmac, and was at St Regis. Hey, I was suddenly in Montana again, following another river bound for Paradise. It was neither a case of paradise lost, nor paradise found. It proved to be a nondescript place, the naming of which showed either an overactive imagination or one hell of a sense of humour. For the pioneers the numerous rivers and lakes would have been a paradise after travelling across the endless, dry dusty plains further east.

Once past Paradise the scenic byway, bound for the northern tip of Flathead Lake, completely failed to live up to its name, or am I being too picky? Slightly lumpy cattle country spread out on each side of the road, small numbers of cattle were to be seen, grazing on dried out pastures. Being fair, it was all quite unspoilt, development was low key with no obvious blots on the landscape.

On a more constructive day it would have been recorded as wide open spaces and rolling hills. The highway itself was straight and boring, slight rises now and again gave the illusion of not being absolutely monotonous. Of the surrounding countryside I could only describe it as pleasant, in a characterless sort of way. It may be an unfair description, but compared to the last six thousand miles or so it wasn't inspiring, maybe it was grossly unfair to make such comparisons, or maybe nothing could shine through the mood I found myself in.

It must have come from somewhere but I never noticed where. Late afternoon, just pottering along to conserve fuel, a sudden upwelling of emotion burst free. One second frustrated and bored, the next a blubbering wreck, veering across the road, struggling to control the bike through my inconsolable tears. OK, I should have pulled over. I did at least keep within the confines of my own lane. The cars behind, waiting to overtake, must have thought I was a complete arse. At that moment I could see no point to life at all, having lost Cai nothing else held any importance, nothing of value remained. Completely hopeless, that's how it felt. Weaving around my lane made me realise how easy it would be to stop fighting against the tide. All it would take was to veer in front a truck, BOOF, end of story. With such thoughts I got a grip on reality, it wasn't the solution, I wasn't about to throw away my life, I don't consider myself a quitter. Instead I called it a day, pulled into the first campsite and drank myself into a stupor. It only took half a bottle of Bushmills.

Surprisingly freshened, the following day went without incident. It was close though. Never keen on being evangelised, the occasion could have taken an unpleasant turn, had I possessed any residue of anger. Unexpectedly the culprit was a Native American, who'd come to convert his heathen brethren. Each to his own, I don't try and force my opinions on others, and appreciate not having theirs forced on me. I'd only stopped to take a photo. I was admiring the scenery and if God created it, then I was paying homage to his creation. The most appalling aspect of my meeting with Shane was his acceptance, his justification even, of the massacre of his own race by the white man. I'd pointed out the wars and death throughout history that were down to religious intolerance, an explanation as to why I followed no religion. I even used his own people as an example, but no, I'd got it wrong. The Native Americans were savages, needing to be subjugated. It was the only way for them to accept the word of God, the love of Jesus. Whoa! Was I hearing him right? The Indians, apparently, needed to be educated with religion otherwise they wouldn't enjoy union with the realms of heaven. Jeez, that was one fucked up Indian! I explained my inability to accept the death of my son. How an all-powerful, all-seeing, understanding, forgiving Supreme Being couldn't expect me to praise him after allowing Cai to die. I could accept such things happen, as part of a chaotic world, but not to be told God knew what he was doing. Some random fruit cake was telling me Cai had died due to divine intervention, he was in the company of Jesus, that he was lucky to have been taken, that I shouldn't question the actions of the Lord. Maybe I should believe in God, because somehow that Indian wasn't knocked to the ground and beaten shitless. In truth though, it was just a sign of how truly devoid of anger I'd become. My loss was so great everything else paled into insignificance, even that raving idiot!

Despite heavier traffic and ugly areas of development the remaining ride north was tolerable, taking me within about forty miles of Eureka again, before turning east, towards the Continental Divide. A huge area of wilderness barred passage to the Continental Divide without any trails or tracks for motorised vehicles, the closest I could manage was on State Route 83, the other side of Flathead Lake. It proved scenic and enjoyable, though a constant deluge drastically reduced visibility, limiting what I could see of my surroundings, and meant my camera stayed safely under wraps. Being quieter than the opposing lakeside made the day more enjoyable than the previous one, passing a series of smaller lakes, log buildings and thick pine forests in virtual isolation settled me even further. Open spaces were smaller, more compact, grazing was restricted to fenced in enclosures, occupied partly by cattle, but mainly by horses. It was altogether more beautiful, up close and personal, with an overwhelming impression of rustic, old world charm. A Welsh flag was spotted flying from a log cabin, I actually turned round and was going to knock on their door, to introduce myself as a bold Welsh adventurer. I felt stupid before I reached the house and continued on my way instead. It was only an excuse to get invited into a proper log cabin, those I'd seen being built before were fakes, sheathing ply houses with a cladding of pine. There was no doubt about the authenticity of these, winding my way between the lakes the majority of buildings were of solid log. All phases of construction had been seen, even a guy stripping the bark, by hand, in the pouring rain. These were built in situ from the raw materials, no flat packs in that neck of the woods.

During lunch in Ovando the rain finally eased off, replaced by bright sun and blue, almost cloudless sky. The heavens smiled down on me as I planned the basis of a route, from there it was to be mainly unpaved road for the rest of the day. Looping round to the south, then west, I'd travel back into the Bitterroot Range. A stretch of Route 93 would take me across the Idaho/Montana Stateline for the third but definitely not the last time. The tarmac would carry me over Chief Joseph's Pass which crests the Continental Divide at an elevation of seven thousand two hundred and forty one feet. Off-road rarely meant rough dirt, forest tracks and unpaved road more often involved loose gravel, with various degrees of sand or rocky substratum. No two sections were the same, I much preferred them to tarmac as they needed a higher, more sustained level of concentration. Without fail they were much quieter routes, not necessarily any more beautiful but the experience was definitely a more profound one. All those sections took me through sparsely populated areas, rarely would I encounter other people, there was less to intrude on my private communion with the natural world.

From Ovando to Helmville the track was washboard all the way, a corrugated bed with a loose scattering of dust on the surface. It makes for a very rough ride the vibrations shake every bone in your body loose, and there is only one method of overcoming the discomfort. With the correct speed you can skim over them, that speed depends on the depth and distance between the ridges. A minimum of 50mph was needed, so I fair flew along at 50-60mph, avoiding the physical discomfort at the cost of a massively increased heartbeat. In contrast to the morning's ride it was wide, open pastureland, I would have supposed cattle country but with a complete absence of cows I doubt it was. I noticed a Rodeo arena across the fields, complete with stalls and terraced stands for the crowds. Cows or not, it was definitely cowboy country. After Helmville the corrugations stopped, replaced by a more uniform base, under a deeper gravel surface, with a wide central tyre-track almost clear of gravel and dust. Obviously, the clearer line was the best, so I stayed in the middle of the track. With deep gravel the bike tended to slew around a lot, keeping on the power is the only way to curb this. Changing between surfaces is a worrying experience, it completely changes the dynamics for controlling the bike. As the front wheel entered deep gravel it started to slew, made worse by a reduction in speed, pulling over to stop, or make way for the infrequent on-coming pick-ups freaked me out. The tension it induced only made the situation worse. Despite knowing this, I just couldn't relax sufficiently to overcome the problem, it was one aspect I had yet to come to terms with. Happily motoring along at over 50mph was a doddle, as soon as I saw the tell-tale plume of dust ahead I knew what was to come and tensed up in preparation. Pulling over to stop and take photos was worse, making me feel completely out of control, it was always a relief when finally coming to a standstill. Rather than discouraging me, it egged me on, each scary moment boosted my confidence, allowing me to relax a little more. Whether tense and scary or not, it never made me shy away from the next excursion from solid tarmac. The sense of achievement gained was worth every minute.

With the scenery and road conditions constantly changing there was no time to get bored. From rough, open tracks to tricky, twisting tarmac and intense mountain trails the going was a joy, the diversity delightful. I could have taken Route 93 all the way from Eureka, and saved myself three days of riding, though I would have missed so much. Our goal had never been to take a straight route through The Americas, it was to discover all the little highways and byways, to search out the remotest routes, to explore the more inaccessible places. Criss-crossing the State line meant traversing the Bitterroot Range time and again, huge loops carried me between the Rockies and the Bitterroots, rising over the Sapphire Mountains en-route. Days were spent without conversing with another soul, yet I gave it no thought whatsoever. There was no other place I'd rather be, only one other person I could wish to share it with. But that didn't plague me excessively, it saddened me greatly, yet also strengthened me and gave me the courage to continue. Camping along the more remote mountain passes seemed to bring the greatest pleasure, and the greatest pain. These were the places our hearts had been set on, Cai would have adored being there, roughing it in the wilderness, we'd have been reluctant to move on each day. Alone, I felt a pressing need to occupy my mind, I needed to fill my days with change and challenges.

Roadside campsites around the States are orderly and plentiful, facilities good and access easy. Well-maintained sites, with clearly marked pitches; often screened from each other by trees or bushes, gave a degree of privacy. They were hardly inspiring though, in comparison wilderness campsites were in secluded and isolated spots, it took effort to reach them, which deterred all but the hardier outdoor types. With only basic facilities there was no chance of anything but a toilet, the more remote the simpler the method of waste disposal. You would still find a shack to preserve some degree of decency, yet inside would be little more than a hole in the ground but amazingly they would still have a roll of toilet paper.

Sitting at seven thousand two hundred and sixty feet my camp at the Shalkaho Pass was small, secluded and basic, only once or twice was I disturbed by the sound of a passing vehicle. Riding in was under hot afternoon sun, waking the following morning it promised to be bright, but initially was damp, misty and very cold. Not wishing to pack a wet tent, I sat huddled, fully clad, with my hands grasped round my coffee mug, desperate for warmth. A hurried start may have gotten me out the misery quicker but I preferred to nourish myself and prepare for what the day held in store for me. By the time I set off I'd at least stopped shivering, so my attention could be on the ride, not my discomfort. The trail through the Sapphire Mountains excluded all vehicles but those with off-road capabilities. The rough, narrow track was incredibly steep, with some of the tightest hairpins imaginable and hair-raising drops. Cut round the edge of the mountain some magnificent views were to be beheld, deep wooded valleys to the south and plenty of bare rock, sporting crystal clear waterfalls, to my right. The conditions weren't excessively bad but it was hunting season and the hunters were out in force. The narrow track and tight bends made it impossible to see what might be coming around the corner, there wasn't much margin for error. It was a pleasant ride out though, and before I knew it the bike and I trundled safely into the town of Derby, another mountain pass having been successfully negotiated.

Chapter Fourteen

If I'd hoped for a bright sunny day it proved to be a vain hope, by the time I left Derby it was pouring with rain. A promising forest route over Horse Creek Pass, then through Shroup and Cobalt was ignored, the quicker and more direct Route 93 would make better headway. Torrential rain guaranteed any appreciation of the scenery to be a non-starter, only a vague awareness of my surroundings was possible. And there was no let-up either, by the time I topped Chief Joseph Pass it worsened. Rain turned to sleet, the blackened clouds turned afternoon into evening and the sleet lay as mush along the road. The going was treacherous, wasn't I glad the higher forest trail hadn't been taken. My waterproof gloves weren't, they worked better as sieves than weather protectors. Wet and cold, my hands felt as if they were in buckets of Slush Puppy. My visor steamed up, unless fully opened which still meant I could see nothing. I plumped for the warmer option and kept it only half open. Never before have I felt elation at the appearance of an articulated truck, bearing down on me from behind. I allowed it to pass, duly following it, desperate to cower behind and take what shelter its bulk could offer. Extra wide, double wheeled axles dispersed the worst of the slippery slush, using its rear lights for guidance I followed in its wake; far enough back to minimise the impenetrable spray it kicked up.

Just as I thought the nightmare couldn't get any worse, my engine started spluttering. I knew it wasn't running out of fuel, thought it could be altitude but wasn't convinced. My other alternatives were a sodden air filter or the ignition system shorting out, both due to the veritable wall of water trying to pound us into submission. Whichever maybe the case, stopping wasn't an option as I could do nothing at the roadside. Barely coaxing the bike along, the truck gradually pulled away, leaving me exposed and struggling to keep in motion. I was so glad to be descending, even happier to find a roadhouse within spitting distance of the incline flattening out. I'd expected the bike to cough and wheeze to a standstill as I pulled in, but no. Damned bike, and damned if I cared right then, all I wanted was food and warmth.

Cold and sodden, a pool of water spread around me as I peeled off the layers. All eyes swung in my direction, concern and sympathy the order of the day. 'You poor thing, just what are you doing out in these conditions?' How else could I reply? 'Riding the Americas, hell bent on riding the length of the Rockies before winter catches me up.' Oh, how I lapped up the attention and sympathy, gobbling down mounds of food and gallons of coffee. Nothing seemed too much trouble as they lavished copious amounts of good old American hospitality onto me. It was a typical roadhouse really, canned smiles, fried food and an endless supply of coffee. Hell, they even had Huckleberry pie! Within ten minutes of getting back on the bike though the cold had crept back into my very bones, the respite had done nothing to dry me out either. Night drew closer, camping was not on the agenda, I deserved a bit of luxury so took the more expensive option of a hotel in Salmon. It was heartrending to turn into the car park and see two KLRs, one red and one black, parked out front. That should have been Cai and me.

Bad news comes in threes, and for the third day running the clouds were dark and gloomy, threatening rain wherever I went. Route 28 ran parallel to the Continental Divide, my route back into Montana meant taking either the Lemhi or Bannock passes. The hills were obscured by a bank of thick, low-lying cloud, an ominous sign if ever there was one. The plan had been to take the Lemhi Pass, a more precipitous but lower level choice. Fate played its hand, I missed the entry point and followed Eighteen Mile Creek over the Bannock pass instead. Within a couple of miles I regretted the mistake, the surface was atrocious. I seriously considered turning back. An earthmover busily spread a new layer of sand/gravel over the track, along the centre line laid a continuous mound, half a metre deep, separating the two sides of the track. Abandoned machinery and the old compact track bed lay on the other side, leaving a fresh surface of thick, loose aggregate for me to contend with. This also coincided with entering the cloudbank. I wasn't happy, biting cold, zero visibility and the treacherous surface was testing, to say the least. When the Stateline appeared I was shocked and elated to have got so far. It was still freezing cold, the mist still dense and the track still awful; it wasn't all bad though, the rain had held off so far. Bolstered with a fresh sense of achievement, the second half of Eighteen Mile Creek was handled so much more competently. I shook the gloom from my shoulders, picked up the pace and rode out to face the world.

With renewed confidence the temptation was to go the whole hog, to try and ride the entire way to Yellowstone on dirt tracks. Theoretically it was possible, one tank of fuel would be sufficient, and the tracks were there, it would only need a short distance on tarmac to connect them. Yet for once it was the pull of tourist attractions that got the better of me, I really wanted to see the Ghost Towns of Nevada City and Virginia City. The last few days I'd passed countless ranch entrances sporting huge timber arches and frames, decorated with an assortment of horns, skulls and other western paraphernalia. Large wooden barns stood alongside homesteads and rickety wooden fences, stretching for miles, demarked each range. Ranch land filled with cattle lined my route, deer frequently sharing the pasture and horses corralled nearer the buildings. It all seemed too clichéd but I wanted to complete the picture. I wanted to visit an old west Ghost town. I wanted to pull up at the hitching post, saunter past the saloon, to actually experience my image of the Wild West. Most of all I wanted to see the real thing, not a tacky theme park with mock gunfights and fake Indians. I didn't care that the buildings were closed or the streets deserted, being there and letting the imagination run free was fine.

Still determined to maximise my time cruising dirt tracks, I cut across country from Dillon on a gorgeous trail. Fairly compacted sandy clay, with no gravel, loose enough to dig into, so good for grip. Winding across the Ruby Range, following the contours of the land, the rich red soil track led me through yet more beautiful upland pasture, then along the large expanse of water forming the reservoir. Dipping and weaving with the land made for an enjoyable ride, each bend slightly banked, making for effortless riding. For a day which started with such trepidation, it was sure going well, I was gutted it only went on for about fifty miles. But all good things come to an end, and as I rejoined the highway at Alder, it was with a feeling of deep contentment. With only a short way into town

I was soon transformed into a dusty drifter, rolling in from way out west. And Nevada City was a ghost town, with no sign of any inhabitants and no tacky tourist treats. I was left to let my mind roam free, completely alone with my imagination. Almost audible was the piano tinkling and the glasses clinking from the Dance Hall, looking through the window of the general store suggested it was merely closed for lunch. Well, I had to be moseying along, to find ma'self a boarding house.

I guess it had to be a log cabin, it was a natural follow on from my day. In fact it was all so strange, as the afternoon drew to a close there it loomed, "LOG CABINS", within striking distance of Yellowstone. And that night in the next-door bar, a couple of old timers, proclaiming to be true cowboys, graced us with their presence. Both were from out of town, giving it large, name-dropping events, people and places where they'd competed. Of course by 'cowboys' they meant they had ridden in rodeos, I thought a cowboy was someone who rode a horse, worked the ranch and herded cows. They were a good laugh at first, then got more and more outrageous, eventually to the extent of being ludicrous. Another customer, a young guy, showed clearly the institutionalised respect demanded of authority figures in much of America by addressing an older man, or a figure of authority, as *Sir*. Hell, even sons call their fathers *Sir*. How weird! But the old guys lapped it up, they had a captive audience. I was given an invite to go stay with one near Denver, I couldn't imagine taking up the offer. My attention had been drawn to a younger, local couple. We ended up taking the piss out the 'cowboys', before getting bored and going into the back room to play pool. The beer flowed freely as pint after pint was poured down my throat. The rest of that night is a complete blur!

Lashings of coffee and a belly full of food saw off the inevitable hangover. By 10 a.m. my head was as clear as the bright sunshine and there was no holding me back. With only sixty miles until Yellowstone I could think of nothing but Yogi Bear and the legendary National Park. So much so, my fuel went onto reserve after only a measly few miles, unperturbed, I put my trust in the gods of gasoline and continued ever onwards. Perhaps it was more a case of carrying on regardless, blind faith overcoming common sense, a stubborn refusal to backtrack. However it panned out, the intention was to enjoy the day, after abysmal weather for days the outlook was bright. A rocky corridor lead me towards the Park, the road dipping and winding between lakes and reservoirs, snaking alongside rivers, glinting in the sun. Bands of enclosed pasture changed into huge expanses of open plain, as the mountains released their squeeze, sweeping over to the distant horizon. Groups of antelope scattered liberally, often watched over by the dominant stag, a lone sentinel silhouetted against the skyline. A steep drop of fifteen metres plunged into a defunct lakebed, perhaps this was the body of water, diverted by natural disaster, to create Earthquake Lake. With relief a gas station appeared, a rural single pump affair with extortionate prices. Obstinacy ruled the day, refusing to be ripped blind I set off again, begrudging paying such an inflated price, even for a single litre. A sign declared eight miles to Yellowstone, I'd barely let out my sigh of relief when the last dregs of gas drained from the tank. No amount of coaxing helped, the tank was bone-dry, and I freewheeled onto the verge. SHIT!

Being only a few miles from the park entrance, all was not lost. I was on the main highway to the west park entrance, surely a good Samaritan would be along any minute. Actually, a couple of cars in five minutes failed to raise my hopes, I'd thought the likelihood of a lift was high, an easy way out of my dilemma. And then, for the first time that day, the fog lifted from my dulled senses, the obvious solution dawned on me. All my fuel requirements were interchangeable, Zippo lighter, camping stove and bike, I still had a full canister of fuel in my saddlebag. OK, it was only half a litre but it was better than a poke in the eye. Worst-case scenario, it would get me close enough to push the bike the rest of the way. As it happened, I cruised jubilantly onto the gas station forecourt. I knew the single fuel option had been a good idea, and boy wasn't I glad I'd remembered. I felt foolish enough as it was!

After the mad clamour of tourists at Yosemite, expectations were high for Yellowstone. School holidays were over, the average American family safely settled back into their humdrum lives, summer season was over. The almost deserted approach road was encouraging, there were no queues at the entrance, maybe an uninterrupted trip round the park could be enjoyed. I only wanted to ride round, take a few photos and appreciate the grandeur of America's oldest wildlife reserve. I almost tingled in anticipation at the thought of herds of bison, packs of wolves and foraging bears. My ears awaited the deep bellow of moose, my skin itched to relax in hot sulfurous springs, and my fingers twitched to happy snap a multitude of delights. Yet my excursion round the park left me irritable and grumpy, my patience with the rest of humanity was terrible. Only my attitude spoilt it really, there weren't that many people, and the traffic rarely came to a standstill. It was recognised as a selfish, intolerant mindset, one I couldn't shake off, luckily the exceptional beauty shone through my dour mood.

Spectacular sights abounded, far-flung vistas of empty wilderness spread to the furthest reaches, viewpoints afforded incredible vantage points, showing a world of wonder, totally un-spoilt as far as the eye could see. Steep climbs round amazingly oblique turns carried me through Canyon, over Dunraven Pass, past Mount Washburn and Druid Peak. Narrow canyons plummeted, seemingly for thousands of feet, wild water surging along the gorge's floor. Crowning the ridge were weird basalt pillars, formed eons ago by the contraction of cooling lava. Hot springs bubbled happily, devoid of bathers, kept clean and clear by their exclusion. Sulfur lakes, also benefitting by this prohibition, sat steaming despite the burning sun. Whichever way I turned my head another delight awaited, with hindsight I cannot imagine how I maintained my foul disposition throughout the day. Of the wildlife, there was little, and nothing new for me to marvel at. But Yellowstone was not created for me alone, there was plenty to delight the majority of people. An occasional bison would nonchalantly stand blocking the road, elk grazed the verges, nonplussed by cars screeching to a halt by their side. By every animal sighting a bottleneck formed, crowds of tourists swarmed around, cameras clicking. I'd sneak past to enjoy a stretch of open road, unhindered by the otherwise constant tailback. Reaching Old Faithful within a half hour of eruption was a chance not to be missed, a front row seat was great for taking pictures. As the minutes turned to seconds the crowd waited, with baited breath, and the countdown began. Would I have expected anything else? Not if I'd given it any thought; the eternal cynic won through, and on zero nothing happened, me and Old Faithful had the last laugh.

The most pleasurable experience in Yellowstone proved to be the simplest. Early the next morning I spent over an hour stalking deer in the forest, I got some lovely shots, realising that it took more patience and skill to capture them on film than to blow them away with a gun. Strangely they were happy to wander in close to the tents, but wouldn't tolerate human attention. I'm sure if they hadn't been familiar with humans they'd never have made an appearance, they'd have been gone in an instant at the slightest sight of me, never to be seen again.

Though initially veering away from the magical line demarking the Continental Divide throughout Wyoming, I followed it south, keeping it in sight, whenever weather permitted. And it was the proximity to the Divide that generally determined my route, it certainly wasn't the most direct, nor the quickest. It did however take me into some exemplary wilderness areas, along some dynamic trails. Surrounding Yellowstone are numerous peaks, few below ten thousand feet and many over twelve thousand feet, basically the height of the passes in the area cut Yellowstone off during winter. As I forged my way south again the weather was good, that was taken to be indicative of the way ahead, and a leisurely pace was set. With the Teton Range to my right, and the Big Game Range to my left, the road was the last place my attention was focused. Big, blue sky above and jagged peaks lined up, one after the other, on both sides, the moment was one to be savoured. Grand Teton stood out, tall and proud, above everything else. I like to think there'd been some conscious decision over the direction taken from Jackson Lake but there wasn't. I followed my eyes which were firmly glued on Grand Teton, and found myself slap bang in the middle of the very busy town of Jackson. Gridlocked right through, loud, noisy, polluted and full of stores selling tat. Yuck, tourist hell! Quickly followed by highway heaven.

Chapter Fifteen

Nestled between the Snake Range and the Gros Verdes Range, Route 191 wound down a narrow valley floor, enticing me to relax and glide round fast, sweeping bends. Since starting out late in the morning I'd dawdled for most the day, few miles had been covered and I felt desperate to leave the flow of traffic plying its way along the Scenic Byway. Being late afternoon it was too late to make up for lost time, so I struck out for a quieter route instead, following the Hobeck River, in search of food and shelter. Normally reluctant to classify burger and chips as food, it was a pleasant surprise tucking into the American national dish at a country kitchen, some way before Bondurant. Waiting for my order I acquainted myself with a couple's friendly hound, as he'd helped break the ice, I asked for help to locate an elusive campsite. I should have passed it but no sign had been noticed along the roadside. And indeed, I'd sailed past the unmarked turnoff, understandably oblivious to its undeclared presence. Only too pleased to help they gave clear instructions, in minute detail, including distance, directions and a description of relevant landmarks. They were local ranchers who ran a place I'd passed a few miles back. An interesting couple who still managed to ranch using older techniques e.g. horse power for haymaking. For my part, I spoke of my journey, the original plan, my route and mileage so far. I also expressed my attitude to the hordes of tourists I'd encountered in Yellowstone, they both understood and agreed with my feelings. A Park Warden that morning had corrected me, during a whinge about tourists, and he had pointed out that not all people were horrid, selfish and ignorant. How true, as Paul and Barbara Elwin were so kindly to prove. Wishing me well they departed, leaving me to tuck into a mound of fries and half a cow between bread. So content on stuffing my face I hadn't noticed their failure to actually drive away, five minutes later they returned. Almost apologetically they excused themselves for intruding, without wanting to seem untoward they wished to offer me a bed for the night, but would understand if that seemed a bit strange. They assured me I would have my own space (they had a spare cabin) and be left alone to enjoy the place in peace. You could have knocked me down with a feather, I was lost for words, so moved I was nearly in tears. Don't lose faith in humanity, there are many amazing people, if you only remain open to meeting them. Reassuring them how grateful I was was all I could do, being so overwhelmed by their generosity. So they waited patiently in the car, while I finished eating, then lead me down the road, along tracks crossing pastures, through dried creek beds, until finally arriving at their homestead. And what a homestead it was!

A modern, log-built house took central stage, with a cavernous barn to one side. On the opposite side, to the front stood two log cabins, each big enough to allow ample space for a family. Further away, we'd passed it on our way in, another, slightly larger, log cabin stood apart from the rest. All the cabins looked well weathered but in immaculate condition. There was no other sign of human habitation to be seen, however far you looked, in whatever direction. But it was dusk, and the surrounding territory was indistinct, promising a better look around in the morning, my hosts made every effort to help me settle in; without fuss. There was no need to make room in the barn, the doors rolled open and my bike rolled in, into a space big enough for a light aircraft to taxi into. Bloody luxury, since the day it was wheeled out the showroom it had never seen the inside of any building. And I was introduced to my abode, the solitary log cabin, some hundred metres or so from the rest. A sturdy wooden rocking chair took pride of place on the raised porch, with any place to lay my head I would have been happy for the night. But there was so much more to behold, it just got better and better. Under normal circumstances the lounge would not be exceptional, a couple of sofas, coffee table, bookcases, hi-fi and a TV/VCR. The kitchen was compact (two would hinder each other if trying to prepare a meal) but it lacked nothing in the way of facilities; washer, dryer, cooker, fridge, toaster, kettle. Cupboards with general domestic supplies, and the ingredients for making a choice of drinks, completed the picture. Two double bedrooms, both made up and ready for use, gave me a choice of where I slept, or which bed I found most comfortable. Finally, a bathroom, with fresh towels, and a complete stock of toiletries. There was even a super soft, luxury bathrobe to laze around in. If I hadn't known better I'd have thought I was dreaming. 'Make yourself at home,' said Barbara. 'I'll bring you a couple of bottles of beer from the house.' So there was such a thing as heaven after all.

With on tap luxury, the first thing I did was to strip off completely and throw every article of clothing into the washer, motorcycle trousers and jacket included. With that taken care of, it was a simple matter of scouring myself clean, every inch and every orifice. I wouldn't describe it as cold, but the deluxe bathrobe was preferable to parading around naked. Clean and fresh, all there was left to do was sit back in the rocking chair, cradling an ice cold beer, stare into the star studded sky and ponder.

The preceding days had unfolded an ever-changing stream of, virtually, unspoilt wilderness. Faced with such enchanting sights, my spirits soared, my every sense became saturated with sensory overload. This may have been achieved from the relative comfort of highways alone, it wasn't purely the sights I beheld, they could have been enjoyed sitting astride a two-wheeled armchair, staying in plush hotels, or viewed from a luxury tour bus. Just how deep is your appreciation when life is handed to you on a plate? Inclement weather and demanding trails had been tough on me, very challenging in many ways, yet ultimately rewarding. Whatever the elements had thrown at me, I'd endured, whether wet and cold, loose and rough, or downright scary. I'd not backed down, not given up. Rather than weaken me, wear away my resolve, it had created a sense of achievement, fortified me. None of it had registered as hardship, just par for the course really, had it been a stroll in the park I'd have felt dissatisfied. Physical challenges are meant to give you a buzz, the more challenging, the bigger the buzz. The harder the obstacles overcome, the greater the achievement. I was actually starting to feel proud of my efforts!

Physical hardship is one thing, emotional trauma another matter entirely. During those days of glory, grief had taken its toll, and that proved a harder taskmaster than either weather or road conditions. Plagued by images of Cai lying, in agony, in the middle of the freeway, my real battle had been dealing with that pain and frustration. Cai had been reaching out to me, desperate for me to hug him, imploring me to hold him. Demands to leave him be riled me at the time, did the guy have no idea the strength of bond between us, did he have any notion how deep our love was? He certainly didn't appreciate how important that contact was for us both, him and the other members of the emergency services had no regard for us as individuals, what mattered most for us, at that moment. No, their only concern was procedures, this was the way it must be done, regardless. I had commands barked at me, rights refused and freedom threatened. No wonder I felt bitter, it was no surprise that memories of that fateful day were tainted by unfeeling, impersonal actions. I never did get another chance to tell Cai how important he was to me, how much I loved him. With bitter regret and a heavy heart, exhaustion got the better of me that night at the Elwin's, yet I found a semblance of peace in the quiet tranquility of the Dell Fork Ranch.

Roused from my slumber by rubbing and rustling proved disorientating, but not for long. Horses had returned from their overnight pasture, gathering close to the homestead in anticipation of breakfast. These were horses that appreciated routine, turned out to pasture each night, they'd make their own way home each morning, eager for a tasty treat before a day of work. Being only 6 a.m. the sun had yet to appear over the mountains, it was clear but still chilly. What a lovely place though. To begin with the land sloped gradually away, punctuated in the distance by a boundary fence. To the northeast the Gros Verdes mountains dominated the view, elsewhere it appeared to be empty pasture. An array of wildlife guides lined the bookcase so, armed with my binoculars, I was content to peruse my surroundings for any signs of life. A harem of antelope graced the nearest hill, fourteen of them, just off the access track. Too far for a detailed photo they were still a delight to watch. A Harris hawk flew past, the broad white stripe across its rump made identification easy. Systematically scanning the fields proved fruitless, it made me realise how much land there was out there; then, across my field of view, flew a Bald eagle. Not willing to risk losing sight of it, my camera stayed by my side, relying on binoculars and memories rather than pictures.

It transpired over breakfast that the Elwins sponsored groups of Nepalese to travel over and work on their ranch. They fully utilised the three log cabins, they weren't kept as show pieces. One was actually the original homestead of Will Faris and his mother, who staked their claim in the early 1920's. Barbara still held the original title, complete with the American President's signature from that period. The mother made the wagon journey from New Mexico, in her late 60's. Not liking getting snowed in each year, she got her other son to come and fetch her again. Extraordinary hardship, logged in a published book I read over-night by Jessie, Will Faris' wife; who only died in 1995. In those pioneering days, all you had to do was build a cabin, fence off the permitted one hundred and sixty five acres and work the land. The US government would then gift the land to you and issue the title deed, no wonder the Native Americans still feel hard done by. Hence ranches tend to be in one hundred and sixty five acre plots, who in their right mind would claim less under the circumstances. Everything about Dell Fork Ranch struck chords of harmony; the place, the people, and the history all impressed me. I can only imagine what the snowbound winters are like, thoughts of skidoos and wild adventures in the snow come to mind. Truly a place with a tremendous pull, a place I found difficult to leave.

Armed with information on two highly recommended side trips, an early(ish) start was made. Intended road miles were low, for once a full day's riding was pre-planned. Two excursions would carry me first towards Gannet Peak, the highest in the Wind River Range, at more than thirteen thousand feet. From Green River Lake, almost astride the divide, the two highest peaks could be seen looming above. And then onto Elkheart Park where, from about nine and a half thousand feet, I could view the entire range directly in front of me. A campsite in the park was still open, though I wasn't expecting many other campers. Nigh on two hundred miles would be ridden, even though my actual southerly advance would be little more than sixty miles. Both excursions were dead ends, which rarely featured in my itinerary, I was putting my total trust in Paul and Barbara's suggestions.

Through Cora Route 352 proved curvaceous, being not too bendy and not too fast, that is to say I kept my speed down to a maximum of 70mph. Another corridor through mountainous terrain, passing a couple of isolated lakes and little besides. Just my machine and me, in perfect union with the road. A ninety mile round trip is quite far, just to look at one particular mountain but it was more than that, the whole route was recommended. The twenty five miles of tarmac reached only up to New Fork Lake, another twenty miles of track would carry me to the base of Gannett Peak. As soon as my wheels hit the gravel surface the whole bike started violently juddering. It was the washboard effect, that rough corrugated surface that almost shakes your joints out their sockets. My kneejerk reaction was to roll off the throttle but I resisted, I'd already slowed for the transition from tarmac to dirt, besides there was no point. A degree of uniformity was beginning to show with corrugated gravel in the States, once more, hit 50mph and it tended to smooth out. Plain sailing all the way, only it wasn't! A change in depth and pitch of corrugations caught me unawares, the bike started bouncing out of control, like a bucking bronco set on vibrator mode, at 55mph. To say it scared me shitless would be an understatement, beyond doubt I was coming off, and I didn't have the guts to open it up even more. Standing onto the foot pegs, I managed to regain some semblance of control and cautiously eased open the throttle a touch more, which helped. I'll never know what possessed me, it was unpleasant and the speed gave zero margin of error but I went for it, and got away with it too. Completely focussed on the track and controlling the bike, I have no idea exactly what speed I reached, at the time it was best not to know. Ignorance was a long way from bliss, but it was, without doubt, preferable. Ludicrously, the whole episode was for two quick, rather boring photos, and then I had to face the return journey. There was no alternative, so I just went for it again, making better time and caring less. An added complication of heavy rain clouds behind spurred me on, the way ahead seemed clear, as the first few drops spattered my visor I attempted to outrun the deluge. The rocky heights of the Divide had been bathed in bright sunshine, while the last few miles to the highway saw a light scattering of snow on the verges, which hadn't been there on the way in. Coming every which way, it was unlike any weather I was used to, I failed to accept it as normal. But freak weather front or not, I won through, it was one of the only times I felt relief when reaching tarmac again.

If I'd thought Pinedale to Elkheart Park was more trail riding, it would have been disappointing. However bad the morning ride was, it hadn't put me off and I had a sneaking suspicion little would. As it turned out, smooth tarmac climbed steeply, through a rapid series of sharp turns, taking me quickly skyward. Under the illusion that nine and a half thousand feet was pretty damned high, I'd have thought this to be above the tree line, it came as a shock to find the campsite hidden away in a thick pine forest. A track circled the site with parking spaces lining the way, placed every thirty or so metres. Evidently a quiet, low-key affair, each pitch was separated, sheltered from sight by the dense woods. It gave the illusion of seclusion, only the faint whiff of wood smoke gave away the presence of others. It was nice to greet the select few, braving the onslaught of winter, without intruding upon each other's isolation. Questions of sanity had to be considered, if not my own, certainly of the guy from Michigan. Doing routine checks to my bike, I heard a commotion from the toilet, banging and shouts for help. Dashing down to find the door locked, I hammered on it, calling to him to ascertain what the hell was wrong. 'Jest checking!' he exclaimed. I couldn't be bothered to relate the story about the boy who cried wolf, maybe he'd get the point anyway, when a bear called at his tent and I ignored his screams.

Only three stalwart campers graced the site that night, all single males, it was inevitable we'd at least introduce ourselves, maybe share a beer and a smoke. But rain stopped play, forcing us back into our individual shelters. And didn't it just rain! Having the foresight to pitch the tent on a slight slope meant I didn't become swamped by rainwater, I hadn't bargained on so much water streaming down the slope though. Armed with a trenching tool, at 2 a.m. I was out in the storm digging a trench around the tent. I couldn't stop the torrent of water falling from the sky but I could redirect it. Working fast and furious, I dug a 'v' shaped trench pointing uphill, with channels along the sides, using the excavated soil to form an inner earthworks, as a secondary line of defence. It worked a treat, I enjoyed a lovely warm, and perfectly dry nights sleep. So much so, that the morning saw me reluctant to rouse myself from the comfort of my sleeping bag. Wasn't I the lucky one? Mr Michigan's tent was in tatters, shredded beyond belief and every item he possessed was drenched. He'd spent most the night, cowering in his car, shivering in a sodden sleeping bag, if only he'd "jest checked" his equipment.

Thankfully, the morning proved dry, even if very nippy, too cold to waste time hanging around camp. As the coffee boiled, half a roll of toilet paper made short work of the wet flysheet, there is no point packing a soggy tent into my camping roll, unless there is no alternative. With hands warmed by my coffee mug, and a cheery wave to Michigan's finest, I was on my way. Another day of discovery lay before me and I was up for the challenge. A prominent feature of my roadmap was a dialogue box warning, "INQUIRE LOCALLY FOR CURRENT CONDITIONS BEFORE DRIVING ON UNIMPROVED ROADS SHOWN ON THIS MAP". Featuring prominently on the map is the Wind River Range, stretching for over sixty miles along the Continental Divide, forming the eastern barrier to the Bridger Wilderness Area. From a nine thousand feet viewpoint it was clearly an impenetrable barrier, the lower reaches rugged with sparse patches of trees. The upper reaches of sheer, bare rock having gained a light coat of snow overnight, they were anything but inviting. But the divide represented the central line, the backbone of the Rockies, my point of reference for route planning. Stay off freeways, unless essential, and make the most of unmaintained trails; simple guidelines that weren't always easy to follow. Already having had a taste of the Bridger Wilderness Area the day before, I knew it could be a rough ride. I hadn't been put off though. I was ready for more. On unimproved roads, I could loop across the wilderness to the foot of the divide, then follow it southeast on a parallel track for a further twenty or so miles. I'd stopped calculating distances to cover off-road, it was obvious if they were within range of one tank of fuel. Food, fuel and water were essential items, at all times, not just for excursions into the wilderness. Theoretically I could stop and cater for myself at any given point. I didn't foresee being forced to do so but predicting the future is not really my forte!

It was disappointing that Route 353 from Boulder was tarmac. For some obscure reason I'd fixed the idea in my head that the trail started from there. I checked the map, it clearly showed a paved road. The route ran from Boulder to Big Sandy and was tarmac all the way. A fixation on dirt was clouding my judgement. It didn't make sense; they provided plenty of heart-stopping moments, frequently made me tense and uncomfortable, and regularly convinced me I was about to come off. More important though, they gave me a huge adrenalin rush, brought a wide grin to my face, and left me feeling elated. The tiny hamlet of Big Sandy heard a loud cheer from me as the tarmac came to an end. And what was the landscape I beheld? Big and sandy, what else? An enormous area of open, high altitude plain spread before me, in the distance hazy mountains lined the horizon. Winding into the distance, the dull red track made for the hills, clearly seen amongst sparse, low-lying scrub. Ah, real dirt again, sandy mud, fairly well compacted, yeehaa! Gunning forward, I wasted no time clicking through the gears, snicking it into top gear I saw the needle hit 65mph. Some degree of caution was upheld, the frequent dips and rises would see me easing off the power, as would the sharper bends I encountered. There was little to obstruct my view, which inspired confidence, impeccable grip from the tyres boosted it even more. The panorama really was immense, infinite, and totally empty of any sign of mankind. That world belonged to me, as I sailed across the top of it, alone and unhindered, I felt invincible. Life has a tendency to catch you unawares, it happens most often when you're not paying attention, luckily I was. A short, shallow series of ruts appeared and I barely checked my speed, the bike got very twitchy passing through. That was a mistake, a small one, with a valuable lesson, don't let down your guard. All it needed was to give more respect to the conditions, slow down a touch and apply a liberal amount of power as you pull through. And then came the soggy patches, churned up areas filling the entire road, again, not too deep but unstable as I went through. I slowed down more as I approached those wet sections, they were easy enough to see, and then accelerated carefully through. Few and far between, the obstacles posed no great problems. In between, the trail was pretty flat and straight by then, but I'd cooled my heels and kept a slightly more sedate pace. Until I came across a pickup, I don't know what came over me. Unwilling to sit behind, being blinded by its dust trail, I hammered past and kept going. An approaching muddy patch didn't deter me in the least, I gave it a handful of throttle and blasted through, full pelt. WOAH! The bike threw such a wobbler, I thought it was about to ejaculate and in an instant it was over, before I could do a thing. It gave me heart palpitations, and had me laughing hysterically. It was so scary and such good fun, though I would not want to repeat the experience. I was still laughing a mile later, where the trail came to an abrupt end at the highway.

And down came the rain. Satiated with excitement, I went into business mode, time to get more miles under the belt. I could have struck out into the Great Divide Basin, there's a plethora of trails criss-crossing the area. Had it not been for the rain I might have but the word basin combined with torrential rain, spelled disaster. So to Farson and Rock Springs it was. A horribly wet and very cold ride, what I lacked in enthusiasm I more than made up for in endurance. Trying to appreciate the scenery was pointless, it was hard making out road features, what chance had I of sightseeing? Rock Springs, yet another boringly drab way station, its sole purpose as an interchange between Route 191 and Interstate Route 80. It seemed to comprise of nothing more than a cluster of gas stations and cholesterol boosting fast food stores. Whether I liked it or not, both the bike and I needed to refuel, and I needed to consider my options. So I filled the bike, and then found a suitable establishment to play havoc with my blood pressure. Poring over the map proved a simple affair, go east or south. Whilst the Divide swung east, I wanted to avoid the freeway, so decided to head south and cut across the northeast corner of Utah, before turning east myself.

As the rain eased off, my throttle eased on and mile gobbling speeds ensued. From approximately seven and a half to eight and a half thousand feet there were long, open views and wonderful vistas. The sun tucked itself behind the hills and the chill factor increased substantially, too much to consider stopping to marvel at the landscape. It was beautiful, delightful to regard but it was the geological wonders I most enjoyed. Numerous forms and features of rock lined the way. Huge slabs of basalt, atop soft crumbly mudstone/sandstone; natural erosion undercutting the softer material, leaving large overhangs of basalt. Other outcrops had ripples formed down their flanks, as one might expect lava to set in mid-flow.

As the last light left the sky, a tight succession of switchbacks plummeted down the hillside, spewing me out far below, into the environs of Vernal. Utah received the briefest of visits, all I did was find the road out, Route 40 straight over the state line into Colorado. But only just, entering Dinosaur I was on my last legs, I'd struggled for miles with tiredness, riding was becoming a desperate affair and I had to find a bed for the night. Enquiring at the first convenience store I came to, I was devastated by an apparent lack of hotels in town. Their only advice was to try the next town. Somewhat confused but immensely relieved, the Dinosaur Inn stood prominently by the main highway, not one mile from the convenience store. Remember, always check for local knowledge.

Chapter Sixteen

Waking to a steady downpour wasn't inspiring, and the sky showed no signs of improvement. Stepping out of bed goosebumps covered my body, God it was cold! 7.30 a.m., wide-awake and shivering from the cold, I clambered into my thermals. With bright skies and radiant heat I would have relaxed, enjoyed a leisurely breakfast and not got going until mid-morning. In miserable weather, I was more inclined to set out quickly, not allowing the inclement weather a chance to weaken my resolve. After a strong coffee I kitted up and set off. It was a good one hundred and fifty miles to the Divide, with luck I could have lunch with my old friend. A short fifty mile stint got the ball rolling, by that time we both needed replenishing. A belly full of breakfast and tank full of gas meant uninterrupted riding for the majority of the day. For four and a half hours, I kept my head down and rode through endless rain. It was horrid weather, miserable, depressing, not fierce or exciting, as severe weather can be, just monotonous. I could do nothing but put up with it, only my hands actually got wet, the rest of my gear worked well. But the biting cold slowly crept in, stealing my precious heat, robbing me of my comfort. At least the landscape wasn't completely hidden from view, what I could see impressed me, a jumble of sedimentary rock, multihued, jutting from every conceivable angle, forming weird and wonderful shapes. A couple of occasions, when the cold penetrated too deep, I stopped briefly to admire the scene, jumping up and down, swinging my arms about to warm up. Town after town came and went, their only significance a slacking off from my relentless pace.

Only Steamboat Springs stood out from the rest, it marked a lull in the persistent rain, apart from that it was just another tourist hub, a place of little interest to me. And it was only a lull, before long it resumed its dreary tirade. It could easily have consumed my whole day, but as the road rose towards Rabbit Ears Pass things were about to change. Rain changed to sleet, sleet changed to snow, the road changed to slush and the temperature dropped even further. Now that couldn't be described as boring, more than ever frequent stops had to be made, to force warmth into my freezing body. Using the heat from my exhaust system, I tried to warm my saturated gloves, as I ran up and down the verge. In an attempt to bolster my spirits, I sang loud, raucous songs as I rode, to the bewilderment of stationary vehicles.

Camping was out of the question, I enjoy a challenge, but I'm not a masochist. All day I'd doggedly headed east, towards the Divide. Rabbit Ears Pass, at nine thousand four hundred and twenty six feet, crested the Divide itself. We'd been reunited, but it didn't mean we had to jump into bed together. I plumped for the relative luxury of a hotel, I had a feeling worse was in store, and preferred to be snowbound in a hotel than my tent. All the way around Canada the dread of approaching winter had dogged my passage, since entering the States it hadn't been a consideration, I'd weaved my way around without thought for the weather, once again it forced my hand. A notion to ride round the Rocky Mountain National Park was forestalled as snow drifts over a metre deep blocked the road. By spending the night in Granby I would be ideally situated to make the detour if the roads were cleared for the morning. With snow falling thick and fast that night, the signs weren't very good. I wasn't hopeful of setting off anywhere the next day, let alone the lofty heights of the national park. A wander to a sport bar that night almost turned into a battle with a blizzard, the talk of the town was of "diggin' out them snow chains."

What a transformation in the morning, no snow, bright sunshine and sub-zero temperatures. The luggage left on my bike had frozen over, preserving the only snow in sight. If it was so cold, where had the damn snow gone? Not that I was complaining, I had a vain hope the national park might have cleared; it was a short lived hope. Further drifts were unlikely to be cleared, all passes over nine thousand feet could be affected, and that could pose a slight problem. My route south laced through numerous high passes, not least was Berthoud Pass crossing the Divide at an altitude of eleven thousand three hundred and fifteen feet, a lot higher than most in the national park. I could have dithered, and revised my plans any number of times, but there was one sure way of finding out. If the road was closed, I'd have to turn round and find an alternative, the area was a winter tourist destination, of course there'd be a way through. I needn't have worried, I saw no snow at all, the trees glistened with frost but the road was clear. Boy, was it cold, it froze my breath to my scarf!

Layer after layer formed a decent defence against the encroaching cold; thermal vest, thermal polo-neck, a wicking layer, micro fleece, windproof layer, cashmere scarf and finally, my bike jacket. I should have felt like the Michelin man, but they were all thin, specific layers, any combination of which should guarantee comfort, whatever the weather. Sitting exposed and immobile on a motorbike does not generate any heat unless you have an independent heat source, e.g. heated grips or clothing. Gradually the cold penetrates, millimetre by millimetre, leeching out your precious body heat. It is only a matter of time; it gets there in the end. You can delay the inevitable, small movements help keep the blood flowing, carrying heat to the extremities. Once feeling the cold, it's hard to ignore, and so begins the downward spiral, the colder you get, the less focussed you become, and the more at risk you are. A lot of thought had gone into my layering to cope with any conditions from blazing desert heat, to freezing conditions or wet and cold driving rain. The only failing was in my gloves, my fleece lined, thinsulate, 100% waterproof, winter gloves; the one's that allowed water to flow freely in, and my body heat to flow freely out! They failed abysmally whenever it rained, but that morning, in freezing but dry conditions, they did me proud.

A slightly convoluted route was required to gain access to the longest, most scenic way through Colorado. I even had to scoot along the freeway for fifteen miles. It was a small sacrifice for the glorious landscape beyond, even the short ride there took my breath away. From the top of Berthoud Pass the view was phenomenal, being the highest point around, you could see for untold miles. After days of rain the clarity was striking, after many miles of following the divide far below, gazing in awe at its inaccessible peaks, the range of vision was awesome. A gift only the highest of peaks can present, a top of the world experience. Surveying the world below from high above, detached, absorbing the immensity of nature, observing the frantic activity of mundane existence, how could one not suffer delusions of grandeur? I was not a part of that world, I could exist within it, or step out of it, the choices were mine, and mine alone. Happy with the world, the rapid descent was a pleasure, not even the frantic freeway could faze me, the quick jaunt among mere mortals humoured me. A leafy, local road bypassed the outskirts of Denver, making me a happy bunny indeed. Entering the environs of the city would surely have knocked the smile off my face. Instead, I dawdled through El Rancho and Evergreen, stopping to savour a huge cup of the most delightful coffee, taking the opportunity to top up my dwindling reserve. When I joined Highway 285, at Conifer, I was at peace with the world, happy to share it, ready to join the serried ranks of tourists, snaking down the scenic byway.

Through quiet grassy slopes, amongst fields littered with rolls of hay, I approached the awaiting rock. The smooth surfaced, tarmac road wound up the mountainside, its broad expanse allowing easy manoeuvring round the incredibly steep 180° bends. Letting the bike wallow into a switchback, I'd see just how low it would lean, before winding on the throttle and powering out the bend. The gradient, camber and degree of turn were great fun, I could lean enough to scrape the foot pegs whenever I so desired. At altitude the road would often level out, offering fast open bends, around beautiful turquoise lakes, glistening in the sun. Crowns of crumbling sandstone topped gentle slopes of fine screed, jagged buttresses, worn and misshapen pinnacles, victims of erosion, creations of chaos. Threading its way between peaks of ever increasing height, the highway rose and fell over a succession of high passes. Kenosha, Red Hill, Trout Creek and finally Monarch pass crossing over the Divide, back to its western flanks. The mountains themselves reached lofty heights, many in excess of fourteen thousand feet, if I thought I'd already seen the best the Rockies had to offer, I was sorely misguided. Routes 285 to Poncho Springs and the 50 to Montrose were second to none. Each ascent was rewarded with euphoric views to the end of the world, the mountain lakes shone the deepest, deep blue, and the densely wooded valley floors, shaded havens, laced with roving rivers.

Dodgy middle-aged creeps stood no chance of breaking my reverie. I'd caught up with an open-topped jeep, cheesy rock tunes blaring, driven by a guy with back to front baseball cap, mirror shades and, believe it or not, the campest moustache since Freddie Mercury. It put the Village People to shame. I followed for the briefest space of time, noting driver and well-preserved jeep, dismissed them both and overtook, happy for a clear road in front.

A few miles later, at a convenient roadhouse, I pulled in for lunch. And who should pull in behind me? It isn't a sign of weakness, I try not to be put off by appearances, give people a chance, he might just have had poor dress sense. Commenting how far I was from home, he asked to join me at my table, I agreed. I wished I hadn't. He proved to be pushy, creepy and full of shit. The invitation back to his place didn't faze me in the least, his refusal to take no for an answer, irritated me. He tried to convince me that Mexico was highly dangerous, that I shouldn't, under any circumstances, try to ride my bike there. In fact I could just hole up at his place for the winter, 'yeah right.' I assured him I'd plenty of experience riding, through many countries, under a huge variety of conditions. The guy would still not desist, insistent that I go back to his place, to check it out on the Internet, to phone the US embassy. What a freak, he got to the stage where he actually angered me, trying to frighten me out of a journey, a very important journey to me, for his own devices. He was either suffering from acute sexual frustration, or had a hole in the woods he wanted to bury me in. I excused myself and left, feeling so angry with him, yet proud of myself, for staying calm, for maintaining an air of decorum.

My trusty steed had found the going tough that day, as I climbed steadily higher the smooth, reliable torque started to struggle. Gone was the crisp acceleration. No longer did it pull like a tractor instead it wheezed like an old man, struggling to catch its breath. It wasn't misfiring, it wasn't trying to cut out, so I ruled out any fault with the ignition system, or fuel starvation. How long was it since the air filter had been cleaned? Three thousand miles, that wouldn't be helping, considering the dusty duels off-road. That wasn't it though, once descending from the high passes it seemed fine. It was a lack of oxygen at the higher elevations, auto-altitude sickness, the air/fuel mixture required adjustment, it needed to be leaner. A simple adjustment would have improved it, what a shame Kawasaki sealed in the air mixture screw behind a plug of solder. Short of dismantling the carburettor and drilling it out, there was nothing I could do, except add it to the list. A growing 'to do' list that would eventually get my attention, when I reached Ojai for my next break. Daily checks were routine chores, to ensure nothing untoward was likely to happen. And indeed, once over Monarch Pass, descending towards Montrose, it never missed a beat, never hesitated in the slightest.

Owing to an absence of campsites in the latter stages of the day, I found myself entering Montrose as dusk fell. Tired, yet jubilant after a spectacular day's ride, I resigned myself to another night in a hotel, the second night on the trot. In the early days, a lifetime before, a hotel was a well-deserved luxury. Other times they'd been a welcome relief from incessant rain, shelter from the storm. For those two nights in Colorado they felt like prison cells, I felt cut off, alone. During the times camping in the wilderness, much of the time many miles from other humans, I had never felt so desperately cut off. Sitting on my own, ensconced within a hub of humanity, I felt more alone than ever before. In Granby, I'd gone in search of a bar, unable to bear my own company. As soon as I closed my hotel door, the four walls closed in, my world folded in on me and my grief erupted. I couldn't stand it, so I went traipsing through the snow, looking for a diversion. For sure, I'd grieved in the wilds, shed tears while sitting by the campfire, even felt a bit lonely. But this was different, only feeling on my own amongst crowds of people did I feel totally cut off, the ultimate despair of loneliness. It brought to mind normal, everyday existence, questions of my life, a future without Cai. Before me lay a deep chasm filled with doubt and uncertainty, lined with fear and foreboding. I wasn't strong enough to dwell on that future, brooding on my anguish was counter-productive. I had to take each day as it came, live for the here and now, busying myself with mundane tasks, occupying the mind, kept the despair at bay. The evening wore on into night, my washing hung around the room drying, my boots sat waxed and polished, my body squeaky clean and finally I lay down my head, closed my eyes and relaxed into a peaceful sleep.

Chapter Seventeen

Morning eluded me, after rising late and utilising the local library facilities, it was 2 p.m. before I got my arse into gear. Spurred on by chatting to a local motorcyclist, my planned route changed, no longer taking the more direct road to Cortez. He'd been most emphatic. I should continue along the 550 all the way into Durango, claiming it to be the best biking road around, before swinging west to visit the Mesa Verde National Park. And who was I to argue? With little chance of making it all the way to the Mesa Verde, I was in no hurry. A critical decision had been made, if I was to visit the Grand Canyon, my ride west would be the point at which I turned my back on the Continental Divide. Purgatory; the town at which I bid farewell to the backbone of the Rocky Mountains.

Narrow bands of rich pasture, gave way to stands of broad-leaved deciduous trees, before rising into a darker green scrub of the foothills. Patches of darker conifers punctuated the hillside, completing a picture of ever-darkening green. In the foreground, horses and cattle grazed amongst stacks of hay bales, perfect images of a lazy rural retreat. In the background, sharp ragged rock stood against the skyline, snow-pocked crevices gleaming in the mid-day sun. Tranquil valleys lead to steep, zigzagging ascents, hewn from the bare rock narrow roads tightly hugged the mountainsides. Veering round rocky projections, unprotected verges overhung deep chasms. Swinging first left, then right, left again, continuously twisting this way then that, it aroused a passion to push ever harder, cried for enthusiastic use of the throttle. A sharp, narrow right-hander swung close into the rock face, cutting through the bend my tyres skimmed along the verge. Looking to my right was shocking, my head and upper torso leaning out, giving me an uninterrupted view down a precipitous drop. Curbing my urge for excitement, I reined in my enthusiasm. Instead of being spurred on to overtake all and sundry, I pulled over and made the most of photo opportunities. Groups of Harleys rumbled through, fully dressed tourers, hogs, low riders, and the plainly absurd. Ape-hanger handlebars and highway pegs, arms and legs stretched far forward; how can that be comfortable? Surely a position suitable only for posing! Tailing them proved tempting, my fingers itched to rip the throttle open and blast past. But even then I let them go, stopping instead to admire the far-reaching vista of gargantuan, geological glory.

Finally, descending towards Durango, I rode alongside the ornate carriages of the Durango-Silverton narrow gauge railway. Smoke billowing black, whistle tooting, it rattled its way along, resplendent in its gaily painted colours, filled with wide eyed, happy, smiley faces. Enter stage left, man and machine, packed to the gunwales, tucked tight amongst the plethora of luggage, a man on a mission. I like to think I painted a pretty picture, not just another guy on a bike, a bold adventurer out to conquer the world. Clamouring for attention, they lined the windows franticly waving, the kids bobbing up and down in excitement, their fathers grinning inanely, maybe lost in romantic dreams of their own road-trips. Whatever image I portrayed, it made their day to attract my attention, to have their enthusiastic waves returned, to gain recognition of their existence. And I was happy to oblige, it gave me a buzz, an anonymous fanfare, well overdue!

Entering Durango at gone 5 p.m. should have signalled a halt to the day's proceedings, but no chance, I wasn't about to encage myself in another hotel, not for the third night on the trot. I decided to play catch-up, wound on the throttle and flew along at over 80mph. If I didn't make it to the Mesa Verde, it wouldn't be for a lack of trying. A brief stop, for a bottle of tequila was the only delay. The long open road made overtaking effortless, nothing hindered my progress. As darkness fell the tent was pulled from my camping roll, and by torchlight I made camp. And what a difference, warm welcomes, sincere requests about my journey and friendly invites to share campfires. Now you don't get that in many hotels!

Hangovers are inevitable after polishing off a bottle of tequila. As a haze of liquor still clouded my mind, coffee sufficed for breakfast. My aim was to survey the ruins from the cliff top, then get the hell out before succumbing to the full rage of alcoholic excess. Mesa Verde, green table, refers to the high plateau sitting atop an extensive landscape of sandstone. Seen from the southwest, a vertical bluff rises from the valley floor through slopes of loose debris, hundreds of feet high. From the road it dominates the landscape, for many miles, from the Mesa it's a different story. Deep chasms formed sheer cliffs undercut by erosion or slippage, large caves litter the cliff faces. Into these the Anasazi built increasingly complex buildings from the profusion of natural stone. Using the area for thousands of years, they'd initially dug pit-houses in the Mesa itself. Over time they became more settled, the basic shelters of hunter-gatherers didn't offer the protection or security to safeguard permanent settlement. The older buildings were single storey, as they mastered their techniques round towers and multi-storey houses were added. From the safety of the cliffs, they would ascend to the Mesa each day, to tend their crops, returning each night, secure from animals or other enemies. Little more than pockmarks in the stone, the toe and finger -holds were the means by which they climbed up and down. They must have been awesome climbers, one slip would have meant certain death.

From the Mesa top the long-range views were exceptional, spreading for miles the edge of the Mesa then plunged straight down, into a sea of sand. Overlooking a vast expanse of desert, it was easy to see why the lush plateau had first attracted the hunter-gatherers. The dwellings themselves could only really be seen from the opposite cliff top, sites made accessible if you paid for a guided tour. The appeal of traipsing in full motorcycle regalia, down a long dusty path, exposed to the scorching sun, was lost to me. I'd ride, as close as humanly possible, to each accessible point, and leave my jacket and helmet draped over the bike as I wandered around taking photos. It was true, my jacket contained all my travel documents, my wallet and credit cards. I refused to be overly concerned, to pander to paranoia over travel security, I couldn't be bothered. They are all material things, they could be replaced. Besides, not inundating yourself with worry over possessions is actually quite liberating. A bit of trust in humanity can actually go a long way. My concern at the time was more my own head state.

Wracked with guilt and thoughts of how Cai's death could have been avoided were foremost in my mind. There is no magical formula for dealing with bereavement, guilt is just one aspect of the process. Thoughts churned over and over in my mind, constant questions, whys and what ifs. Why did I ever introduce Cai to riding motorcycles? What if I'd never ridden myself? Why did we not collect the bikes in a pickup? What if I'd had the red bike? Why hadn't it been me? Once open to this train of thoughts it can be never ending. I knew Cai was doing what he most wanted to at the time, the huge grin on his face minutes before the accident said it all. The freedom and independence he'd found since having a bike meant so much to him, he revelled in riding, just the same as I always have. He'd had a couple of spills, don't we all? He knew the risks, it's all part of the excitement. Maybe it was easier to dwell on the past than try to make sense of the present; compared with thoughts of the future it was a walk in the park. I could still see no point in a future without Cai, was still afraid to contemplate how I'd cope. Riding round the cliff top loop of Mesa Verde, alongside sheer drops of many hundreds of metres, I again recognised how easy suicide would be. A simple matter of steering my bike off the road, plummeting hundreds of feet to the canyon floor. With an image of freefalling past the cliff dwellings, the thought held a strange appeal, a dramatic yet majestic end to life. How destructive though, how selfish, how thoughtless. As I knew so well, it's those left behind who must deal with the pain, whose suffering continues. How could I do that to those I love, those who'd shown so clearly, through care and support, how much I meant to them? My family and friends deserved better than having to deal with another death. And what about the archaeological destruction, am I meant to care about such things too? The process was both natural and necessary for me, the questions needed rational responses, not belittlement. Reprimanding myself, telling myself I was stupid, would have been counterproductive. I needed encouragement, strength and a clearer understanding. Isolating myself as I had left the task to me, and it was coming along, slowly.

A pounding headache accompanied me for the long haul across the Arizona desert, my hangover had caught up with me. Sunglasses hardly gave any respite from the burning sun. Already dehydrated, it was difficult getting enough fluids into my body. Preconceptions led me to believe Arizona was a boring, uninspiring, monotonous melting pot. How far from the truth that was. The road was indeed flat, straight and boring but the rock formations were spectacular. These were not endless cliffs lining the road, no gaping chasms a wheel-width from the verge, and no breath-taking views from lofty peaks. Dotted haphazardly across the endless plain, solitary formations thrust out of the desert floor, each distinct from any other. Colours ranged from the lightest beige to the darkest brown, with yellowy orange, red ochre, and every imaginable shade in between. Oblong chunks like immense obelisks stood tall and proud, the size of a small tower block. Poking from steep sandy slopes, as though forced through the desert floor, making a molehill from the overlying desert sand. Jagged peaks reared a hundred feet from the scrubby sand, rough and sharpened points jutting upwards, their blackened points menacing against the skyline. Towering above a small hamlet, a Mitre loomed large, as befitting a very big-headed Bishop, its edges battered by the elements. On one of the rare hillsides two figures squat, back to back, sentinels over the Hopi Indian Reservation, like relics of primitive clay sculpture. Swirls and whorls form incredible shapes, reminiscent of a child's frantic attempts on a potter's wheel. My intention was for a high-speed blast, straight through the desert, next stop Grand Canyon. The compromise was to stop only when sure of a good photo, then to play catch-up, belting along at 85mph. With nothing to block my view obstructions were not a problem, traffic was passed in a blur, my throbbing head kept me wide awake.

On through Navajo and Hopi lands, the road ran as straight as a die. The few stops I made left me alienated and confused, feeling responsible for the wrongs dealt to the Native Americans, tainted because of the colour of my skin. Making eye contact invariably led me to acknowledge the person, a simple nod, a *hi* or *hello* will do. Nothing! And the second encounter, nothing! Boy, did I feel out of place. Was this really the flipside of white hostilities? It was a relief when a guy actually approached me, friendly and talkative, what a shame it was only as an opening to request money. I couldn't blame them for loathing whites, what had they ever got from us but strife? The only exceptions to this were found to be those in the service industry, the hotel reception staff, cashiers and servers in a café, invariably young women trained for the tourist trade. It didn't make for a comfortable night, camping round the back of a hotel, I felt exposed, out on a limb.

On the road out of Tuba City, road signs advertising snack stalls and tourist souvenirs declared them to be, "Friendly Indians". That was reassuring, I could relax; it wasn't anything personal. Apparently, a Navaho returning home after a prolonged absence might sit with their family on the first night, with barely a word spoken. Their culture does not use the spoken word to the same extent we do. It makes sense, enabling a deeper, more relaxed acceptance of people, not hiding behind a barrage of bullshit.

A blistering pace had been set since Durango, since the mountain roads gave way to continuous straight highway. It reflected a growing frustration, an attempt to outrun the emotions broiling inside. Eventually the dash and desperation got to fever pitch. An eruption of tears almost halted me in my tracks, the release was much needed, bringing a more composed approach to my riding. I took time to ride down to the Little Colorado River Gorge, deep yet narrow, I was content to continue along its lip. I had the place to myself but the track only allowed excursions from the road to set points along the rim. Looking longingly into the gorge would not get me to strike out over open desert, it was reservation land which needed to be respected. So I turned tail, reluctantly setting off for the Grand Canyon, and the biggest accumulation of tourists so far. I wasn't looking forward to it really.

Tourists or not, it is one of the 'must see' parts of America. Met by a vast area of empty asphalt, the car park for the Desert Viewpoint raised my hopes. There were plenty of vehicles parked, I'd not really expected it to be empty, but it was less than half full. A large group of German bikers raced up and down, trying out each other's rented Harleys, hammering down the length of the car park, in jeans, T-shirt and shades posing for photos. Thirty or so of them congregated in the main car park, whilst smaller groups plied the access roads along the southern edge of the canyon. They weren't menacing or threatening towards other people: they were loud, leery and obtrusive, making their presence known to all and sundry. It was a bit much, hairy arsed bikers showing complete contempt for their own, or anyone else's safety, the less savoury aspect of motorcycling. I've done stupid things with bikes, especially in my youth with a group of us together. Boys and their toys, showing off, trying to impress. Understanding their enthusiasm was one thing, imagining a kid running out from between two cars was another. I rode sedately past without a flicker of acknowledgement, putting on my, "I am not amused" boring old git guise. I didn't want to associate myself with the over exuberant display, the public don't appreciate it. I was actually surprised no park officials put a stop to it.

One benefit of being a single bike is the ease of parking, any little slot will do, whether or not it's a recognised parking bay. It allows you to park closer to viewpoints, so an eye can be kept on your possessions. I still left my jacket and helmet with the bike, even though it was out of sight for a fair while, if I'd had to carry it I wouldn't have left the bike. As it was, the jumble of people crowding out the vantage point almost made me turn round and not bother. I had to have a look though, I'd diverted specially for this, a quick look and a photo were all I'd need. Until I got a clear view, then it was a different story, others stood no chance if they thought they could squeeze me out the way. Politely but firmly I wriggled my way through, before finally being confronted by the vastness of the Grand Canyon.

From four to eight miles wide, over a mile deep and supposedly two hundred and seventy seven miles long, it fills your whole view, and then some. At first sight it seems infinite, an immense landscape of spectacular proportions, it literally takes the breath away. Thought to have taken seventeen million years of erosion, the Colorado River and its tributaries have exposed approximately two billion years of geological history. A million different stratified layers, cut and shaped beyond belief, ridges, ledges, overhangs, pillars, walls and much, much more. An array of colours that blur into the haze, only on closer inspection does their variety come into focus. On one buttress muddy brown veins separate the white sand from the deep ochre, another displays bands of the deepest russet red imaginable. I stood bewildered, trying to absorb the scene I beheld. Only some minutes later did I notice the Colorado River threading its way through, a minute detail amongst the surrounding enormity. Try as I might I couldn't take it all in, it stretches to infinity. Pictures can only detract from the magnificent view, no description, no photo can capture just how amazing the Grand Canyon looks. One look is not enough, each standpoint is incomparable from the next. If I thought a couple of photos from one place would suffice, I was quickly proved wrong. Heading west along the southern rim, each glimpse made another stop imperative. Every angle was totally different, the formations change constantly, a myriad of hues highlighted by the sun, walk a hundred metres and another vista opens before your eyes. I spent four hours marvelling at the views, never dissatisfied, never irritated by the peasant hordes, mesmerised the whole time. It could have been a lot longer, almost with regret

I turned south, bound for Route 180, then Interstate 40 for the long slog back to Ojai.

Approximately seven hundred and fifty miles from Ojai, I got it into my head to make it back that day. It was 1 p.m. when I left Grand Canyon Village, all I could think about was the welcome back at Alasdair and Lauren's, a respite from days in the saddle. There really was no stopping me, with the throttle wide open my cruising speed rarely fell below 80mph, 85mph was maintained wherever possible. Three stops were made, each for fuel, I'd fill the tank and force feed myself, before swinging my leg back over the beast and ripping it wide open again. Hot desert air damn near seared my lungs, sticky sweat made the slightest move unpleasant. I rode with my jacket tightly zipped, ever conscious of the extremes to which I pushed myself. It was a blessing when darkness descended, but coolness soon turned to chill, and layers needed adding at each stop. At my last stop, I took enough time to exchange greetings with a Suzuki Virago rider. For him, the glory days of Harleys Davidson were over, he was more than happy to save money and gain reliability with his Japanese Harley lookalike. For him leather chaps were the solution to the encroaching cold, I preferred an extra layer under my jacket, to strut my stuff in a pair of chaps is a little too camp for my liking.

Closing in on LA the traffic was horrendous. I'd wanted to swing west, north of the city, avoiding the congestion and mayhem of LA freeways. My tired, befuddled mind struggled to navigate through the chaos, anger consumed me, blaming anyone and everyone for contributing to my loss. Without the energy to stave off those unwanted thoughts and emotions, I fell prey to the confusion, bewilderment took over concentration. In the darkness my map was useless, I relied on my memory, the junction I wanted, the route number and the next destination. Ending up on an unlit, single-track, country road didn't fill me with confidence. My visor was dirty, visibility severely affected, and I was cold. Mile after mile I rode, convinced I was heading in the right direction, the road seemed endless, with few side roads, those few shed no light as to where I actually was. None of the signposts corresponded with my map, at any possible point of reference I had to stop and use my torch to check. Cold and dispirited, I actually considered lying down at the side of the road and sleeping. Literally on my last legs, I found enlightenment in the form of Route 14, my link road, my saviour! It bolstered my spirits, re-energised my weary body and gave me the strength to complete the last, familiar, miles from Santa Clarita to Ojai. And into the welcoming arms of my hosts! It felt like a homecoming, familiar faces, familiar places, truly a home from home.

Chapter Eighteen

It was as if I'd never left, I settled easily and valued the care and companionship of the whole family. But it was so much more, their friends and neighbours were familiar, as were the roads and shops. Not exactly devoid of memories I know, it was the last place Cai and I shared time together, but it helped to some extent. It didn't have the all-encompassing grief I'd felt at home in North Wales, it was where I'd first had to deal with the loss, where I'd first found sanctuary. With the amount of support and understanding of everyone around, is was the safest haven I could have found. It gave me the security to face my fears, assess my life, the present and the future. For the first time, I brought my grief to the forefront of my thoughts, applied myself to the task of accepting a life without Cai. And, as with all interludes in my journey, it gave me the chance to pay more attention to the upkeep of my bike.

Ten thousand miles on the clock, and the replacement Avon tyres had proven much better wearing than the Dunlops. Three thousand miles with hardly any sign of wear, front or rear. I could have left the next service for another two thousand miles, there was no point, why leave it to be done in uncertain conditions? In Ojai, I had a secure environment to work in, and a host of extra tools to use. Having complied with Kawasaki's warranty conditions, I was free to service my own machine, approved dealers must do the first two services. I trust myself, a service by dealers can be a hit and miss affair, you never know until it's too late. I also enjoy working on my bikes, as much as riding them. Regardless of any other reason, it improves your understanding of your machine and makes you mechanically self-sufficient. Having pin-pointed each flaw, in design or setup, it was time to put my personal touches to it. My 'To Do' list consisted of sensible upgrades, an attempt to increase reliability, performance and security. Originally we'd bought soft luggage, with the two of us security would have posed few problems, one could always watch the bikes while the other shopped, went to toilet, etc. Without fail, everyone's opinion reflected a huge problem with theft throughout Central and South America. I considered a more secure luggage system vital for my solo journey through Latin America. Spare parts could no longer be guaranteed, local sources would be scarce and the postal services unreliable. I also wanted better fuel economy, the Kawasaki drank fuel compared to my old Honda XL, alterations to airflow, carburettor and exhaust would improve that.

A frenzy of retail therapy ensued, I restricted my consumerism to sensible upgrades only, the range of after-market parts for KLRs is huge in the States, so some restraint was called for. Double locking aluminium panniers and top box were the biggest priority, with the addition of a wire mesh lined tank bag, security would no longer be an issue. Hi-flow, reusable air and oil filters reduced the number of spares to carry, whilst improving the fuel/air delivery. A Supatrapp exhaust, allowing adjustments to the backpressure, produced a cleaner, crisper pickup from low revs; a smoother power delivery should mean less wastage of fuel, it also sounded more raucous (my type of bike). Maximising the efficiency of the inlet and exhaust would improve fuel efficiency; changing the gearing of the sprockets would mean lower revs at cruising speed, optimising consumption (though this would not be done until new chain and sprockets were due). Drilling out the lead plug from the air mixture channel gave access to the screw itself, which I replaced with a custom screw, ending in a T-bar. This allowed instant adjustments to the mixture, no tools required, hop off the bike, turn it one way or the other, hop back on and away I go again. In case that wasn't sufficient, I also bought a leaner pilot jet, I was determined that altitude wouldn't pose any more problems. What I considered essential spares would be carried, throttle and clutch cables, brake pads, new chain and sprockets, and a full set of bulbs. Barring a major mechanical failure, I was prepared for any eventuality.

Compared to the standard exhaust system the Supatrapp was incredibly light, the removal of the California spec fuel evaporation emission control system further reduced weight. Offset against the heavier luggage system, net weight gain was negligible. Handlebar controls were refitted, using newly drilled locating holes they sat exactly where I wanted them. The rear of the panniers and top box were emblazoned with GB and CYMRU stickers, in an attempt to clarify I was not American, despite riding a Californian registered bike. Put simply, Latin Americans can have a very poor attitude to Americans.

It wasn't all bikes and bits though, I'd hurried back partly to join the Coyne family on one of their renowned hikes into the Sespe Wilderness area. The irony wasn't lost on me, Cai was keen to go on a longer hike earlier in the summer, and I hadn't been, even to the extent of using a weak knee as an excuse not to go. Yet there I was, full pack on, wilting under a fierce sun, with a three-hour hike ahead, and that was just to reach base camp. The chances of rain were zero, or so I was told, so we camped in the open, on a sandy bank by the creek. Cooking and hot drinks were prepared on an open fire and our water filtered from the creek, to reduce the ever-present risk of Giardia. With so little equipment to set up we settled in quickly, hiking in was the easier part of the weekend. The following day, Saturday, was to be a full day along the riverbed, uprooting invasive Tamarisk bushes. Apparently, once they start to get established they spread like wildfire, completely choking the gorges, eradicating the native species. A bit like Europeans in their endeavours to conquer foreign lands, once they got a foothold there was no stopping them, until the native population was completely subjugated. Our attempts at keeping the foreigners out waylaid us a bit, the hike to Devil's Gate took six hours, the return only three. Enormous boulders, rolled hither and thither by the winter's raging waters, provided a continuous obstacle course. Scrambling over, squeezing through, shimmying round or simply wading across the creek, the choices were infinite. Rarely was our party in an orderly line, playing follow the leader. Sometimes Iain and I would venture off alone, traversing narrow ledges in pursuit of a promising jump point, praying to find the perfect plunge pool. The going wasn't too tough, hot and slow going maybe, but the frequent plunges into the creek kept us cool and kept dehydration at bay. And that was the fun part, crystal clear, freshwater to hurl ourselves into. Find a deep enough pool, climb as high as you can, and jump. Simple things please simple minds, and I was easily pleased! The water wasn't warm though, by any stretch of the imagination. The first bold leap left me breathless, what a shock. I'd thought that flowing through a parched environment, baked by the sun for months, the water would have got a lot warmer. After three or four dips into the water I'd started to get used to it, to some extent anyway. Once dried and overheating again the temperature difference still took my breath away. But excellent fun! Iain, at eight years old, loved the thrill of it, even more so having someone who appreciated the childish delight to the same extent as him. And Sunday was much better, we pretty much lazed around camp, enjoying the sun and playing in the water. There was plenty of choice for amusement, hidden pools with water chutes into other, deeper pools, rock arches to dive through, and some awesome high jumps. All too soon the weekend was drawing to a close, the ferocity of the sun waned and it was time for the hike out, uphill all the way.

After a three week stay I felt settled, secure. It wasn't all fun and frolics, the emotional turmoil didn't miraculously vanish, my grief was still a constant companion. I'd been feeling pretty low generally, but working on the bike had been therapeutic, joining in the fun and games of the family doubly so. But still there was little to rejoice about, my thoughts filled with memories of Cai, my mind wracked with guilt. I woke most mornings with thoughts of Cai, memories sprang to mind at the drop of a hat, throughout the day. It didn't mean I was always falling apart, or breaking into floods of tears. Those occasions were the exceptions, I'd become more self-contained with my grief by then. I'd started to live with it, my journey wasn't only about dealing with bereavement, it became more to do with me, my life, my enjoyment. I nearly decided to go home for Christmas, I'd enjoyed the time with my Californian friends so much. But I still wasn't ready, didn't feel like facing the barrage of memories awaiting me in North Wales. I was in no doubt that continuing would benefit me most. So once the bike was ready, it was time to go. I hung about for one last weekend amongst friends, for one last celebration with my adopted family. After that I ran out of excuses, however tempting further delays might be, I wanted to set off, to face my excursion into Spanish speaking realms.

Chapter Nineteen

A late start and several detours for further spares, saw me finally on Interstate 5 heading out of Los Angeles at gone 6 p.m. Not long after clearing greater LA the sky became darkened by smoke, almost blocking out the moon. It was really dense and got thicker by the minute. It was so surreal, thick smoke obscuring everything, ash highlighted in my headlight like flurries of snow, the cloying taste of burning thick on my tongue. A rider of the apocalypse, ash raining down, surrounded by the glow of wildfires littering the hillside. By the time I approached Spring Valley signs declared Highway 94 closed, bang went my hopes of making Tacate that day. I stopped at a retail park. The fires spread across the horizon, only a few miles ahead of me. I hadn't realised the extent or seriousness of the wildfires, the car park was full of RVs and campers, people who'd been evacuated. It appeared more like a community outing, cooler boxes and hampers open, gossiping with neighbours. People sat on picnic chairs in the back of their pickups, watching the progress of the fires, a grandstand view. They were jostling for the best photo shots. The flaming hillside did look impressive, but my mind remained focussed on ways around the flaming barrier. I was desperate to find a way past the fires without resorting to the Tijuana border crossing. I couldn't face the seething cesspit of humanity I believed the place to be. High, shifting winds compounded the problem, the authorities unwilling to risk passage between the various fires, so haphazard was the chance of them spreading. Route 8, re-joining Route 94 beyond the fires, re-opened, restrictions on motorcycles were lifted; a sufficient enough drop in the wind for the fire services to declare it passable. OK, it was passable, because I got along it! It was a hairy ride though, at relatively slow speed, constantly battling with gusting cross winds. If I went any faster than 55mph the instability was a real problem, below 50mph and I didn't have enough speed to maintain a straight line against the wind. There was no foretelling which direction the next gust would come from either, nor how strong it would be. I struggled for an hour, then resting at a gas station, chatted to a couple of border guards. They told me the 94 from the east, to circle round the roadblocks, was in fact closed as well. Holy shit, what choice did I have left? I continued to the junction of the 94, with no other choice I booked into a hotel. It was late, it had been a long day and I was wound up. Time to take a breather, give myself time to calm down and reconsider my options.

I woke early, breakfasted and packed by 9.30 a.m. With no sign of a roadblock onto the 94, I thought my luck was in, but not for long, after twenty miles, up popped a sign, "road closed". There was no police blockade, so I decided to ask locally about the situation, still hoping to reach Tecate and cross the border. No chance, two miles further along was a police roadblock. And then I meet two local guys, with the solution to all my problems. 'What sort of bike are you riding, is it a street bike?' Oh no, not a discussion on the merits of street versus dirt bike! Absolutely not, with a dirt bike it was simple, up to the roadblock, turn left and strike out across the desert. Continue until reaching the border fence, then turn right and follow the fence, all the way to the Tacate border crossing. Wow, what a treasure; I do believe in miracles. It appealed to my sense of humour, approach the roadblock, watch the police move in anticipation, then indicate left and ride off into the desert. Not even giving them a chance to say a word, or signal for me to stop. They stood watching me veer off, a look of bemusement on their faces. A straight forward trail, easy to follow, led directly across the desert. Before I knew it, a twelve-foot high metal barrier stretched from east to west, as far as the eye could see. Wow, that is some border fence. It put the security fence at Glastonbury festival to shame. It wasn't my problem, hang a right, next stop Tecate.

It turned out to be a reasonable track, not too loose, and not too much gravel. It was compacted sand, well used, with some steep, rocky sections. Uphill sections were treated with caution, low revs, up on the footpegs, slow but sure. Steep downhill sections made me ride with the utmost caution, still up on my feet, low gear and low revs, covering the rear brake at all times. Of course, it was the track used by the Border Patrol vehicles which plied their way up and down the wall, all day every day. Having passed a couple of them it didn't seem a problem, I wasn't on restricted land, and I wasn't doing anything illegal. The third one stopped me, asking where I was going. Again, no problem, he wished me luck and left me to continue on my way. Easing over the lip of abrupt drops into sandy ravines, picking my way carefully up sudden inclines, I took my time. Overcoming each obstacle as it came, I never pre-empted problems and I certainly wasn't blasé about the terrain. An empty desert, twenty five miles of torturous track, it was tricky going and I loved every minute of it! Far from being featureless I enjoyed a whole host of desert delights, sandy sinkholes, rocky ridges, slippery switchbacks and crucial climbs at impossible angles. Only the wall hinted at the presence of humans, there was nothing else but sand and rock, my bike and me; it felt like my own personal playground. It provided a perfect practice session for future feats of riding prowess, for real desert crossings.

I was within a few miles of Tacate, and who should I run into? One of America's finest, a border guard on a power trip. I was met with disbelief, he obviously wasn't impressed to see me, and sure as hell wasn't about to be helpful. Demanding to know what I was doing there, how I'd got there, and why, he made it clear he did not want me there. Obviously, tolerance and indulgence were character flaws in his book. He also claimed the border crossing at Tacate was closed, telling me to turn around and go back. I didn't believe him, assuring him plenty of his colleagues had seen and spoken to me, they'd had no problem with my presence there. He wouldn't believe me which left us at an impasse, a Mexican standoff. Neither of us was about to concede on any point. I didn't mind staying a night at the border, he claimed there was nowhere to stay there. In my eyes I was doing nothing wrong, there was little he could do about it, he must have realised that too. Expressing a few last words of displeasure he left me to it, returning the way he'd come.

It must have been the rush hour, as I sat contemplating, the first guy I'd spoken to reappeared. I couldn't believe it, after confirming the closure of the border, he told me to find a hole in the barrier and go through. OK, turn around and change tactics, except I'd only just turned around when Mr Obnoxious came back. Followed closely by the helpful one, complicated or what? Luckily no, a quick discussion between them and a note was taken of my details. Mr O turned and just advised me to get across the border anyway I could. They merely wanted me out their hair, didn't want me to be their problem. It suited me fine, next stop Mexico!

If only life were so simple. Following the border it was clear there were breaches in the wall. All I needed was a point to get the bike through, so I rode slowly, carefully inspecting any gaps as I went. Once more I had the desert to myself, or so I thought. Stopping for a closer look at one gap, I noticed a 4x4 trailing me on the other side of the border. Bugger, a Mexican border patrol. I could imagine their delight at catching a Gringo skipping across the border illegally. A visit to a Mexican prison was definitely not on any agenda of mine, with hindsight a small bribe may well have seen me safely across, instead I turned tail and ran for Tacate. True to their word, everything was closed, the only personnel present were the border guards, and boy were they disgruntled to see me. Once I'd explained the situation, they were fine, maybe a bit perplexed at my adamant reluctance to cross at Tijuana, but otherwise fine. Of course, they felt obliged to do a complete check on me, without malice or hostility, they were actually apologetic, but my presence at the border post had to be duly recorded. And then I was sent packing, not back across the desert, but east on Route 94, straight through the frontline of the wildfires. Then retracing my steps, along Interstate 8, all the way back to San Diego, before heading south again, only to be spewed out towards the dreaded Tijuana. No bloody way was I relenting, not once an alternative border crossing for commercial traffic was found, six miles further east. I rode straight through, astonished at not being stopped, no sign of officials. I just pulled up at a red light, it turned green and I was through. My own disbelief caused me to stop and check, no, no sign of a customs office or immigration, so I carried on my merry way. Somewhere, in the back of my mind, I recalled someone saying Import Tax and Tourist Tax could be bought in Ensenada. After hearing horror stories of police corruption in Mexico, I didn't really want to travel without the correct paperwork. My impatience was stronger though, at that stage I was beyond caring, the day had already been complicated enough. I'd get the hell away from the border and overnight in Ensenada, the paperwork could wait till the morning.

My emotions obviously couldn't, unexpectedly my whole world came crashing down upon me. A hotel proved the language barrier beyond my abilities to breach, a dozen words of Spanish wasn't enough to communicate effectively. Wi-fi came with the room price, the room was out of range though and expressing my dissatisfaction was beyond me. Such an insignificant detail, with such a drastic response, feeling a rush of anxiety, I made a mad dash for my room. I lost it completely, a full-blown panic attack left me quaking in my boots. Fighting for breath, trembling with fear, I desperately rummaged through my pack. A double dose of Rescue Remedy helped, taking a further dose helped even more. It was hardly the start I'd envisaged. After mere hours of entering Mexico, I sat crying like a baby, afraid of what lay ahead. It robbed me of any self-assurance I'd gained in the north, leaving me with severe doubts of coping south of the border. Completely drained of strength, physical and emotional, I finally succumbed to a troubled sleep. Tomorrow was a new day, hopefully it would bring with it new reserves of strength.

Doggedly, I went through the process of legitimising my presence in Mexico. Immigration in the town was primarily as a seaport, the $23 Tax could be paid there, but at a price. A penalty of $5 per day was imposed for failure to procure Tourist Tax at your point of entry. For the lack of queuing, and a hassle free entry it was worth double the price, I felt I'd ripped them off. With grumpy delight, the immigration officer informed me I had to pay the fine at the bank. I noted the satisfaction with which he gave the directions, as if the mile trek there and back was of great hardship. Though in all fairness, it probably was for a lazy lard-arse, who spent all day sitting behind a desk pushing paper and making life difficult for Gringos. For me it saved time, an ATM was to be my next port of call and I had no idea where to find one. There was no need to pay temporary import tax for the bike either, it wasn't due until I left the Baja Peninsula, for the mainland. I tried insisting on obtaining it there and then, but he was having none of it. It humoured me, pushing to obtain what I didn't need, and no doubt gave him pleasure to deny my persistent request. It was only a game, at that precise moment I wasn't even confident of making it to mainland Mexico.

A pattern was forming. Troubled days clouded my thoughts, and weighed heavy on my heart after a break in the journey. I still hadn't recognised it, still tended to fold under the pressure. Entering Latin America compounded the problem, the language barrier set me aside, another Gringo ripe for plucking. I felt so out on a limb. With a head full of my own problems, I withdrew from my surroundings, oblivious to the beauty, insensitive to the degradation. The coast down to Ensenada had passed without comment, the filth-ridden shanties of Tijuana received not the slightest criticism, run down fishing coves went scarcely noticed, clear blue skies reflected in azure seas failed to impress. My only concern had been to reach the comfort afforded by a hotel, had I lost all sensibility? Since when had hotels provided emotional security?

A second day was spent stubbornly pressing on, filled with a desperate desire to turn around and return to Ojai. All I wanted was to be around friends, to have their support, their comforting words. I cried bitterly, each mile adding to my distress, calling out to Cai, pleading him to give me the strength of my convictions. The journey seemed too much of an undertaking on my own. I didn't want to be alone. I didn't want to face the trip on my own and I didn't want to face life alone. My grasp of Spanish was appalling. I couldn't communicate with local people. My only hope was to meet other English speakers, to meet other travellers to bolster my motivation. I couldn't face the isolation, I needed people, needed interaction. I forced myself to make an effort, saying hello in Spanish, trying out a few words, a few phrases. Failing to make myself understood, all hope was lost. On the verge of turning round, indecision stopped me, my despair so acute I couldn't even face the return trip. Unable to continue, too afraid to return, the only alternative was to stop and get a grip of myself. Sliding surreptitiously into a phone booth wasn't an option, gone were the days of blubbering down the phone in private. An international line was only available at the open counter of the local store, but I had to hear a friendly voice. So I sat quietly, on the main street of a village, attempting to contain the tears and struggling to do so. Oblivious to the stares of passers-by, my only concern was getting my shit together to make that call. I was teetering, precariously balanced on an emotional tightrope, scared of how far a fall might take me. At the limits of enduring the pain, a gentle, calm approach was essential, any more pressure was unthinkable. Focussing on the breath, breathing deep and slow but not forcing it, slowly but surely letting go of the tension, releasing the fear, I gradually gained enough control to face other people. Setting off and facing the world again wasn't on the agenda, I was still fraught at the prospect of continuing.

Soothing and calm, the voice of reason pervaded my irrational thoughts. The gentle voice of Lauren crackled down the line from Ojai, patient and understanding. Reminders of previous days, the trauma of setting off originally, reassurances as to my own strength, my accomplishments so far. Probing questions, gently put. How would I feel to give up at that moment? Would I feel I'd failed? Wouldn't it detract from the effort already made? Maybe a couple more days might make all the difference, wouldn't that at least let me feel I'd tried? And realisation dawned, I did remember how overwrought with grief and fear those initial days had been. The words brought to mind the battles fought, the hardships overcome, how essential that had all been for me. Recognition of the importance of my efforts came clearly to mind, I knew giving up would never be forgotten, never be forgiven, not by me. It was for myself I rode, for the sense of achievement gained, the strength of mind it induced, to vent the emotional turmoil. To give up so readily was to give up on life, it was to belittle the loss of Cai. It mattered to me, and it would have mattered to him. How could I wimp out with so little effort? None of those thoughts fortified me, they didn't lighten the load. They simply made me dig my heels in harder, gave me back a degree of determination. Much as I'd like to say the way ahead urged me forward once more, it didn't. With reluctance I straddled the machine, pointed it away from sanctuary, and headed south.

Road grades took on a whole new meaning. The term Freeway meant nothing more than a single carriageway tarmac road. A "Highway", a single-track tarmac road, if you were lucky there might be passing places, though on the bike they were irrelevant. Next category was "Gravel Tracks", the occasional one led from the Freeway to a designated port. More common were "Graded Dirt Roads", I believe there was supposed to be a semblance of smoothness to them, in reality there was little difference to ordinary "Dirt Roads", there were likely to be rutted, washed out sections at any point, without warning. Last but not least, the "Poor Roads", which form many hard sections of the Baja 1000, the infamous desert race, running the length of the Baja Peninsula. Looking at route maps for this gruelling race it appears to be largely made up of "Dirt Roads" and "Poor Roads".

From Ensenada, Mexican Federal Freeway 1 plied its way through a succession of hot dusty towns. Once leaving the urban sprawl access to the coast involved using dry dusty tracks, in fact, once venturing off the tarmac of Mexico 1, everything was dry and dusty. "Graded Dirt Roads" proved the most common to reach the various coastal villages and occasional small-scale resorts. More often than not they would only link to other "Graded Dirt Roads" by "Poor Roads", making circuitous detours via the coast fairly extreme. Compared to my jaunt along the Mexican border fence, the trails to the coast shouldn't have posed too many problems themselves; the link roads could well have proved problematic. But I wasn't even in the mood to attempt it, trying to complete sections of the Baja 1000, on my overloaded Enduro wasn't appealing.

I rode from Colonet to San Antonio del Mar on a "Graded Dirt Road", meandering for seven miles between the Freeway and coast. An ever-worsening road, but by the time it got to the sea it was fairly well compacted dirt. It was alright really, nothing to write home about, and nothing to cause any problems. Unfortunately the beach was non-existent, only a shallow cliff was visible, with a rather glib looking tourist compound a mile further along. I didn't bother checking it out, my interests were with beaches and dirt riding, and I hadn't exactly come up trumps. All was not lost though, an idea to "what "Graded Dirt Road" meant" was invaluable. I wouldn't hesitate to choose that category of road in the future. Satisfying my curiosity, I could move on, it was getting late and a suitable campsite had to be found. A recommendation of the Parque Nacional Sierra de San Pedro Martir had been heard in Ensenada, an authorised campsite suited my mood. It was gone 5 p.m. and over sixty miles had to be covered, on an increasingly rougher road. It was a breeze, averaging over 60mph, mainly on tarmac; being depicted as dirt was misguiding, it was better than the graded road earlier.

Time and again preconceived ideas let me down, wasn't Baja California a one thousand mile spit of desert? I expected it flat and lifeless, nothing but sand, maybe a bit of rock dotted here and there. A ridge of mountains form a backbone to the peninsula, sometimes dominating the west coast, later seen as a central feature to the peninsula, swinging hither and thither, unpredictably, to either coast. A rising ridge carried me inland towards the National Park, as I gained altitude the panorama opened before my eyes. More mountain visages than I'd imagined, bare rocky peaks reared above softly folded mounds, rolling down to sandy desert plains. Ahead lay a profusion of Pine trees, ringing the highest peaks, the tree clad slopes belied its desert location, certainly not what I expected.

It was gone six by the time I got there and nearing darkness when I set up camp. I actually managed to understand the gist of park rules and motorcycles. There are no bikes allowed within the park boundaries. Of course there are always ways around rules, the guy took me round a sandy track, where I could park my bike and camp. With dark closing in fast I didn't bother with the tent, merely unrolling my sleep mat and sleeping bag, happy to sleep in the open, under the stars. With plenty of wood to burn a campfire was a must, the aesthetic quality of my campsite was perfect. Cooking on an open fire completed the picture, and produced a wonderful vegetable stew. Bloody luxury, my first camp food for weeks. Gone were the extremes of despair, I felt a degree of loneliness but my resolve was strengthened. Lying back with bloated belly, fire flickering by my side, staring into the star-studded sky, it could only help but relax me further. Loosing my thoughts into the cosmos released pent up emotions, gently filling me with memories of Cai, profound love for my son. It was a teary goodnight, directed sky wards, but not without a degree of contentment.

Blistering sun by day and damned cold at night, the desert is a place of extremes. Daylight had arrived but the sun was yet to appear over the mountains, I lay curled in my doss bag patiently awaiting its warming rays. At first I took the approach of a throbbing engine to be another motorbike, raising onto one elbow in anticipation, a bright yellow slug-bus appeared instead, stopping abruptly at the sight of the bike and me. I guessed it to be the Aussie who'd booked into the park the day before me, and sure enough, as soon as he opened his mouth my suspicions were confirmed. Wow, he seemed so pleased to see me, initially I thought there must be a problem. But no, not physically anyway, Davo felt the same isolation and loneliness as me. Having travelled six months round North America, he'd enjoyed the companionship and hospitality of the Americans. Now south of the border, he suffered as I did, actually not quite, he was almost shivering with cold. Offering strong, hot coffee was the only decent thing to do, and so we started our acquaintance. One that was to last a number of weeks, over many miles and countless hours of fun, finally leaving me fully prepared to strike out alone.

Chapter Twenty

Everything in life has its pros and cons, and travelling companions are no exception. By and large we worked well together and appreciated each other's company. If I thought I had problems with the language, Davo was linguistically crippled, absolutely hopeless. So, armed with dictionary and very basic phrases, I got more than my share of practice which I was more than happy about. We bolstered each other's confidence, taking routes and sleeping places we may easily have avoided if left to our own devices. For endless miles I followed his progress, letting the VW Camper dictate the pace, a sedate 50-60mph. Frequently I'd stop, for a photo, or just a closer look at one particular scene or an interesting feature. I loved prolonging the wait, allowing Davo to increase the distance, then setting off like a bat out of hell, playing catch up. If an especially winding stretch of road appeared, I'd overtake, cranking it through the bends, whooping with joy. Disappearing for miles, I refused to forsake those aspects of my trip I cherished most, those which filled my soul with joy. Waiting cheerfully for the slug bus to chug into view, I'd often roar off again before he could even acknowledge me. Generally I was more considerate, checking all was OK before zooming off, looning about on my own. As a rule, we stuck together, communicated well and enjoyed the companionship. Riding is a solitary occupation, without two-way radios conversation is impossible, you're left to your own thoughts, regardless of Davo's presence my world was my own. At night the company was appreciated, campfires and daiquiris ruled the roost, more often than not I'd sleep in the open whilst he snuggled in the van.

As a prelude to our journey south, we visited San Vicente and a contact of Davo's, Larry, one of a pair running Off-Road bike tours of the peninsula. Enjoying a few days respite, their compound offered security from the wandering palms of local kids. At least when my stuff got stolen he managed to recover it, both times, from the same kid. Rides in throaty Toyota pick-ups and souped up VW Beetles thrilled us no end. An afternoon jaunt into the desert took us over and through endless mounds, ridges, ditches and dykes. Surrounded by a rich ochre landscape, we criss-crossed for hours, through a veritable maze of endless trails. Jacked up by extended suspension struts, with twin choke carbs and straight through exhausts, the Beetles seemed capable of going anywhere. Inside they were appalling, as passengers we were shaken and thrown all over the place. Eduardo, Larry's young Mexican protégé, accompanied us on a Honda XR250.

Stopping at the foot of stupidly steep, high slopes, Larry would point it out and call, 'Eduardo, ride up there, to the top.' And away he'd go, not even bothering to wind around the track, he'd stand on the pegs, point it straight at the summit and go for it, never once faltering, never once failing.

The Beetle itself amazed me, pushed to the limits it never gave up, defying gravity itself, or so it felt clinging on for dear life inside. It had an unbelievable centre of gravity, half in half out of deep ditches, leaning at impossible angles. I was convinced it would topple over. Cresting the top of awesome slopes the front end would leave the ground, threatening to flip right over, but no. No way, it was a VW Beetle for God's sake, hooray for Herbie! The grin factor was excellent, the scenery beautiful, and my backside was battered and bruised. It proved a good distraction, with a good crowd, it did my spirits the world of good.

Mainly mounted on XR250's and 400's, the off-roaders were unanimous on one opinion, they wouldn't like to tackle much off-road on my over loaded KLR650. We sat down and pored over my maps of Baja, Dave and me making suggestions as to possible routes across the desert. Their feedback was disappointing, they really didn't rate my bike as capable of much at all. They scoffed at the idea of me managing anything beyond "Graded Dirt Road", I had a lot more faith in the bike, but I knew how much it had already seen me through. The biggest problems I faced were sections of deep sand, the KLR was by no means a lightweight machine, and fully loaded it was verging on the obese. I wasn't about to be deterred from having a go, though I took note of the routes they particularly warned against. Ironically, our first night out we both got stuck in deep sand, not in the desert either, at the beach.

Striking out along a dirt road, we left the highway just past San Quintin. A promising start, on compacted sandy dirt, deteriorating into ruts and potholes as we neared the beach. I led the way, to avoid the spume of dust kicked up from Davo's camper. The fine, gritty cloud obliterated my view, coated my lungs and found its way into every slit and orifice imaginable. Leaving my eyes near blind, my nose blocked solid, and me hacking and coughing trying to spit out the grit from between my teeth. Whatever our routine on the highway, my place on dirt was out front. It gave me the benefit of uninterrupted views, unhindered progress and the feeling of being alone, yet with backup following, just in case. A gritty orange track surface gave way to bright, dazzling white sand. The open sea was still distant, little more than a mirage, shimmering between low-lying bars of sand. At first seemingly featureless, the blinding expanse stretched into the distance to both sides, low, drifting dunes bordered the endless beach, forming sandy spits that curved round, creating shallow lagoons. A peaceful, quiet place to camp on the beach was what we set out to find, it looked like we'd found it, we just had to find our own little spot. At my invite the camper set off, swinging left just short of a rising lagoon, with the tide encroaching we kept above the high tide mark. Mistake number one! After all of fifty metres, the slug bus sank up to its axles in sand. Realising Davo's situation, I rode on to give assistance. Mistake number two! I swiftly followed suit, sinking far enough to get off the bike and leave it upright, without the kickstand down. At least with a quick push I was freed. With gentle use of the throttle, paddling along, the bike was turned round and firm ground reached. Nothing so simple for the slug bus though, it'd sunk right up to the chassis. Rocking backwards and forwards achieved nothing, pushing only knackered me in no time. Wedging timber and matting under the tyres for traction, was a waste of time. He was well and truly stuck, there was no alternative, it meant clearing space beneath it, jacking up the damned thing, letting out the tyre pressure, and repacking sand under the tyres. Armed with my trenching tool, Davo got to work while I got cooking. By the time food was ready, he'd finished, and to enormous relief the effort was successful. After that aborted attempt at traversing the beach, we decided to stay put. Davo enjoyed the relative comfort of his camper, whilst I plumped to enjoy the fresh air and distant sound of surf. Mistake number three! It left me exposed to the ravishes of the notorious Mexican beach bandits, "*los poquito mosquitos bastados*". Waking up my face closely resembled that of the Elephant Man, I'd been stung around my eyes, cheeks and nose, my face puffing up beyond recognition.

Some days we made little progress, lazy starts and early finishes, expending more effort in finding the perfect spot on secluded beaches. Scouting ahead I'd often investigate a promising dirt road, checking out deserted sandy bays, or shallow cliffs overlooking miles of golden sand. With Davo as back up, my confidence soared, I grew more relaxed under increasingly difficult terrain, I really making the most of the opportunity to push ever harder. Unfazed by the terrain I'd take off along rough, dusty tracks, with the knowledge that if all went wrong, I wouldn't be stranded; wouldn't be left to claw my way, busted and broken, across miles of desert. Little regard was given to recorded road grades, if a spot looked promising, either on the map or from the road, we'd venture forth. Inevitably each evening would find us on a lonely beach, marveling at the natural delights before us. The west coast bestowed upon us the most wonderful sunsets, topped by bright blue sky, swirls of brilliantly lit cloud spiraled towards the sun. Multiple hues of blue and gold, cascading inwards, ever brighter, merging into a ball of the purest, white light. Faded midnight blues formed a hazy halo, on the outer edges. Vibrant orange tails whirled into the midst of vivid yellows, streaked with subtle flaxen locks, flecked with rich reds. Pastel shades of pink edged rusty ochres, diffused with a hint of purple. Below, gently lapping waves glistening, with deep, rich tones of amber, spilling as molten gold across the wet sand.

Whether east or west, a host of ornithological wonders never failed to impress. Enormous flocks of shore birds crowded sheltered lagoons, taking flight at the slightest threat, forming a solid contorting mass, dipping and diving along the shoreline. I would sit for hours watching the pelicans, never ceasing to applaud their antics. Diving from up high, plunging vertically, folding their wings at the last moment, emerging with gullets engorged by water. Skimming the waves above the breaking surf, silhouetted against the sun, groups of a dozen or so would form a ragged line, plying their way up and down the coast, synchronising their wing beats.

When the lead bird ceased flapping, the rest followed, when he resumed gliding, so did they. I was amazed, having thought them to be solitary and quarrelsome. There was no mistaking the nature of vultures, querulous, grouchy beasts, beautiful in flight, scabrous, ugly brutes up close. Their mere presence is enough to fill me with dark foreboding thoughts, they deal only in death, delight in the misfortunes of the living. Waking to the morning sun shining on my face, flinging open my sleeping bag to feel its warming rays, three pairs of beady eyes watched my every move, glinting with evil intent. Not the nicest start to the day, the brothers Grimm sizing me up for breakfast. I much preferred their majestic, effortless flight, riding the thermals high above. Though they do make for an impressive sight, sitting atop a cactus, wings spread wide, soaking up the morning sun.

Stretching from Tijuana to La Paz, Mexico Freeway 1 was the only sizable road along the peninsula. Initially hugging the west coast, it was straight and boring, approaching El Rosario it got much more fun. A leaky petrol pipe, squirting fuel onto the camper's exhaust called a halt to the proceedings; luckily Davo had smelt petrol in his cab before being engulfed in flames. Lucky for me too, I had a solo blast into town, savouring the first winding road for days. Swinging away from the coast, the sticky black highway cut through the arid landscape. Ferociously gunning the motor, I kidded myself there was some kind of hurry, it was only an excuse to have fun. I wound between scrub covered mounds of shale, revelling in the furious pace I set, cranking over hard through the bends, marvelling at the traction from the soft tarmac. In no time the town was reached, a length of pipe procured and back I went. More motorcycle mayhem ensued, throwing the bike over, left then right, yanking open the throttle, the Supatrapp exhaust barking with delight and me cackling with glee. Little stood in my way, even less slowed my pace. Only one military checkpoint blocked my path, and they waved me through unimpeded, preferential treatment of motorcyclists is definitely what the doctor ordered. In virtually no time I pulled up alongside the VW, handing over a new length of rubber fuel pipe, but it wasn't the last of the poor camper's troubles. Being old and tired was a setback for the slug bus, frequent losses of power needed a touch of TLC, first resetting the valve clearances, next dressing down the points and resetting the timing. At least all the mechanical demands could be meet by Davo himself, if I was lucky there would even be a spot of shade for me to shelter under, as I lounged around admiring my new, trouble free machine.

The Arizona desert had been a barren desolate place, pierced by up thrusting rocky outcrops, punctuated by escarpments of molten muddy brown sandstone, weird and wonderful formations that made the mind boggle. Sparse, tufted grass spread across flat desert sands, a precious green veneer over otherwise lifeless plains. Baja California was not comparable, so distinct were the two regions. Both were victims to the blinding glare of a merciless sun, the searing heat that scorched my lungs, and left me awash with sweat but there any similarity stopped. Gone was any grassy cover, clumps of tumbleweed and other tenacious scrub dominated the Baja desert, thinning as sand gave way to bare rock emerging from the sandy plains. As we turned inland from San Rosario, dense bushes of flattish cacti fought for space amongst the crowded sands. At first there was barely an inch to spare, so dense was the scrub. At any hint of a clearing, fast growing, ground hugging, foliage staked a claim, rushing to establish itself, before being overshadowed by taller growing vegetation. Thick, bushy trees lined dried riverbeds, resplendent in their dark green foliage, their extensive root systems fighting to defy the hostile arid conditions. Behind small wooden huts, well-tended patches of land cultivated broad, flat ears of cacti in neat ordered rows. Initially confused, I later discovered it to be prickly pear, a local staple.

Leaving the coast further behind, the black streak of Mex 1 snaked through the central plain. As we wound our way deeper into the heartland, the scenery changed. Dense scrub struggled against the intense heat, losing their precarious battle for water. Drifting sand lay in all directions, encroaching upon the highway, deadly traps waiting for the unwary. Deeper-rooted shrubs dotted sparsely between mounds of rocky jumble across the desert floor, struggle for survival, their foliage varying between dull green and brittle brown. Tall cacti stand proud, single, hairy trunks tapering as they reach for the sky. Thicker trunked species, branching into a profusion of limbs, reaching heights of twelve to fifteen metres, towered above me. Dense clumps of bushy cacti sit in sandy hollows, forming an impenetrable barrier of spiky table-tennis bats. Always in the background, hazy mountain ridges rise and fall, a distant barrier between desert and skyline. Suddenly the land, broken by plants and rock, flattens out and empty sand stretches to the horizon, with only the mountains to block its advance. A wall of heat descends, cloying, suffocating, literally sucking me dry. A carrying capacity of twelve litres of water was calculated as sufficient for four days, in the fierce heat of the Baja desert it was reduced to two, three at a push. Jacket flapping open and no gloves, I tried to reduce the effects of the heat. There was no cool breeze. The passage of air over my skin did make the ride more bearable though. My visor concentrated the sun's rays, blistering my lips and burning my nose. I'd have loved to remove it completely, but the dust and grit played havoc with my eyes. Maybe it would have proved wiser to travel early morning and late afternoon but we'd established a pattern of relaxing in the cooler periods of the day, enjoying our free time, not cowering in the shade.

Bearing east through the featureless plain, we detoured off the main highway, heading for Bahia de Los Angeles. Shifting sand gave way to a veritable forest of giant truncated cacti before climbing to the crest of the mountain ridge, where scrubby shrubs cling desperately to meagre deposits of sandy gravel. At the crown of the ridge, the Sea of Cortez sprang into view, its turquoise waters scarcely surrounding a string of islands, giving the impression of a lake rather than sea. The near shore sports almost a continuous line of buildings, despoiling our hopes of finding an easy campsite before reaching the town itself. Not becoming disheartened, I posed for a rare photo of myself before winding our way downhill, in search of food and water. A typical sleepy Mexican town, serviced only by the narrow single-track road, it held little of interest for us. Lying on a narrow strip of sand, between a low volcanic ridge and the Sea of Cortez, it consisted of little else but a rundown hotel and busy little *Mercado*. To our amazement purified water could be bought on draught, between us we managed to replenish our entire range of containers, over sixty litres. Our dilemma was over, we could drink to our hearts content, happy in the knowledge there would be plenty for the days to come. It also meant we could carry on around the coast, find an isolated beach and set up camp. A lumpy, pot-holed dirt track lead out of town, turning away from the coast it became undulating, loose gravel. Avoiding the turnoff heading into the desert, we re-joined the coast expecting to find no sign of houses. And there they stood, one after another, American holiday homes. Unsure of the extent of development, we actually stopped to enquire where we might find a quiet spot to camp. And with typical

American hospitality, we were invited to park up and camp beside the guy's house. It wasn't really my image of camping on a desolate beach, hidden from the prying eyes of others. We sure appreciated the free beers and the use of a power point though.

Rather than backtracking, our plan had been to cross the desert, taking in an old mission, San Borja, on our way. We'd been given contradictory advice. Larry claimed it would prove to be too rough. Another bike rider, Eric, said it was stony with some sections of loose sand, but passable. So what the heck, we decided to give it a try. As an extra, we decided to visit a canyon near the base of Volcan San Evita, to view some ancient rock paintings, a side trip reported to be only a couple of miles off our route. It turned out they were six miles off the track, a twelve mile round trip, and it was all very deep sand. I was distinctly uncomfortable riding there, the front wheel kept slewing off to the side. I went as slow as I dared, putting my feet down whenever I felt it going. This technique was how I was told to tackle deep sand, paddle through, keep your feet out in readiness, in case you fall. Pah! It exacerbated the problem, with my feet out it caused more of a balance problem. Keep them on the pegs, dabbing them down only if, and when, needed.

The Canyon itself was a bit of a let-down, the paintings were very faint being no more than a few squiggles and basic geometric designs. I wasn't impressed, I hadn't enjoyed the experience riding in, nor did I fancy turning immediately round. So we stopped and had a coffee, using two rocks to grind our own coffee beans. If nothing else it gave me a chance to gather my wits, which worked, I rode faster, and with more confidence on the way out. It showed. I fell off twice, but only at relatively slow speed. Davo was there to help lift the bike, it didn't put me off, quite the reverse. Afterwards the track was a real gas, I whooped it up, loving the sheer joy of riding rough shod across open desert. I'd let my tyres down, to 17psi and it worked a treat. With the added traction, I just rode as fast as I liked, reaching unimaginable speeds over whatever surface presented itself. Stony gravel unwound before me, with sharp edged rocks poking out, posing a constant threat. The presence of wobbly cobbles didn't perturb me in the slightest, faced with steep inclines of bare rock I didn't falter, deep sandy hollows failed to slow my progress, I just throttled through the lot. Constantly twisting and turning through abundant flora, it hardly felt like desert. Scrub, shrub, bushes and trees lined the way, stunted palms competed with towering cacti for space. The lower pressure gave so much more control, despite the bike bouncing all over the place it never felt out of control. I launched myself from hump backed mounds, leant at stupid angles through horribly dusty bends, without fear.

Thrilling, is the only word to use, I couldn't stop enthusing about it to Davo. After each rip-roaring ride, I sat and waited, in total silence. Sooner or later the distinctive chugging of the slug bus could be heard, and then he'd appear, a cloud of dust in his wake. Poor guy, I was almost demented with joy and didn't give him a chance to rest himself. Throwing caution to the wind I'd stamp into gear and take off again, relishing the feeling of total isolation, spurred on by the backup he provided. Even the pockets of sand were tackled with a new confidence, powering through, almost with gay abandon. I had a bit of a slide, which slowed me a touch, until I hit the rough stuff, then it was balls out again. It wasn't just the speed the whole experience was such a rush. Out in the wilds, at one with this awesome environment, and not just coping but loving every minute of it. It was truly awesome, such a brilliant ride. Out of all the roads, all the days, and all the rides, that experience was the epitome of motorcycle travel. I was buzzing, as high as a kite, my enthusiasm was in orbit. So when my companion suggested we camp out in the desert, it was a done deal.

Finding a site was easier than ever before, spot an area of bare sand, pull off the track and roll out my bedroll. Looking around, the presence of so many plants, in that place, seemed a contradiction of terms. It was supposedly desert, yet the biodiversity and abundance of plant species was phenomenal. Camel dung may be the fuel of necessity in the Sahara, but manure of any sort was in very short supply. However, there was a plenty of dead wood scattered about, it would have to do. Carefully lighting a fire, a ropey meal of pasta was cooked and devoured, washed down with a bottle of Daiquiri. In the blink of an eye darkness descended, we lounged by the campfire, replete. Who could ask for more? Without the faintest whisper of wind, the slightest sound could be heard, but there was only silence. Lying back, we gazed into the biggest, emptiest sky ever. At no point did the amber glow of civilisation pollute the horizon, not a single point of light penetrated the desert night, there was absolutely no sign of another living soul. Marvelling at the enveloping blackness, the stars sparkled bright and clear, undisturbed, no planes despoiled the view. For the briefest moment I actually begrudged sharing this scene with my travelling companion, so intense was the sense of solitude, so unique the perception of participating in the ways of an infinitive universe. At some point David retired to his camper, I was still wide-awake yet lost in my own thoughts, adrift in a host of heavenly dreams. So vast was that night sky it could contain anything, it was easy imagining alternative universes, mirror images of our own. Places inhabited by another Les Kay, another Cai ap Leslie, where events had taken a different turn. Another Baja desert where father and son lay together staring into the night sky, in awe at the enormity of creation. Maybe they too explored such possibilities, maybe they could enjoy a long and fruitful life together. I hoped so.

The sun rose early, finding us engulfed by a thick band of mist. I woke up damp and cold in a sleeping bag saturated by dew, to the glorious view of a tabletop mountain shrouded in mist. Comprehension dawned, there were no secret sources of water lying beneath the sand, the magical moisture came airborne, a daily dosing to sustain the plentiful variety of plants. All there was left to do was wait for the sun's rays to magic away the moisture from my doss bag, and then the fun could begin again. We had a ride out of about ten miles, but within the first mile we entered thick mist, it was cold and I had to ride without shades or visor, as the combination of mist and dust formed a gritty paste. So to begin with I took it easy, I was being safe, I didn't want to blast off and come a cropper. It wasn't too long before enough confidence was gained to up the pace again though. Another ride over constantly changing surfaces, another chance to prove my worth, and I loved it all. There were many more sandy sections, some fairly deep. It didn't really slow me down too much though, with a bit more momentum the front end didn't slew about as much. I felt more in control, giving it more throttle once I hit the sand. And there lay the problem with the ride to the canyon the day before, too slack a pace, and way too much hesitation powering through. What a shame it was only ten miles, I could have ridden like that all day. I felt so disappointed when, all too soon, we reached the highway.

What a boring stretch of road too, for over one hundred miles there was no sign of the slightest bend. Our painfully slow progress was too much to endure, attempted excursions to the coast were fruitless, only wasting time and fuel in the aborted attempts. Locked gates and uncooperative guards blocked our path, deprived any chance of whale watching or sizzling sunsets. We ploughed on regardless, deciding to make a bold attempt at reaching Mulege and finding a deserted cove called El Coyote. Already being late morning, we were faced with a gruelling distance of two hundred and sixty miles with little more than seven hours of daylight. At only 50-60mph, a long day's slog lay ahead. The road relentlessly stretched before us, straight as an arrow, an endless black line narrowing into a pinpoint on the far horizon. It was tedious. I tried to make the most of it, noting the slightest change in scenery. For a long time it was devoid of anything interesting, flat barren sand for as far as the eye could see, dead scrub being the only blemish on a featureless plain. The line of mountain ridges ran parallel to our course, vague shadows on the horizon. But then it suddenly changed, and I do mean suddenly. With no apparent change in altitude, topography or temperature, cacti appeared, a multitude of them. A variety were scattered randomly, of all shapes and sizes, but a tall branching type dominated, sprouting only two or three limbs off the highest central trunk. Many sported high opposing branches, giving the appearance of arms, while others could only be described as phallic. With a branch growing from just below their midsections, protuberances thrust heavenwards, they so closely resembled erect penises. Combined with arm like projections they were uncannily humanoid. Soon another cactus dominated, this was more like a shrub, actually, more like a marine creature than a cactus. Irregularly truncated, short fat branches sprouted any which way, knobbles dotted every surface, like polyps on coral. At one stage it spread so profusely nothing else grew between the towering giants. Mostly the mountains remained distant, though as Mex 1 entered Baja California Sur, it veered east to the Sea of Cortez, heading directly for the wall of rock. The last stretch before the coast was unbelievable, a whole host of various sand/mudstone formations with the road swinging round to the left, then sweeping gorgeously to the right, twisting around the slopes. How I craved to thrash around it all, to forget Davo and have a blast. Instead I marvelled at the glorious sight, cutting through soft golden hills, formed into rivulets of sand, the sea glistening through the gaps between peaks. Revitalized by the cool, fresh sea breeze, it was a pleasure to meander down the hillside, savouring our reunion with cooler coastal plains, golden sands and beautiful beaches.

If only this had not been spoilt by the town of Santa Rosalia! What a dirty, dingy pit, a festering festival of filth. It put me off before I even entered the place, I could see from a couple of miles away what it would be like. The beach was fenced off, and needed to be, to save people from polluting themselves. The trash on the fore shore was everywhere, not flotsam either, industrial waste. Rusting piles of metal, derelict mechanical hulks and foul smelling heaps of rubbish, filthy with oil/tar residue. Worst of all, it was dusk, we had no supplies left, and we were shattered. Our need for food and accommodation was first and foremost, and couldn't be ignored. Fuel was another top priority, and much as I wanted to ride straight through town, I wouldn't get far without refuelling. It was dark, and my golden rule was not to ride after dark. Gone were our hopes of reaching Mulege and the fabled beach of El Coyote. So food came first, sustenance to replenish our dwindling reserves of energy, during which we weighed up our options. Enquiries about accommodation drew a blank, neither of us fancied spending time traipsing around such a shithole, so my golden rule went out the window, after refuelling we hit the road again. The map showed a dirt track five miles out of town, short of many alternatives we could drive a couple of miles up that, pull over and park up for the night. Not the nicest option, but what we settled for. Using the VW as a screen, I parked out of sight, sleeping between the bike and camper, in the open, bear spray to hand. Why the paranoia, I couldn't say, Santa Rosalia had unnerved me, I felt vulnerable. Oh well, it could have been worse. We weren't waylaid, mugged, robbed or hassled in any way at all. A kangaroo rat visited me though, he just popped out of a hole in the ground and, curious and courageous, approached me. A dose of bear spray would have taught him a lesson, but I'm much too kind-hearted for that, besides it was really cute.

The mind boggles as to how many catholic saints there seem to be. There certainly was no shortage of towns named after a plethora of saints, San Lucas, San Marcos, San Jose de Magdalena, I hear there used to be a saint for every day of the year. In Baja alone I think they had to share many days, I wondered if each saint warranted a public holiday. No wonder it's always '*manaña, manaña*'.

A narrow strip of pale, coarse sand flanked to the west by a jagged ridge of mountains kept us close to the coastline, until San Bruno, where overgrown, sandy plains once more became the norm. A few sidetracks led temptingly into the deserted hinterland but we remained on the highway, fast tracking to our beach destination. I don't think Davo was over- keen on another jaunt into the desert. The few opportunities that arose were blithely ignored. If I studied the map I could come up with endless routes, of all grades, to keep me amused. But I was also content to make straight for El Coyote, a bit of R&R wouldn't go amiss. I'd vowed to slow down in Latin America, take a bit of time out to relax.

A mercilessly short ride was all it took to arrive in Mulege. There had been no let-up in the searing sun, so the palm fringed canal running through the town, gave the pretence of cooler climes. A brief psychological respite was all it was, climbing steeply out of town our way curved continuously round to the right, cutting closely into the mountainside. To our left, brackish coastal plains lay far below, with wet, sandy tracks criss-crossing between God knows what, they looked more like fun trails than access routes. It didn't take long before the road wound back down the mountain, overlooking a beautiful sea and quiet sandy coves. Thin crescents of sand carved into the base of steep sided rock marked each bay. Facilities were sparse, access to the beaches often gained only through Spartan resorts, frequented by a mish-mash of mixed nationalities and local fishermen. If it hadn't been for a detailed description, El Coyote would have passed us by. Only by following the shoreline through an empty RV park, across an open expanse of soft sand and through a gap in the rocks, did we finally behold our promised paradise. Facilities did not exist. There was no water supply, so no showers and nothing to drink. There was a stall made of tin perched above a hole in the ground, our toilet. I'd seen plenty worse, at least we had a plank to sit on whilst relieving ourselves. Dilapidated *Palapas* lined the shore, open sided huts of palm fronds hanging off broken wooden beams. Most were battered beyond use, failing to provide even a rudimentary windbreak. Of those with walls and roof, a ragtag dribble of Americans was already firmly ensconced. Little choice remained, little more than a lean-to gave us a space to call our own, although it was plenty for a couple of nights. But the beach, that heavenly beach! Golden, soft sand arching round the bay, sloping gradually into the tropical, turquoise water, cool enough to refresh, warm enough to luxuriate in. If heaven relied on McDonald's and modern facilities, welcome to the infernos of hell. I could tell I was going to enjoy my stay. To celebrate our arrival, we bought a kilo of tiger prawns and set to with the makings for a barbeque. Finally Davo crawled into the camper and I laid back, satiated, after gorging ourselves on succulent seafood, and chilled daiquiri.

Four others were already in residence, they obviously occupied the most intact of the *Palapas*. Davo had his camper, so it was irrelevant for him. Although none of the *Palapas* offered any form of security I still wanted to spread my things out, create a bit of personal space. So after a couple of days, when someone moved on, I took possession of a piece of prime real estate, a *Palapas* with three and a half walls, an open doorway and a roof. It was to be my home away from home, nine square metres, just enough space to lay out my bedding and place a few other non-valuable possessions. For David it was the furthest south he intended to go, so after a few days we were parting company. Our time together had been fortuitous, for both of us, we'd found travelling together easy, and we'd complemented each other's inefficiencies. My riding was up to scratch again, my Spanish had improved, I was ready to face the world on my own again. More than ready, I looked forward to travelling alone, to follow my own itinerary, and worry only about my own desires. And for the time being, I wanted nothing more than to chill out in the sun, to soak up the rays and float in the beautiful blue waters.

Chapter Twenty One

For more than a week I did just that, luxuriating in the sun, bobbing about in the sea, and making occasional excursions into Mulege. Each day locals would come along and ply their trade, Tamales, Chilli Pasties, fresh seafood, weed and water. Most evening meals consisted of veggie stew, or a pasta broth, now and again riding to the next bay, El Burro, for a cold beer and some fast food, American style. Other travellers passed through, some good, some bad, and some indifferent. By and large I kept to myself, though another lone biker took my email address, maybe we'd meet up later, he was heading south too. Riding a CB750, Andrew was taking a more "by the skin of his teeth" approach. I liked his style, and my ears positively pricked up at his proposed route on reaching the mainland; Mazatlan to Durango, "The road of a thousand turns." Now that was an opportunity I would not be missing!

Many miles north of the border had passed in a blur, my days filled with riding, on and on and on. Sometimes driven by fear, often filled with thrilling rides and awesome landscape, but always driving myself ever onwards. I hadn't wanted time to analyse too closely the full implications of what life held in store for me. I fought to steer clear of imagining a life without Cai, my immediate needs had been to deal with the crushing loss that threatened to swallow me whole. The tools to tackle that task were long gruelling rides, mind-blowing scenery and lots of personal space. I knew I could still do with more of the same, yet I was also ready to give myself time to think. I was ready to start facing my demons, up until then I'd only been gaining the strength to do so.

Sitting and staring at the night sky, a falling star left a blazing trail. My only wish was that Cai did not die, I had to accept that that was one wish that could never come true. However desperate I felt to talk to him, to hear his voice, it was no good, I had to force myself to accept the futility of such desires. However difficult it was to accept, even comprehend the finality of that fact, sooner or later I would have to. Torturing myself with bad memories was going to get me nowhere, it was time to erase the negative memories, those associated with my intolerance or shows of frustration with Cai. I am only human, I found parenting hard at times. We all do. Cai understood this, and accepted it. It was time for me to do the same. Unable to change the past, I had no other choice, unless I wished to persecute myself for evermore. Whiling away the days in the sun calmed me down, stilled my troubled mind. Relaxed and at peace with the world, I was kind to myself. Hours were spent reading, watching the Pelicans dive-bombing the abundant fish stock, swimming out in a vain attempt to reach a pod of Dolphins. Mainly the time was spent releasing pent up frustration, letting go the tension, pacifying the turmoil.

With Davo gone, I was happy with my own company, but over a period of a few days opened up a bit and spent a while with some of the other guys on the beach. Admittedly, I'd first judged them harshly, a bunch of loud, brash, aging Americans, which they heartily agreed with. They were also generous and hospitable, inviting me over to share spaghetti and meatballs, washed down with a bottle of beer or two. The trip was like an annual pilgrimage for them, each year they'd drive down, meet up and enjoy a month or two of fun in the sun. For the rest of the year, they lived in far-flung corners of the States, all in semi-retirement. Regardless of an edge of bitterness over failed relationships, and an overly keen eye for hot totty, all four proved their worth to me. Considering I'd spent two days keeping my distance, they quickly showed how askew my judgement had been.

In those two days I'd spent time with a Canadian guy and his four year old son. They'd been like a magnet to me, so reminiscent of Cai and me travelling together. When first approaching them I'd been close to tears, almost deciding to steer clear, but it was normal behaviour for me, parents travelling with kids had always caught my attention. Of course, it had filled my head with endless fond memories, given me a chance to relive life with Cai, how he grew with that lovely open mindedness of his. Something I'd always attributed to his experiences in foreign lands, around alternative cultures, as he himself did! If it achieved nothing else, it gave Eric a bit of relief from Harvey's constant demands. We dug and made castles in the sand, collected shells and generally amused each other. Their father son bond was pretty much thrust upon them during the holiday periods, during the normal course of events they lived some distance apart. Their relationship was slightly forced at times, I took the opportunity to reassure Eric it was quite normal, it could be a strain at times travelling alone with your kid. I also made it clear how it provided the perfect setting to strengthen the bond between them, relating my own experiences as an example. Over time Eric asked me how old Cai was then, what was he doing while I was travelling, questions I clumsily ignored. For my own peace of mind it was the wrong tactic, it felt as if his existence was being denied, and it weighed heavily on my heart. Not wanting to pour my heart out to whoever I meet, I'd not yet found ways to avoid blurting out about his demise. For sure I wanted to talk about my son, the wonderful years we'd enjoyed together but didn't want to burden every one with my grief. Talking of past travels, of happy times in life, they invariably involved Cai, and I refused to live in denial. To rectify my show of ignorance, I approached them later and explained the situation, apologising for the tactless manner I'd dealt with the situation. I should have trusted my initial gut instinct. After a brief statement of sympathy, awkwardness descended, it ruined any interaction completely. Before, we'd enjoyed an easy-going flow of intercourse, a bond of mutual understanding. Afterwards, we exchanged little more than short, strained sentences. I still tried to indulge Harvey, but more often than not Eric would interject, chastising Harvey for hassling me. I got to feeling like a leper, an unwelcome presence to their already strained existence.

But it wasn't going to stop me talking of my life, my son. He'd been an integral part of life for eighteen years, they still formed the happiest days of my life, my most treasured, even before his death. If losing him caste me outside the realms of acceptance for some, it opened the hearts of others. Some innate sense generally saw few mistakes in who I shared my grief with. I was learning to trust my instincts. A bunch of cantankerous old farts would seem the last to understand my plight, but no, with tear filled eyes they opened their hearts. The warmth and sympathy they exhibited was so touching, it made me ashamed of my initial reaction to them. Without fail, they all welcomed me into their fold with outstretched arms, insisting on another round of beers and a heartfelt toast to Cai. Indeed, we live and learn!

An easy camaraderie settled amongst us, no bluff, no bullshit, a deep felt feeling of mutual respect and understanding. They really felt for me, really felt the pain they knew I must have been going through. They were struck by my strength to continue the journey, and convinced that if I didn't carry on for as long as I could I would regret it. Invigorated by their support and encouragement, I prepared for departure. Andrew had emailed me inviting me down to La Paz, to join him on the ride to Durango, I had a feeling we'd enjoy whooping it up, through all one thousand bends. But before that, the guys, Errol, Gino, Tony and Dan planned a hearty send off. El Burro was a convenient venue, so we piled down in two cars for a lunchtime feast of burgers and beer. Followed by more beer, with interludes for swimming to sober up. Had it not been for my assertion, that I really needed to buy a good quality bottle of Tequila, we might have made it through the day relatively unscathed. The next thing I knew about was waking early in the morning, my mouth parched, reaching blearily for water. Quenching my thirst, I gingerly staggered to my feet, noting first my camera, left unattended in the open since midday the day before. Next, the naked figure of Errol, swaying as he wandered aimlessly around the beach, apparently missing his set of false teeth. Lastly, the two cars stood neatly by the guy's camp, I preferred not to dwell on who, or how, they'd got us back. Worst of all was the slowly dawning realisation, I had a long, hot ride down to La Paz ahead of me.

Chapter Twenty Two

Rising swiftly off the coastal strip, the road curled round a short series of sea cliffs before meandering along, between mountainous ridges. A barren corridor, winding through steep walls of bare rock. If only I'd been in a fit state to appreciate it, even fuelled by a gallon of coffee, it was a miracle I could keep my eyes on the road. Rare opportunities to refresh myself were gladly taken, drinking Red Bull or coke, anything to keep me awake. An absence of pull-ins meant few chances to stop and take photos which suited me fine. It was much too much effort anyway. Gently swaying, from side to side, was enough to negotiate the bends and lull me into a contented stupor. Sections along the cliff edges gave spectacular views of isolated fishing camps, and the desolate offshore islands of the Loreto Bay National Marine Park. Empty roads and hot, sleepy towns induced a state of dreamy semi-consciousness, there was little to concentrate on, making the ride thankfully effortless. Swinging back inland, cutting across to Ciudad Insurgentes and all the way to Santa Rita, the road was dead straight and extremely boring. My concentration was particularly low, still the excess of tequila dulled my senses, it was fine to cruise along at 70mph though. Through flat, empty desert, the highway never deviated from its course. To both sides wide-open plains supported no life but the giant cacti, prickly sentinels breaking up the horizon, if not the monotony. Nearing La Paz, formations of flat-topped, shale hummocks finally broke the monotony, once more forcing the band of tarmac to wind around the broken landscape. Where the route cut through the mounds, you could see stratified layers of semi-compacted sand, mud and stones. What I was most glad to see were the city limits, at only

3.30 pm I'd made good time, about three hundred miles in five and a half hours.

Navigating around foreign cities is bad enough on foot, difficult in a car, and bloody awful on a bike. Getting within a few blocks of the ticket office, I secured the bike and set off on foot to buy my ferry ticket to Topolobomba for the following morning. Most impressive, I purchased a ticket, in Spanish, without much problem. Next on the list was a suitable hotel, I guess camping out of town was an option but not having slept in a bed for over two weeks, I preferred the prospect of some comfort. More importantly, a shower was long overdue, it had been over ten days, I couldn't stand the stench any longer. Andrew had recommended a cheap place, but again finding my way through the inner city maze of crowded, one-way streets wasn't how I wished to spend the evening. I thought it was close when the streets diverged, two were dead ends, the third led away in totally the wrong direction. By pure chance, stopping to enquire at a street café, I found a secluded haven, the quirkiest place imaginable. Hotel Yeneka, accessed through a narrow passageway, which opened into a secluded courtyard, festooned with an eclectic collection of junk. An ancient car took pride of place, driven by a moth-eaten, stuffed monkey. From the walls hung antlers, whale vertebrae, blocks, tackles, scissors, saws, crucifixes, horseshoes, hats, harnesses. Shelves were stacked with hand irons, hand driven sewing machines, hand drills, augers, typewriters, pots and pans. Tables and display stands were cobbled together from steel wheels, pulley wheels, motorcycle wheels, car wheels, traction engine wheels, gear wheels, even flywheels. A countless assortment of irrelevant junk, roughly sorted into relevant groups, filled the courtyard. Maybe the bike's modernity made it stand out from the antiquated chaos, but at least it was safely out of sight, no mean feat amongst the busy city streets, private parking was hard to come by.

Keen to get away early, I rode straight to the port, rather than riding to the other end of town to refuel being confident of finding a petrol station on the way. By the time I approached the dock gates, it was obvious I'd totally misjudged Mexican business acumen. There wasn't a single source for fuel within twenty miles of the port. I was already on reserve and was reluctant to trust to the situation improving in Topolobomba. Being two hours early, the answer seemed simple, turn round and fill up before boarding. It was a nice road to town, good tarmac, clear views and refreshing sea breeze, definitely better than waiting in the sweltering heat of the port area. So back I went, passing pristine white bays, with thatched sun shelters and shaded beach bars. Banking hard round craggy outcrops, I could then lean leisurely through a long, sweeping bend continuing for a couple of miles, as the coastline bowed inwards to meet a sandy creek. More tight turns followed, scraping round rocky promontories, overhanging sheer, inaccessible drops littered with rusty ruins, victims to past highway calamities. Marinas and plush hotels lined the way into the outskirts of La Paz, a poor road surface curtailed my fun, as I reined in the power, behind a slow moving truck. As decent tarmac was once more approached, I checked behind me, apart from the car on my tail, it was all clear. I signalled, glanced to my side and pulled out for the overtake. BEEEEEP.......SMAAAASH! I careened out of control, finding myself shunted towards the back of the truck. Braking had no effect, other than to worsen the viciously oscillating front end. Realising a collision was unavoidable, the only thought that went through my mind was, *Is this the end, is it all over?* The next thing I knew after being rammed into the truck was the bike going down, with me enwrapped in it. Survival instinct? I'm not sure. All I know is that I rolled clear, coming up at the side of the road. Sitting in the road, my next coherent thought was the trip is over. I had the perfect excuse to pack my bags and return home.

Miraculously, I realised I was still in one piece, amazed there was no apparent damage to myself, I stood up to check the bike, and my knee gave way with a jolt of pain. So I hadn't got away unscathed. Only then did the pain strike, I had to sit back down and assess the situation. Unzipping my trouser leg revealed nothing, no apparent disfigurement, no contusions, no broken skin, a good, but careful, feel around the joint further reassured me. With the truck driver, there were eleven people surrounding me, looking frightened and trying to help. Eight climbed out the car, a group of four youths with their girlfriends, and two American passers-by who offered their services as translators. The girls were freaking out, the Americans wanted to call an ambulance, three of the guys stood around looking crestfallen, while the fourth had the nous to pick my bike up and wheel it off the road. I was surprised by the lack of damage. One pannier was contorted sideways, the rack for the other side had been sheared in two and badly bent, and its pannier hung off precariously, though didn't seem too damaged. All in all, a very lucky escape! At that point I felt deeply ashamed of my instant willingness to find an excuse to go home, and my innate stubbornness kicked in, I would be fine, I would continue, nothing was going to stop me. The intention then was to jump back on the bike and make it to the ferry on time.

None of the locals spoke English, maybe I should have kept the Americans there to assist with the language barrier. Instead, I assured them I was OK and would sort it all out when I got to the mainland. I also assured the guys and girls there was no problem, they seemed extremely relieved and made a rapid departure. Only afterwards did I realise the accident would have been attributed to them, as I had clearly signalled my intention to pull out. But this is the enigma in Mexico, drivers wanting to show the road ahead is clear to overtake use their left indicator, and people will then overtake them. How the hell can they distinguish whether you are overtaking, turning left, or showing they can overtake? I guess they can't which is why this car full of youths, floored the accelerator to overtake and nearly wrote off El Gringo and his machine. They were probably shitting it at the thought of the crap they were in, the car was a brand new Toyota, I guessed a parent's car, so they'd still have a lot of explaining to do. And me? Climbing aboard the bike again wasn't easy, riding it would have been foolhardy, taking my weight on the right leg wasn't an option, and the fairing had also been badly bent, making it impossible to turn the handlebars. Making the ferry was a poorly conceived idea, even getting back off the bike posed problems, so as I was already on it, I limped back to the Yaneke Hotel to lick my wounds.

Filled with copious amounts of codeine and paracetamol my knee felt right as rain, I walked round town for an hour, in search of food and refreshment, and even pushed the bike up the steps and back into the courtyard. A slight hiccup to my plans was all, I only needed a few days to straighten out the bike and rest my knee. Until waking up the next morning. My knee had swollen massively, I could barely put any weight on it, and the hotel staff were not impressed by my insistence that it would be alright. The owner, Miguel, was a GP and everyone hassled me relentlessly until I agreed to let him examine me. If nothing else, painkillers were essential, I'd almost run out, having squandered my valued supply of co-proximol. But of course it wasn't going to be that simple, only a fool would have kidded himself otherwise, I bowed before the voice of reason and allowed an appointment to be made with Miguel's sister, a trauma specialist. With Paulo accompanying me, as interpreter, I painfully hobbled to the appointment. Without his assistance I don't know what I'd have done, while being prodded and poked, x-rayed and, finally, having a bloody great syringe plunged deep into my knee joint. The careful explanations, in English, made it all possible. Poor guy went white as a sheet watching the syringe being inserted and 45cc of fluid being drawn out of my knee. It hurt like hell as more fluid was manipulated round the joint, to where it could also be extracted. Once finished, the relief was immediate, whether due to a cessation in the painful manipulation I couldn't be sure. When I stood any doubts went out the window, I could actually walk again. I hardly blinked when presented with the $150 bill. Pledging to follow the specialist's advice, complete rest for four days, it was clear I wouldn't be setting off again immediately. If only I'd known at that stage just how long it would take!

*Pause for thought after nearly losing the rear end - Loggers trail,
Vancouver Island*

Young Orca males - Off Vancouver Island

No star accomodation - British Columbia backwaters

Where the buffalo roam - Watson Lake to Fort Nelson

The land of Oz - Fort Nelson to Jasper

Posing to keep the tourists happy - Jasper to Radium Springs

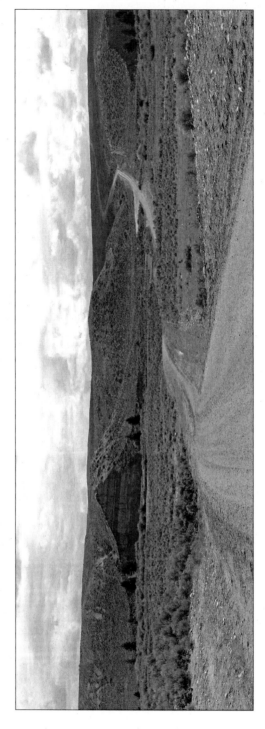

High Plains drifting - Bridger Wilderness Area, Wyoming

Navada City Ghost Town - Montana

Awesome road with deathly dropoffs - Montrose to Durango, Colorado

They don't come much bigger than this - Baja Desert, Mexico

Morning coffee with the villagers - Guatemalan highlands

Life in the slow lane - Nr Salama, Central Guatemala

Living close to the margins of poverty - Rural Honduras

Adrenalin fuelled surfing - Massella Beach, Nicaragua

Chapter Twenty Three

However foolish I'd tried to be, the decision to return to Hotel Yaneke was the best thing I could have done. The mixture of staff and their associates proved invaluable, as were some of the other guests. Complete rest for four days were the doctor's orders, if only that were possible. Food wasn't served on the premises, there was no alternative but to leave at least once a day for sustenance, during which time I'd load up with snacks and beer. Ice wasn't easy to come by either, so the regime dictated by the specialist got off to a poor start. So much more could have been done with hindsight, though it went well to begin with. Each day the swelling went down, there was a marked improvement, but the joint was so stiff it worried me. Exercising more and more, it would again swell, the staff would chastise me, constantly encouraging me to sit and relax, bringing me coffee, tea, even glasses of Tequila. Warnings of doing too much too soon followed my every move, but I wouldn't listen. With a pig-headed refusal to rest completely, I stripped down the bike, ready to accept the repaired and replacement parts. It was the last straw though, my knee ballooned again and I was forced to rest properly. A German paramedic explained the situation to me, in no uncertain terms, assuring me that if I didn't rest it adequately then, I'd be facing a prolonged period of inactivity, maybe permanent damage. By this time a week had passed, I was climbing the walls in frustration, but then I made two discoveries. Skype, and a liquor store tht would provide me with bags of ice when I bought a six-pack of beer.

And so I settled down, spending hours chatting to friends on Skype, writing emails and humbly following the advice of professionals. Swinging between depression and rage, the time crawled by. I'd sit, slowly drinking beer, with an ice pack on my knee, pouring out my woes to friends and family, chasing up progress of the legal investigation into Cai's accident. Long awaited news came through, a detailed report of the entire fuel system on his bike. A gelatinous substance, blocking the jets of his carburettor, had been found. Raging anger flooded every inch of my soul. Those bastards, those careless cretins. Nothing more than contaminated fuel had robbed me of my son, one second of sloppiness in the workshop had deprived him of life. For days, any picture of Cai would send me into a torrent of tears. I downloaded a whole host of photos posted on Photobucket, many I'd never seen before, losing myself in a whirlwind of despair. Why is life so unfair, why Cai? But there were no answers to such questions. It was pointless torturing myself, I had to let it go. Some things in life are beyond our control, they just have to be accepted, that's the way life is. Gradually images of his bright, smiling face won through, despite the tears, a smile appeared on my face. Recognition of how precious our lives had been slowly dawned. Of course I knew it before, but progressively I came to appreciate it more and more. It may not have stemmed the flow of tears, but it made me grateful for the rich and varied life we'd shared, for the inseparable bond we'd formed. If eighteen years was the longest I was to enjoy life with Cai, then I'm eternally grateful to have had that time. To have shared what we had was the most phenomenal experience I could ever have wished for. It brought more joy into my life than I could have imagined. The loss may well have left a gaping void in my life, beyond my ability to see past, but those precious years meant more than the loss ever could.

Stripped of all its damaged parts, the bike stood semi-naked, dejected, awaiting my attention. A quick fiddle now and then only left me feeling dissatisfied, any more it left me in pain. I could only rest and practice the ancient art of patience. While resting I at least managed to re-sew the tank bag, order replacement parts over the Internet, and organise repairs locally. Miguel's contacts were invaluable, a welder repaired the aluminium top rack, snapped in two places. Aluminium can be a bitch to weld, slight variations in the alloy can totally ruin attempts at welding, he'd done a superb job though. And then that was it, work came to a grinding halt again, my order from the States hadn't arrived, and I was still pretty much laid up anyway. Another friend of Miguel's helped me with my

Spanish, and Paulo encouraged me to actually use what I had learnt. It lacked depth. I wouldn't give the time to tackle the complicated use of grammar, or the extensive list of verbs. Basic phrases and responses seemed more important, still believing it would only be a matter of days before I made a miraculous recovery, and rode off into the sunset.

Miracles weren't really my forte. Having to rely on patience and hard work, recovery was slow but sure. Gradually, more time was spent on my feet, at first I'd only managed to feed myself from street stalls and local cafes but slowly I extended my wanderings. For hours I amused myself, by taking photos of the daily goings on of the city's inhabitants. Sitting on benches in the square, shooting unsuspecting citizens kept me occupied, if not entirely happy. After about ten days, slightly more prolonged excursions beyond the immediate area, improved my disposition. Gentle walks along the palm fringed Malecon, induced deeper feelings of tranquillity, curbing my impatience. Golden sunsets, silhouetting thatched roofed sun shelters and sculptures of breaching humpbacked whales, encouraged quiet contemplation, easing the frantic thoughts of a troubled mind. Carlos, a fellow guest, took me under his wing, running me out to the beach a couple of times, a chance for some self-prescribed hydrotherapy, some time to relax in the sun. Anything to ease off the stiffness in my knee, whatever it took to sooth away the growing frustration and helplessness.

Quoting delivery within five to ten days, I assumed the USPS (United States Postal Service) had kept their side of the deal that my bike bits were sitting on a customs shelf somewhere in Mexico. I badgered the local Post Office every day for over a week, insisting they must have the package. I may as well have gone and battered a street beggar, blaming him for it, I'd have got more sympathy. All the tracking number could inform me was that it left San Francisco 19 November, ten days after it had been posted. Two weeks later, still with no sign of it, I was livid. Thank god for Skype, I could phone America and be abusive to USPS and the supplier, at virtually no cost whatsoever. The frequent trips to the P.O. had proved one important thing, there was a definite improvement with my knee. So nothing was going to stop me sorting out my bike, I could leave ASAP. So without further ado, I put all my attention into preparing the bike.

Before even starting the repairs, regular maintenance took priority. Twelve thousand miles of wear from the original drive chain was deemed enough, it was time to fit the new set with the improved sprocket ratios. Basically it got a decent service, it was damned near due, it had made sense to do it while I had reasonable facilities available. More important, it kept me busy for a while, stopped me chomping at the bit over my delayed parts. Cleaning both filters and adding new engine oil, were par for the course, everything else was thoroughly checked. Straightening the fairing bracket took no time, half an hour battering it, first one way then another with a lump hammer. Headlight and fairing then slotted neatly into place, requiring one last, well placed, wallop. The panniers were a different story, solid boxes of high grade aluminium made stronger by a 15mm top lip, they weren't about to bend back so easy. They'd been pushed into a rhomboid shape, the hammer would only dent the side panels, a different tactic was required. After spending a long time looking and thinking, the only thing I could think of was to rest one edge against a short section of railway sleeper, then use a second section to bounce into the opposite edge. A nice solid whack, and another, before checking to see the results. WOWEE! That was it nearly sorted, so I turned it around and bashed it from the other side, PERFECT! It was so easy, so I lined up the second pannier, a few bashes and that was dead square too. HALLELUYAH! The lids closed with no interference, and while they couldn't be described to be as good as new, they were damned close. In fact they were better, it showed they'd been places, seen action, withstood the test of time.

And that was that really, one day's worth of work and everything was in order. The only thing still to be sorted was mounting the panniers, which relied on the mysteriously missing parts, the ones that no one would take the blame for. Now, where was that beggar? Alas, a final internet check revealed the package had arrived in Mexico, and cleared customs. Putting away my bovver boots, I made a mad dash to the P.O. Hurray, their computer system agreed with me. So where were they? Having got used to me, they were actually quite helpful, not once had I played the part of the enraged Gringo, at no time belittled the staff or their efforts to help. Once it had got to the point where I refused to accept another casual brush off, I decided that I needed to be more insistent. So in my best Spanish I stood my ground and kept asking where they were, where they'd gone? And in their simplest Spanish, they shrugged their shoulders. And finally it went in my favour, they assured me it would be delivered as soon as they received it. It was due the next day, and they promised it would be delivered by hand immediately. Possibly I was being a bit gullible, not entirely though. I'd a bodged repair to the side rack and was going to set off in two days' time, come what may. Apart from the pannier mounting the bike was ready to roll, it seemed a shame to let it stand there ready but ignored.

Swinging my leg over the bike was cumbersome, whether due to the heavy strapping I couldn't be sure. It made no difference anyway, I wasn't about to ride without supporting my knee. And ride I most definitely would, a test ride at first, to ensure everything was OK. First problem, applying the rear brake proved painful. Unperturbed I continued, and the pain seemed to ease off a touch. Heading along the coast road, I rode past the scene of the accident, checking for any residual nerves. That didn't faze me either. So came the time to assess the machine. Hmm, the handlebars and front wheel weren't quite in line. Giving it a gutful of throttle, I determined to put it through its paces, cranking hard and fast round a few bends showed no twitchiness at the front end, no fault with the steering geometry. Slowing to a crawl, the engine felt a little lumpy, but only in higher gears at low revs. I put that down to the new gear ratio, which I'd get used to. Blasting round the coast road, to the dock gates and back, gave me all the reassurance needed. Hot damn, wasn't it nice to be astride my trusty steed again? Bugger the knee. I could ride, if necessary I'd ride with my bloody leg stuck out front. Unfettered once more, nothing was going to hold me back. Oh, how I wanted to just keep on going, but no, after a three week delay I could wait another couple of days. Besides, too much still had to be organised for my imminent departure.

With only three weeks before Christmas, a yuletide destination was set. Utila, off the coast of Honduras, we'd always planned to celebrate relaxing on a tropical beach. Renowned as a dive mecca, I longed to sink my head beneath the waves, and escape the rigours of the terrestrial world. For fifteen years I'd relished thoughts of discovering the undersea world of the Bay Islands. Being two and a half thousand miles away, it wasn't expected to be a doddle, but I had faith in my ability. There was no reason it couldn't be done, with time to spare. There was no reason to take the direct route either, Durango had an irresistible pull over me, and that would drag me into the heartland of Mexico, well away from the Pan-American Highway, my nemesis. That was the easy way out, the quick way through, which I'd avoided at every turn. I wasn't about to relinquish my byway bigotry so easily!

As repayment for help with my Spanish, I led an English class at Eric's evening school. A bunch of teenagers mainly from privileged backgrounds and of various abilities and temperaments. All in all a successful session, nothing but my home life and journey were discussed. We all helped each other, they with my Spanish and me with their English, leaving us all with a sense of achievement. As I'd found on previous travels, the chance to speak with native English speakers is greatly appreciated. The questions came thick and fast, some easy, and some rather more pointed. Did I find Mexican women beautiful? 'Why sure, thick lustrous hair, gorgeous olive skin, the way they wiggle when they walk, by the way, do you have an older sister?' As if, I was the model of decorum, playing it coy, slightly abashed at such a personal question. Honesty was employed too, pointing out their tendency to put on weight once married, how age and the use of make-up seemed to increase in proportion to each other, how natural beauty didn't need highlighting with make-up. They actually seemed to agree, apart from the apprentice drug baron, sitting there, spouting shite about rap and hip-hop. But I guess even prospective members of drug cartels benefit from learning English, it increases business opportunities, allows expansion into the English speaking world. But he wasn't too bad, not actually hostile, or disruptive, it was just the first time I'd encountered such attitude there. The residents of La Paz had been friendly and warm towards me, it was great to give something back and I left happy to have done so.

If the night class brought happiness, my arrival back at Yaneke found me ecstatic. The bike parts had arrived, my faith in the fickle Mexican god of postal miracles, *Servicio Correo*, had indeed done me proud. My prayers had been answered, the daily pilgrimage to La Postal Officia, his house of worship, had at last borne fruit. In a manic fit of excitement, the packaging was ripped to shreds in an instant, behold the holy relics, a brand new side rack and fitting kit. I would say just what the doctor ordered, but I'd already largely ignored the doctor's orders and, justifiably, suffered the consequences. I'd have loved to jump for joy, do a gleeful jig, but hopping about just wasn't the same. The temptation was to fit it immediately, Paulo offered a more practical solution, Tequilas all round! A long and frantic day had changed everything, yet left me stiff and exhausted. After weeks of inactivity it was too much, Paulo surely had the right idea. And so I sat with my leg up, an ice pack on my knee, my bike bits in my lap, a beer in my hand, and a satisfied smile on my face looking forward to the morning.

Everything just slipped nicely into place. The tide had turned, sweeping me onwards with effortless ease. For over three weeks life had been slow and laborious, I'd endured a great deal of physical and emotional pain, but I felt stronger for it. Rather than being at a disadvantage, with my dodgy knee, I felt more capable of facing the future. I'd started being able to smile when thinking of Cai, when looking at photos of him, gratitude for our lives together filled my heart. There was a long way to go yet, in my bereavement, yet knowing this no longer filled me with fear. Almost using my accident as an excuse to give up travelling had appalled me, it made me feel ashamed. I shouldn't need excuses. If a time came for the journey to end, I should accept this gracefully, because some day it will end. Where and how, was yet to be determined, but some time I must face going home.

Chapter Twenty Four

Farewells to newfound friends, and posing for their photos, couldn't curtail my enthusiasm to get away. Nestled neatly between camping roll and tank bag, I settled instantly into a comfortable posture, as if I'd barely broken my stride. I'd love to say I was gagging at the bit, eager to speed off into the great unknown. Truth was, a calm detachment descended, relieved and relaxed, at last my world again revolved around the bike and me, the road unrolling before me. It was a pity a mere twenty miles would take me to the ferry. I'd have enjoyed more time to savour the flavour of freedom. No longer was Topolobomba on the agenda, no-one awaited me there anymore. An overnight ferry would take me straight to Mazitlan and the notorious ride to Durango. Rather than trepidation, I delighted in the thought of enjoying my own company, it would just be me and the open road.

Documentation for the ferry was a right rigmarole. Triplicate copies of all my documents, weighing in, Import Tax and finally the ticket itself which they won't sell until everything else is completed. Two hours of bureaucratic bollocks, countless queues, numerous officials, all keen on displaying their power to mess you around. Being sent to another window, queue again, get copies from the other official in the same office, return to the back of the queue, at the first window etc. It was hot, too hot to waste on the effort of being irritated, being forewarned of the palaver, I was bemused rather than annoyed. No doubt I wouldn't have been, not if the tickets had sold out before being permitted to buy one. Refusing to allow them to ruffle my feathers, I finally pottered down to the head of the queue for embarkation, and settled in for another four hour wait.

Two wheeled vehicles took pride of place, and a couple of Canadian women touring on bicycles, joined me. Whilst in the next line for the Topo' ferry, a Canadian BMW rider drew alongside. We were virtually all up to the same thing, heading south from Canada, variations in routes and modes of transport being the only difference. Mike had started in Canada making for Tierra del Fuego, the southern tip of Argentina. I enthused about the road to Durango, explaining its notoriety. Without further ado, he zipped off on his bike, returning to announce he'd changed his ticket to Mazitlan, so we could ride together. Yeah, right. He hastened to add, if I didn't mind. Actually I did but felt crap for doing so, and found myself in an awkward position. Memories of my own loneliness and despair came to mind. I couldn't really say no, felt I should at least try. Reluctantly I agreed, but after boarding the ferry took some time alone to get used to the idea. A fish eagle swooped down right in front of me, plucked a fish out the sea and banked away clasping the epileptic fish in its talons. Mere metres before my eyes, a mid-flight shake loosed a fine spray of water from its sodden wings. Gratified by the sight, I remained to witness a glorious sunset, golden banks of cloud lit up the sky, as the bright orange ball slid rapidly below the horizon. The last vestiges of frustration vanished with the setting sun, replaced by tranquil acceptance, a readiness to take life as it presented itself.

A beer soaked evening gave us an opportunity to break the ice, and boy didn't the guy knock back the beers. He'd just been medically discharged from the Canadian Armoured Corps, diagnosed with Post Traumatic Stress Disorder, after serving in Bosnia then Afghanistan. His trip was to start dealing with the emotional aftermath. It put us both in pretty much the same boat. I hadn't the heart to bear a grudge, however much it had initially cheesed me off, it had been my choice whether to accept his company and I'd made my choice. Inevitably we got on fine, even formed a reasonable level of camaraderie, two emotional cripples cast loose upon the world. It could have been a recipe for disaster, giving us carte blanche to pour out our tales of woe, an excuse to release a deluge of anguish, two kindred spirits wallowing in a mire of self-pity. Luckily, neither of us was that way inclined, it instead gave us a deeper understanding of each other, an underlying respect for each other's plight. Having shared our evening with the two cyclists, we both received words of encouragement, displays of admiration over our courage to face life full on. I'd recently come to the same conclusion myself, their words weren't wasted on me though, they reinforced my own sentiments, reassured me that my thoughts were rational and reasonable.

First on, first off! Mexican ferries win hands down in my eyes. A blistering sun welcomed us to the mainland, stopping only to wave a cheery farewell to the girls. Mike led the way, having the benefit of GPS to guide us through the city. Half an hour later, glancing down at my map, I overtook and waved him over. Wrong way, in fact totally the opposite way to what we wanted. Backtracking through the heaving metropolis, we emerged back at the dock gates, where a compass bearing led us south en route to Mexico Route 40, the road of a thousand turns. With no turn offs and no deviations, Mike's GPS was pretty much redundant, thank God!

Durango sits within a horseshoe of the Continental Divide at about three thousand metres. From the coast it's a journey of three hundred kilometres, this averages out at a rise of one metre for every hundred metres travelled but there was nothing average about the road to Durango. It twisted up and down, and round and round, skirting round the mountainsides. Never breaching the crests, it would wind round, climbing or falling, along the precipitous edge of the hillsides. Staggeringly steep climbs wound up each new slope, hairpins sitting almost on top of each other, extra wide expanses of tarmac allowed for extra wide turning circles round the impossibly tight bends. Nothing obscured the views, giving plenty of time to pick the best line, only occasionally would any unexpected truck give cause for correction. The incline on each hairpin was unbelievable, resembling launch ramps more than highways. Levelling off, the road kept tight to the hillside, weaving in and out of rocky promontories, wrinkled escarpments looming overhead, lining our path. To the side lay a jumble of green clad hills, each encroaching onto its neighbours flanks. Their plummeting slopes were choked with dense thickets of trees or bushes, nowhere could we discern clearings, plantations or open waterways. The only signs of habitation were dotted along the roadside, long, narrow houses on narrow strips of land, smallholdings with pigs, goats and chickens, scratching a subsistence living from trade with passing traffic. The land was so lush, a verdant green profusion of inaccessible hills, behold the Sierra Madre Occidental, the Pacific flank of the Continental Divide. It was nice to be reunited with my old friend again, but this time it was only to be a brief encounter. In

Mexico the Divide formed a spine along which, further south, the country's heaviest concentration of people had settled. That wasn't to my liking, I'd wend my way through quieter areas of the country, steering well clear of the overpopulated heartland.

Future routes and possible destinations where far from my mind, Mex 40 had my undivided attention, surely there couldn't really be a thousand bends in three hundred kilometres? I'd have thought it would whip me into a peak of excitement, finding me hustling through the bends, pushing harder all the time, cranking hard over, ripping open the throttle, launching myself out the hairpins, whooping in jubilation. Sadly it wasn't to be, Mike lead at a sedate pace so I sat back and chilled out, admiring the views, waiting patiently for him to settle into the ride and up the pace. It didn't take long to reach the Tropic of Cancer, its whereabouts brought to our attention by a bright, new road sign. We were buzzing, seeing it as a symbol of our progress south, gaily swapping cameras to record the event for posterity. In fact it was the point at which we crossed back over, heading north, proving it to be nothing but an insignificant crossing of an imaginary man-made line. But we weren't to know, it spurred us on, gave us a sense of achievement. So much so that as we pulled away, the floodgates opened, I should have been sharing this with Cai, it should have been us thundering round the bends, grinning inanely with joy. Like most things, we were well matched as riders, our styles and techniques mirrored each other. We'd spent endless hours riding together, had complete confidence in each other. I began to begrudge sharing my ride, plodding along behind someone else, rather than surging forward without hindrance, having to restrain my natural riding style. Bugger that, maybe he thought he was doing me a favour, taking it easy for the guy on his comparatively small 650cc Enduro. So I took the lead, hoping to spur him on a bit, though it only seemed to exacerbate the problem.

Mike seemed to get slower as the day went on, he felt he couldn't negotiate his BMW 1150GS round the bends as easily as I could. Fair play, the KLR loved roads like that, I could throw it around wildly and it never complained. With its high ground clearance, I could lay it down low, scraping the pegs and power round the tightest curves. But if he wasn't as confident, I shouldn't have been pressuring him to exceed his comfort zones. It got really daft though and I had to slow down to less than 30mph to give him a chance of catching up. Riding alone I would be soaring round the bends, launching myself skyward from the incredibly steep switchbacks. I imagined death defying dives into hairpins, swinging wide, banking hard and swooping round, it was so frustrating. It was painfully slow going, and the time took its toll on my knee, becoming cramped and stiff, making me trail my leg straight to relieve the pain. With one hundred and forty five kilometres to go the road got considerably less twisty, I just started hammering it, I was beyond caring. We only covered about two hundred miles that day, and it took over eight hours, it was a nightmare. I felt crap about my intolerance, Mike was a decent enough guy, but neither our machines nor our riding styles were conducive to my idea of having a motorcycle travel companion. I wasn't dissatisfied, I was fuming, my long awaited ride ruined, snatched from my grasp at the last moment. Many times I thought to continue alone, without so much as a cheerio, only a misplaced loyalty stayed my hand.

By the time we reached Durango and found a hotel it was dark. Our initial attempts took us to dodgy looking dives with names like, "Motel Viagra". I could have done without sharing a bed in a knocking shop, at least on that point we agreed. But it was a palaver, constantly stopping and discussing what to do, I'd spot a hotel down a side street but by the time I got Mike's attention it would be long gone. He'd lead the way guided by his GPS, I thought it might need a bit of fine-tuning, with a brick. We spent over an hour looking for a room, eventually backtracking through a maze of tiny back streets, attempting to beat the one-way system and locate one we'd passed by. Finding it was a relief, a hotel with a secure compound, wireless Internet connection and two single beds, phew! Once settled, I discovered I'd left my power lead on the ferry. For me it was the last straw, I couldn't imagine being so careless travelling alone, blaming everything on anyone but myself.

We got on fine socially, spending a rest day together in Durango, time for me to rest my leg and Mike to do some bike maintenance. The evenings were spent sauntering round town, sampling a variety of red-hot Mexican food and ice-cold Mexican beer. It proved to be an easy-going companionship, though tainted for me by the knowledge that I was going to blow him out. Not having made my decision known, I felt awkward. Mike seemed content to continue together, I didn't want to spoil our day of rest. There were no doubts in my mind, I wanted to travel alone, more so when Mike was up at the crack of dawn, ready to set off again. We worked to different schedules, my mornings were slow affairs a leisurely breakfast before venturing forth, his was up and at 'em early, ride for an hour before considering a breakfast stop. Mike wanted to cruise the highways, using the fastest roads, the most direct routes. His aim was to reach South America by Christmas. I had no intention of using main roads, ploughing through the urban sprawl of Central Mexico, of going any further than Honduras for Christmas. It became time to part company, so a high-speed burn along a primary route took us to Fresnillo together, where I'd decided we'd part company. Over tacos and cola we said our farewells, with Mike heading off south, down the Freeway and me pointing east towards Hidalgo in search of a convenient dirt track.

Chapter Twenty Five

Any semblance of road promptly disappeared entering Hidalgo, itself a rundown hovel that didn't even warrant a graded road. Shutters hung off their hinges, paintwork peeling, grime-covered windows hid tatty drapes. I couldn't tell if it was even inhabited, there was no sign of life but the fields around were obviously cultivated. A choice of dusty farm tracks led out of the village, neither showed any sign of where they might go. Catching sight of a battered old bus in the distance, I made a snap decision, it must be on its way somewhere, I'd head in that direction. The dry, dusty dirt track passed between empty fields, at best an amalgam of ruts, ridges and potholes. At intervals bomb craters devoured the track, up to a couple of metres deep with steep banks to contend with each side. Surely a bus hadn't gone that way but there was no other way around, it must have done. What a bus can manage is bound to be a doddle on a motorbike, so ever onwards. *Carefully ease down the near bank, gun it across aaand, WHOOPSIE!* I hadn't meant to go airborne, I nearly soiled my underwear, but it had me laughing like a loon. This was more like it, I quickly forgot about the aborted attempt of the "Road of a thousand turns". Hey, I tried accommodating someone and it failed miserably, if that was selfish then so be it. With an almighty crash the rear end bottomed out, hot damn, maybe taking it a little easier might be a good idea. I swore not to risk off-roading until my knee got substantially better. It was reassuring though, and with only a slight grimace of pain I forged ahead.

I was off the map, neither the track nor the next village featured on it. It was bigger than Hidalgo had been but still a sleepy little backwater, with all the doors and shutters firmly closed. At the far end a lone guy sat at an open hatchway, the village store. Thinking it might shed some light on where the hell I was, I stopped. Apparently I was in Torbio, not that it improved matters in the slightest, it still couldn't be found on the map. Though with only one track in and one track out, taking a wrong turn was nigh on impossible. I left a very bemused Mexican, shaking his head in disbelief, no doubt wondering what the crazy Gringo was doing in the middle of nowhere, without a clue where he was, or where he was going. A mile later the dusty trail turned into tarmac road, in turn culminating at a T-junction. It even had a signpost giving me a choice between two towns, if only either name were to be found on my map. Not that it would have helped a great deal, I'd blindly been following an easterly direction, confident in the assumption that if I ran out of daylight I could pitch the tent. Generations have used nothing but the stars and the sun to navigate by, however, I preferred a compass. And off I rode, from somewhere in Central Mexico, to some other place, further east.

Everywhere I went people seemed dismayed to see me, they constantly assumed I was lost, that I'd arrived by mistake. They may have had a point, but it was only my exact whereabouts I was ignorant of. Obviously I was off the beaten track, people's surprise at my presence made that clear. It didn't help that I often had to stop and enquire as to which town or village I was actually in, few displayed roadside nameplates. But that had been our plan, our whole ethos of travelling through Latin America, to explore the hidden depths of the countries, avoiding the tourist trail. Spending the afternoon winding along unmarked roads, through unnamed villages, induced a sense of being at peace with the world. Rural living in hot countries dictates a leisurely pace, urgency is a foreign concept, lethargy is favoured, it makes far fewer demands. "Sleepy", and "Mexican town" are synonymous with each other, but most places I passed through that day were in a coma, it wasn't a slow pace, it was non-existent. The world had come to a standstill, it was hard to imagine life ever changing, anyone ever summoning enough energy to rock the boat. Being acutely aware of how much it would have meant to Cai, gave me a strong feeling of his presence, he may not have been there with me physically, but he damn sure was in spirit. It wasn't accompanied by grief or guilt, there were no tears, no lump in the throat, it felt reassuring. I treasured the wholesome awareness.

Santiaguillo put me back on the map, from which I managed to find my way to Gonzales Ortega, or Banon as the locals insisted. Sitting at the back of the central square, an old colonial cathedral loomed large, the imposing centrepiece of the town. Does having a cathedral make it a city? If so, it was the smallest conceivable city, with only a hand full of shops, a couple of lanes of adobe built houses, no hotels, and little else but a market area. Town or city I couldn't say, I'd have described it as a one-horse town, due to a guy putting his horse through its paces around a training circle. A gorgeous but skittish, dappled grey beast, trotting happily round, yet snorting in disgust when prompted to reverse direction. Mexican men, especially the older ones have a penchant for the cowboy look. Rather than the archetypal sombreros, they favour straw cowboy hats, often completing the picture with the appropriate boots, chequered shirts and bootlace ties. This guy was a more modern breed of Mexican though, attired in baggy T-shirt, baggy pants, heavy duty work boots and a baseball cap stuck on his head. John Wayne turns gangster rapper, so the world hadn't quite stood still there, but it was still a horse he was training, not a pit-bull. He had an advantage over me as well, he stood in the only shaded spot around, and as nice as it was to stand and watch man and beast bonding, I had to make a move before I melted.

The countryside seemed bare, large areas of tilled soil, yet no crops. Mile after mile the scene was the same, the maize harvest was over, next season's crop had yet to appear. Maybe, that would explain why the fields and villages were devoid of people, lazy days waiting for the next crop to emerge. Gone were the luxuriant western slopes of the divide, now I rode high arid plains, not so much small-scale subsistence farming as large-scale maize production. Very few trees could be seen, a thin, broken line formed a dark edge, far away, to the never-ending dusty, dun coloured soil. Scarcely discernable, little more than a shadow on the far distant horizon, a hazy line of low-lying hills threw a shadow along the skyline. A huge cobalt blue sky overshadowed everything, faint wisps of lacy cloud failing to soften its glaring brilliance. Without a whisper of wind, not even the faintest of breezes, the dust lay thick over everything, only to be whisked into clogging clouds whenever disturbed. A lack of traffic meant it wasn't a problem, I was the one kicking up the crud anyway, and I wasn't about to hang around behind anyone else.

As the sun dipped lower, my entry into Villa de Cos was halted by a funeral procession, the casket in the back of a battered farm pickup, the mourners following on foot. My heart went out to them, concerned for their grief without considering my own. My compulsion was to follow, to show I cared, that I understood. But no, a funeral is not the time for such bold gestures. I remembered all too well my own accusations of voyeurism at Cai's. With silent commiserations I let them go, allowing them their privacy, their right to grieve alone, without confusing it with mine.

All roads lead into the town square, a quick circuit revealed no hotels, so I parked up to make enquiries. Well I didn't have to go far, as I swung my leg stiffly over the bike, I was met with a host of curious well-wishers. First and foremost, they wondered how I'd got so lost as to show up in their town, none believing it could be intentional. A Gringo in Villa de Cos? I must be a mistake. Kids, teenagers, young guys and old men vied for my attention. They clustered round the bike, eyes lit up with wonder, 650cc, a Kawasaki. Detailing my journey so far impressed them no end, I felt like a celebrity. Even women paused in passing, asking who I was, where I came from and why I was there. Curiosity satisfied, most shook my hand and sauntered off, pleased to welcome me to their town. All expressed their pleasure at seeing me there, a few declaring it an honour. Someone produced a drink of Sprite, another some peanuts, the honour was all mine. I couldn't really begrudge them the attention, whether or not darkness fell in the meantime. Being assured my bike was safe where it stood, I set off on foot in search of a hotel, finding one overlooking a lively night market. I'm a sucker for being the centre of attention, I like seeing delight on people's faces merely by my presence, happy, smiley faces and cheery waves. My Spanish may have been appalling but no one seemed to mind.

By the time I'd got some fruit, biscuits, cigarettes, ice and beer, I was shattered and limping worse every minute. No way was I about to go gallivanting. I holed up in the hotel, ice pack on my knee and settled down for the night. Riding hadn't posed any problems, getting on and off the bike was a strain, and it got so stiff after hours of riding. Explosions throughout the night could have been disconcerting, I assumed if there were problems they'd be accompanied by sirens and gunfire. True enough, morning dawned with no trace of running gun battles in the streets or obvious signs of terrorist attacks. It was still a busy little town, packed with early morning shoppers, and café owners more than pleased to serve me up a huge plate of *Huevos Rancheros* and a scolding hot mug of strong, black coffee. All told my bill whilst in town only came to about $14, hotel, food and everything, at prices like that there was little point in contemplating camping. It had been a delightful experience, finding, and staying in small town Mexicana, one I looked forward to repeating en route.

Another two days spent plying my way across the Sierra Madres, all high altitude plains, yielded few moments of mayhem to savour. Flat and boring, the riding itself was straightforward, it was the environment through which I rode that made each day shine. Flat, open plains as far as my ageing eyes could see, squinting against the glaring sun. I saw why the Mexicans have become so invaluable to the farming communities of America. They sure know how to grow things. It doesn't matter what the environment, the crop or the growing medium, they seem to have it cracked. Hard working, they turn the hostile arid plains into a productive land, growing what is best suited for their survival. Nearest the village houses smaller stands of maize grew, with rows of prickly pear in the plot alongside. The cacti grew in abundance, carefully cultivated nearer the village, further away larger plants grew more haphazardly, interspersed with trees. This land was scrub, also serving to graze goats or small numbers of cattle. I wondered why they hadn't turned more of this into cultivated land, then realised it was the only areas for grazing. It boosted their diets incredibly, providing a whole range of dairy products, as well as extra sources of meat, to supplement the pigs and chickens found rooting around every enclave of houses. Also the trees were very important, what other source of fuel did they have?

Villages between Villa de Cos and Arista were dusty, quiet places. Cattle congregated at infrequent watering holes, squelching through muddy banks to slate their thirst. Most buildings were adobe or concrete block. Square structures, largely un-rendered, save for the front which was invariably brightly painted in yellows, purples and blues. Some looked dilapidated, tatty tin roofs held down by blocks of stone, slabs of concrete, even old wheels, others more reminiscent of frontier forts, with cracked and crumbling stone walls, roof timbers protruding from the upper stonework, ancient relics of a bygone age. There were few signs of wealth, just a lot of hard working but happy people. The bike's exhaust note approaching guaranteed getting people's attention, mouths agape, they would watch me wide-eyed. As in any poor isolated place in the world, a wave in acknowledgement would see their faces crack into a smile, as they waved back in happy greeting. I recalled earlier travels feeling too patronising to wave at the poor farming folk as I passed, joyful smiles and hearty hellos changed all that. Almost without fail my solicitations provoked a positive response, at least the kids in Mexico don't line the road to throw stones at you, as in the far east of Turkey. After all, it was rare in such places to see a large foreign bike, loaded to the gunwales cruise through. Kids would run towards the roadside, bubbling with excitement, even the crotchety old men would lift a hand in casual salute. When told of similar, previous experiences, like riding through Turkey the year before, Cai had been enthralled. That was what he'd sought to enjoy, experiencing the real world, being amongst honest folk unspoilt by the flippant wealth of the western world. Being there was the best tonic I could have hoped for, experiencing aspects we'd discussed, living our hopes and dreams. It made me feel closer to Cai, he was never far from my thoughts and it rarely disturbed me during that leg of the journey.

A wrong turn from Charcas came to a dead end at Guaneme. What a waste of time, all the place had to show for itself was an old, rather impressive church building, burnt out years ago. Not a soul stirred, a solitary shop held scanty supplies, and even scantier advice. The occasional flea ridden mutt lay hot and panting, pressed against a wall or the curb, desperate for any sliver of shade, any respite from the torturous mid-day heat. I took a gamble, backtracking to a previous spur in the road, another broken pavement leading to Los Remedios, and hopefully a trail across to Guillermo. On the way stood a bullfighting arena, empty and deserted, but well maintained and ready for use, unfortunately for the luckless bulls. Luck wasn't on my side either though, the sandy trail petered out into mixed scrubland. Confronted by an indistinct trail, through deep sand, I hadn't the gumption to go further, my knee throbbed in anticipation of paddling through the sand. So back I went, riding through oceans of maize, broken by small plantations of Aloe Vera, in long straight rows like tufted islands amongst the otherwise unbroken sea. It amazed me how they did it, ranks of pristine plants without a weed in sight, immaculately kept fields, without anyone seen working them. Maybe it was divine intervention? More likely they spent the early hours slogging their guts out, before the sun reached its zenith and fried them alive. By the time I roused my lazy bones from bed and breakfast, it was generally mid-morning. They could have got a six-hour shift in by then. Siesta lasted a lot longer than a couple of hours in the early afternoon, only late in the afternoon did people begin to emerge.

Nearing the edges of the Sierras I thought it was time to enjoy a night out under the stars. The route across had all been well cultivated land, it hadn't inspired me to camp out, and the need never arose. But it had been weeks since my last night out, a sense of peace prevailed and I just didn't fancy being holed up in another hotel alone. A kindly old gent willingly gave me permission to use the field next to his house. Fortunately, when the actual owner of the land showed up, he didn't object either, only insisting I move the tent a bit, into a more exposed position. For two days I'd ridden the high plains, drifting along, peacefully, filled with happy memories of my son. I'd ridden as if he rode alongside, his presence my constant companion, fortifying and comforting. What changed that is beyond me, it couldn't have been moving my tent, surely it couldn't have been camping in full view of the road that so unsettled me. All I knew was that I suddenly felt exposed, vulnerable and very lonely. Then the world came crashing down around my shoulders. Cowering in the tent, blubbering to myself, powerless against the grief, all strength and determination left me. Sitting, silently screaming, wishing I'd been taken out with Cai, at complete odds with life. I felt too scared to live, yet too proud to die. How was I ever going to deal with it all? What should I do, what could I do? There were no answers, the only solution was to ride the wave, hang on tight and wait for calmer waters. Ashamed of my weakness, I couldn't contemplate giving up, wouldn't consider giving up. Thoughts of returning home repulsed me, I was better than that, besides, without the emotional strength to tackle a bike ride, how the hell could I hope to face North Wales? So in the gathering gloom, I set about recording the day's events, then force fed myself pasta and tinned corned beef hash. As I wrote my last words, by the light of my head torch, the traffic was almost non-existent, an owl hooted from the nearby trees and my head bobbed gently up and down, on the verge of a peaceful sleep. It was the times I felt closest to Cai, infused with his presence, that life seemed almost bearable, it was also those precise moments of time that catastrophe caught me unawares, was most likely to sweep me away on a wave of destruction.

Covering the last vestiges of the Sierra saw no improvement in the nature of the road, it still proved to be tediously straight. The small towns changed though, tarmac would give way to a maze of dusty lanes, leading every which way. Lacking any signposts, the way ahead was never a simple matter of carrying straight on, my map would show only one road cutting through the town. But finding myself arriving at the town square, half a dozen or more indistinct tracks confused the issue, there was plenty of help at hand though. Bustling market towns lined the route, teeming with people and animals, the roads choked with ratty old motorbikes, junk heap jalopies, tiny tractors and a varied host of horse drawn contraptions. Central squares, filled with market stalls, shoppers spilling onto the road, offered not a clue as to the right direction out. Pre-armed with the correct question to find my way was all well and good, understanding the response was nigh on impossible, I resorted to arm waving and reiterating the question. It still got me lost a number of times, ending up turning round in a quagmire, at the bottom of a horrid slope of rubble. With a rapidly expanding audience, I was chuffed at reaching the top without mishap, shame I had to stop for an oncoming horse, my brakes were useless on the loose gravel and steep track, over I went. It never fails to amaze me when I drop the bike, in front of people they're always so concerned, never am I left to pick it up alone. That doesn't make it any less embarrassing, whether or not I laugh it off with the spectators. With busy town life to tickle my fancy, I didn't care about the boredom of the road in between. Every town was unique, some consisted of clapped out taxis, clustered round the market, whilst others seemed abuzz with crappy Chinese 125cc motorbikes. Wherever I went, whatever the local conveyances, I was always under the watchful eyes of dozens of the local denizens. Wanting to cover a fair amount of ground, I rarely dismounted, avoiding becoming inundated with a bombardment of questions. A nod or brief wave would have to do. I was content to be observer and observed, no need to become more embroiled.

Through Santo Domingo and Fernandez to Rio Verde, then joining Route 70 took me all the way to the Gulf of Mexico, finally meeting the coast in the grubby, garbage strewn streets of Tampico. Santo Domingo's sandy lanes rang with the sweet dulcet tones of school kids singing, a horse whinnying its impatience with its owner busily chatting to friends. Cyclists rode three abreast across the dusty main street, laughing and joking without a care in the world, totally oblivious to other road users. Sultry señoras sauntered along the middle of the street, kids in tow, chattering excitedly, keen to keep up with the latest gossip. A more relaxed but livelier atmosphere was immediately evident. Off the high arid plains, as the ferociousness of the sun abated, the lethargy of the locals diminished, replaced with a bubbly enthusiasm for the day's events. Beaming smiles came more readily to people's faces, old and young alike. Life up high in the Sierra Madres is a harsh one, with a severe climate and little respite from the elements, small wonder they came alive when given the chance to socialise on market day.

Fernandez brought an end to the plains, as the road flowed over the flattened top of that world, the expansive areas of maize became a thing of the past. Smaller fields of prickly pear and aloe vera interspersed with stands of corn became more normal. Aloe vera plantations grew in number and size, for a while dominating all other crops. The drop in altitude brought many changes, the diversity and abundance of flora being the most noticeable. Clumps of broad-leaved trees broke up the landscape, their canopies often overhanging the road, providing sun dappled avenues of welcome shade. Palms trees became a common feature, bringing an unexpected hint of the tropics. Lush hillsides sprang into view, a multitude of them, crammed in one on top of the other. Small, fertile valleys shone resplendent greens. Huts of wattle or split bamboo with thatched roofs, stood within busy smallholdings. Pigs, goats and chickens foraged freely, the obligatory stands of maize stood to one side, whilst a bewildering variety of fruit and veg filled the enclosures. It was a vastly different world to the one I'd just left, very Caribbean in nature, truly a tropical paradise. Fruit sprouted everywhere, cassavas, bananas, papaya, melons, mangos and assorted citrus trees. Every compound was a treasure trove of dietary delight, every corner contributed to the production of some food source. Each clearing amongst the thickly forested hills was divided into fenced enclosures, livestock and crops kept separate. As the road tumbled chaotically downhill, larger valleys appeared, offering wider cleared areas, larger scale production. Rolling green hills, dense with deciduous trees, lined long, flat valleys. Grazing cattle chewed nonchalantly on a non-ending supply of luxuriant grass and unlike their upland cousins, these were not scrawny, half-starved beasts. Nor were their attendant cowhands sleeping off the midday sun, sitting proudly astride fine looking horses, with knowing smiles, they waved me on as I thundered past.

Neither as long, nor with the sheer volume of bends as the Durango road, the way to Cuidad Valles was still a blinding ride. Narrower, without open views through all the bends, it was nevertheless excellent. There was no one to slow me down, I was off the leash, and didn't I have fun. Forget tales of speed, it's not about how fast you can go round what bend, there are no medals for the fastest spill, it's all about the dynamics of the ride. How focussed are you, how well do you read the road, how in tune with your machine are you? If all these factors meld together, if you get it all just right, it's heavenly, nothing else exists, it's the road, the bike and you, all in perfect harmony. It's a magical feeling, a natural flowing process, relying on experience, awareness and confidence. On approaching a bend, line up to the outer circle of the arc, easing off the throttle, but keeping the revs up, the engine on the boil, always ready for instant action. With your attention on the furthest, visible point of the road, be prepared, assume nothing, expect anything. Tickling the throttle, keep the gas flowing as you approach the exit, easing off if the curve tightens, whatever the emerging road conditions dictate. And then, when the exit starts to open up, so does the throttle, pulling yourself up and out, swinging into position, ready for the next bend. Every exit leads you into the next bend, in the right position, at the correct speed. There is no mathematical formula, there is no standard, every bend is different, every time you go round. That day I had over eighty miles of constant twists and turns, a helter-skelter through a spectacular orgy of tropical splendour. I had to force myself to stop and take in the scenery, the ride was so exhilarating.

At Ciudad Valles the road levelled off and the land opened out, huge areas of dying grass supported thousands of heads of cattle. Sheds and corrals, covering acres, were full to bursting with steers. Whether intensive beef rearing, or collected for slaughter, the effect was the same, distress and despair, bellowing bovines, beef farming at its ugliest. I wasn't about to waste any time brooding over it, vowing never to eat another McDonald's I hightailed it to El Ebano, and holed up in an hotel for the night. Something had changed, a reluctance to camp clouded my mind. On previous bike journeys, I'd thought nothing of sticking my tent anywhere for the night, as long as it was out of sight of the road. I'd found no problem on the Baja Peninsular, but after only one abortive attempt at camping on the mainland my enthusiasm was non-existent. Unwittingly, a new routine had been established, I'd become more used to hotels, relished a secure shelter overhead. I was happy to pay $10 a night for a hotel room, eat and drink locally, and have an early night.

Beauty, marred by mounds of human waste, dogged my progress. Half-burnt open waste tips lay beside every homestead on the plains, rubbish strewn down the sloping verges of mountain roads, and large-scale waste dumping slap bang in the middle of gorgeous natural wetlands. Black plastic bags, the scourge of the modern world, blown by the wind, snagged on trees and bushes. Egrets vied with refuse for access to the water's edge, herons carefully sidestepping over garbage choked reeds. With hawks and eagles circling, waders stealthily patrolling through the rushes and egrets everywhere, it should have been a wondrous water world. Well it was, but the smouldering heaps of domestic waste and the windblown debris were heart breaking. Maybe it's easy to overlook the belching power plants, the filth of industrialised nations, but seeing an abundant, natural wonderland, befouled in such a way was deplorable. Perfectly reflecting my mood, the dark brooding clouds marked my approach and arrival in Tampico. Finding piles of rotting food blocking the gutters wasn't surprising, somehow it was more fitting to see it clogging the city streets. Standing amongst piles of garbage isn't my preferred venue for eating, when needs must though, it's better than going hungry. And when the deluge came, I savoured the last mouthful of Taco, quickly slipped on my waterproofs and resigned myself to a wet day of mile munching.

Didn't it just rain too, like having to punch my way through a solid sheet of water! Still, my normal approach was called for, hunker down and keep on trucking. Or that's the way it should have been, until the bike coughed and spluttered, and grinding to a halt, stalled. Given no chance to coax any life into it at all, I could only sit and stare, forlorn, up an awfully steep hill. Still, only five hundred metres in front of me stood an escape from the nightmare, a fuel station. Thank God for small mercies eh? Or maybe not, I'd been soundly cussing him ever since that fateful day of July 3. At the lashing rain, the oncoming uphill struggle, my dead engine and God himself, I lifted my head, 'Fuck you, bring it on!' Two hundred and seventy five kilograms of bike and luggage, up a steep slope, with full bike gear on, encased in non-breathable waterproofs, I sorely needed that angst. It may well have been only five hundred metres, it took more effort than riding five hundred miles. My heart was pounding, my knee throbbing, and the sweat ran in rivulets inside my, "boil in a bag" waterproof suit. Was I struck by lightning for my blasphemy, did the ground open up beneath my feet and swallow me whole? No, a young Mexican youth dashed to my aid halfway up, so I let him take most of the strain, merely holding the bike upright and pointing in a straight line being my contribution. And, of course, I rewarded him handsomely for his aid.

Finding the fuel tap in the reserve position, I jumped to the conclusion some tealeaf had siphoned off my petrol. Checking the tank it was a relief to be proved wrong, especially as the gas station had run out of fuel. Although the engine kicked into life when I stabbed the button, I wasn't about to jump aboard and zoom off. There'd been a reason for the problem, so I set about trying to find it. The difficulties at Chief Joseph's Pass came to mind, I was convinced it was fuel mixture or air intake, so proceeded to clean and re-lube the air filter. As an afterthought, I also wound in the mixture screw half a turn, and set off once more, convinced the problem should be solved. Only until the next downpour, when the same happened again, cough, splutter, wheeze and nothing. The sun may not have been shining on me, but fortune was, this time I was pointing downhill, an equally steep hill. Freewheeling, I tried bump starting it! Blaurh, nothing, blaurgh again, nothing, for a mile repeated attempts produced similar results. Traffic started queuing behind and the end of the hill loomed large, I gave it one more valiant attempt, and the beauty burst into life. In a bold attempt to escape the embarrassing predicament, I gave it maximum revs and shot off, leaving all and sundry far behind.

Despite the rain easing off, dark turgid clouds lined the sky. I rode in full waterproofs. The heat and humidity meant I got wetter inside than out. Whilst refuelling at Tuxpan a hint of blue returned to the sky, off came the waterproofs though the moisture laden air did little to relieve my sticky dampness. And as if on cue, out came the sun, in its full glory, revealing another fertile countryside, glistening from the recent rain. Rolling green hills all around, food springing from every conceivable cranny. Hump-backed cattle grazed flattened fields, dotted with date palms, their skinny frames at odds with the profusion of thick, green grass. Goats grazed scrubland amongst bananas and papaya, devouring anything within reach. Orange groves filled whole hillsides, in regimented rows they marched up the hill, their tangy smell filled my nostrils, made my mouth water. Of course, as always, the ubiquitous maize, tall, green patches of succulent corn, liberally spread throughout the landscape.

The road along the Gulf is littered with small towns and villages, every few miles you enter the new environs of yet another town. Sleeping policemen block the way, every hundred metres or so along the through-road, semi-circular strips of concrete twenty centimetres high, forty centimetres wide. They are steep and abrupt, you do not want to be hitting them unawares, or at speed. Traffic always comes to a snarling stop, long lines of vehicles jostle for a quick way through. Engines revving, buses and trucks belch dense clouds of black fumes. Horns blaring, car drivers vie for the chance to force their way past, between the speed bumps. Delivery vehicles don't bother to pull off the road, adding to the chaos, often leaving no room for any traffic to pass. My first experience of this saw me waiting patiently in line, amazed at the lunatics making a dash past a line of waiting vehicles, then swinging back into line, forcing those waiting to move out the way. Because of the lumbering pace of the decrepit trucks and buses, there were often gaps between oncoming traffic, and I didn't need telling twice. Rather than be a sitting target for other drivers, I took the initiative, as soon as there was a gap I was gone. I needed less of a gap, had better acceleration and a sharper brain than the average Mexican driver. Nipping out I could generally overtake the whole queue, before squeezing back in after the speed bump. Fair play to the oncoming trucks, they often made a bit more room for me. Hopefully the entertainment factor made it worth their while. Whatever nefarious techniques I employed, it still meant constant stopping and starting, it was torturous.

Combined with abysmal surface conditions the route proved a bit of a nightmare, the only alternative was to use toll roads when available. I hesitate to describe them as motorways, they're far from it, merely a means to avoid going through every festering piss-hole along the coast. Considering we're talking of having to pay for the privilege of driving them, I think they should have advertised them as adventure routes, it may have attracted more custom. Some sections were no better than farm tracks, huge holes and ruts in loose aggregate. Wow, I'd gone out my way to find trails like that before. When there was tarmac it was likely to be in a sorry state, chunks missing completely, deep ruts and depressions from truck tyres, and a hotchpotch of lumpy repairs, generally making it worse than before. In most ways though driving on the toll roads was a lot better, certainly a lot quicker, the level of driving tended to improve too. If there was only one lane and the shoulder, the average driver moved over and allowed me to pass. This changed when there was a bit of a queue behind a large vehicle, then it became every man for himself again. The rule of the road was "might is right," people will pull out to overtake from the other direction, expecting a motorcyclist to move out their way. Not one to argue, I'd generally oblige, eventually, after a brief show of contempt for their recklessness. All in all though, the toll roads were ideal at the time, they provided a rough but open road, the chance to play catch-up, cover more road miles. When a carpet of new, smooth tarmac unrolled in front of me, I was beside myself, the perfect chance to wind on the throttle and make some real headway.

Crystal clear sky, bright sunshine, gorgeous tarmac and not another soul on the highway perfect conditions for gobbling up the miles. With only ten days left to Christmas and over one and a half thousand miles still to go, I was more than happy to maintain a decent speed where feasible. I was cruising along at over 80mph, enjoying the view, and feeling relaxed, glad to be unhindered by queues of vehicles. Suddenly, right in my line of travel, a groove, gouged out the soft tarmac, appeared. Even as the tyres settled into the groove it shouldn't really have been a problem, being little more than an inch wide, and of similar depth. It didn't cause too much concern, until it suddenly veered off, at 45° towards the hard shoulder. Being nicely settled into the groove, my front tyre followed while the bike's momentum carried it straight ahead. The result, a high-speed tank-slapper, they are virtually uncontrollable. Your front end flips from side to side, easily enough to bring you off immediately. If you fight it, you'll be off without doubt, braking will have the same result. I'd experienced this a few times, on different bikes, each occasion it was more down to pot luck than skill that saved my skin, none had managed to bring me off. You can only really hope to relax and ride it out, maybe carefully try easing off, or rolling on, the throttle. Who knows, ask any biker, they'll all claim something different. Easing off the throttle seemed to worsen the situation, so I tried the other way round. Accelerating up to 90mph with a tank-slapper is frightening to say the least, it may only be 5-10mph difference, but every gram of sense screams at you to brake, to slow down The situation brought with it an unbelievable clarity of mind, everything slowed down, thoughts were precise and clear, complete calmness reigned supreme. And ain't I glad about that, panic would have seen me smeared down the road. Possibly a worthy test for my expensive bike gear, but one I'd rather not put to the test.

Perhaps the weekend had something to do with it, but the traffic only seemed to get worse, and Vera Cruz was a madhouse. Of course, it is the main city on the gulf. There was a particular decadence around the Marina area, high-class, high-rise hotels, very glitzy and very expensive. The rest of the city could have been any dirty, dusty town in mainland Mexico. Endless rundown shops, fronting thoroughfares packed tight with impatient traffic, yet there the roads were two or three lane affairs. It was permanently gridlocked, traffic lights allowed progress in one hundred metre increments, and whenever at a standstill engines would constantly be revved mercilessly, accompanied by a cacophony of horns blaring. Creeping forward, nose to tail, sometimes only metre-by-metre, it was unbearable. Breathing pure carbon monoxide, head pounding from the aural overload, in stifling heat, I could do nothing but sit it out. Unable to roll forward or back more than a couple of centimetres, people still tried edging into my lane, bumper almost touching the bike, beeping their sodding horns at me to let them in. They had more chance of me jumping on their bonnets and pissing on their windscreens. But no, I just flippantly waved them off, without even glancing in their direction. Dickheads! Thankfully I didn't get lost, so the ordeal only lasted an hour, before being spat out on the road to Alvarado. God was I uptight, but faced with an open road again I settled down pretty quick. It didn't matter where I was, what I was riding through, my only concern was how far I got.

It wasn't that the countryside suddenly became boring, only that my mind was concentrated more on the road. Previous reports about the Gulf of Mexico had told of an overcrowded coast, full to the brim with Mexican tourists, I passed endless miles of deserted beach. There were no multi-storeyed hotels polluting the skyline, only occasional low-key affairs, all delighted with my custom during the low season. Images of hammering along the sandy emptiness came to mind, but nothing was to stand in my way, I tried to set a cruel pace. The luxuriant tropical growth still crowded the countryside, fruit still grew in abundance and productive homesteads littered my route. There was no end to totally tropical delight, but with my head firmly rooted up my own arse I rode on, oblivious to any but the most engaging of sights. An inland lagoon stretched for miles either side of Alverado, a long toll bridge allowing uninterrupted passage over its inlet from the sea. It got barely a glance. Little more than registering its presence, I paid my toll fair and roared away from the pay booth, determined to show my contempt at paying the same as a car.

As the road swung south towards Acayucan, my narrow-minded impatience was brought to a hasty halt, as the Parque Nacional Lagunas de Catemaco exploded into view below me. A wonderful watery realm, a placid maze of blue and green, elongated islets stretched thinly across the lagoon, spits of land, talon shaped, arched out from large, lumpy hummocks. Perfectly calm waters reflected the brightest blue sky, mirror the lazy green slopes and tree-lined banks of the interloping land. A convoluted passage of water wound its way around broken and distorted projections of land, yet nothing disturbed the calm serenity of the scene. Yet even that tranquil setting failed to delay me long, only the briefest of photo stops showed any sign of appreciation. Every village was a bottleneck again. It sorely tested my patience, saw me make some very aggressive riding manoeuvres. Once through the snarl-ups, freed of restraint, my only aim was to make up for lost time. The immediate goal was San Cristobel de Casa, a highly recommended old colonial city, within striking distance of Guatemala, my last port of call in Mexico. With my mindset, nothing else would satisfy me, even overnight stops were nothing more than undesirable but necessary, occasions to gather my strength.

At long last I reached my personal El Dorado! Indeed San Cristobel de Casa is a gorgeous city, bright, colourful buildings, sleepy plazas shaded by giant palms and market stalls overladen with embroidered and woven garments, the wares of rural Maya. Narrow cobbled streets, lined with tables and chairs, places to relax with a refreshing drink to watch the world go by. The central cathedral stood proud, painted in rich ochre tones of yellow, orange and red, intricate latticework detailed in white, a truly imposing sight. Small side streets hid understated entrances to quaint guesthouses, once inside revealing sheltered courtyards, encircled by guest rooms, upgraded relics of colonial villas. Too narrow for anything but one-way traffic the streets were an utter maze, leading to total confusion when trying to ride around the city. On a grid-work pattern every cross street was marked to show the direction of traffic, making it easy to know which way to look for oncoming traffic, rights of way weren't so clear. I took the easy way out, the pedestrian way. After trying a few places it was proving not to be an easy task, I'd not wanted to leave the bike, so had gone for those closest to the cathedral, the busiest part of the city. Space was at a premium, none could accommodate the bike as well and I wasn't about to leave it parked on the street overnight. Ranging further revealed quieter sections of the city, secluded coffee houses, more upmarket art and crafts. Only walking along each street could I discern whether or not there were any guesthouses, most did not have outward projecting signs. Whilst I managed to get my bearing a bit better that way, it was a very hot and sweaty Les that finally struggled up the steps with his bike, into the calm, seductive environs of his newly found accommodation.

Chapter Twenty Six

Sitting in a tranquil courtyard, supping a cold beer and writing my journal, the day was at last over, and I finally felt relaxed. Contemplating the last three days, three long weary days, trying to put it into perspective, I realised how intensely frustrating it had been. Before that I'd sat high and proud, touched by the presence of Cai, at peace with the world. Infused with a sense of togetherness, at one with my heart, my thoughts and the surroundings, he could have been riding next to me. But I'd lost that, that tranquillity seemed far, far away, tainted by the turn of events. From the pollution and filth I'd seen around Tampico, the problems with the bike, to the horrendously congested towns. They'd been dealt with at the time maybe, but still left their mark. I'd pushed myself hard, driven by mounting frustration, not for the thrill, nor for the enjoyment. An escalating furore over incessant delays, had whittled away at the pervading calm of days before. Brief respites of natural beauty, between the numerous chaotic towns, had done little to improve my tolerance of other road users. Their only purpose in life was to impede my progress, I despised them, surely they realised I had somewhere important to get to. Rising by 7.30 a.m. each morning, waiting only for a quick breakfast, I'd be on my way. Riding full out all day, until darkness finally descended, stopping only to refuel the bike and myself. Despite the gorgeous countryside, I'd barely noticed it, being so intent of making progress. It's such a blinkered approach to travelling, focusing solely on your destination, oblivious to the here and now. Anyone or anything that got in my way was a hassle, being cussed for slowing me down. I'd been my own worst enemy, creating my own personal, self-induced, mobile rat race.

Self-awareness is not to be sniffed at, it's our chance to rectify our own faults, realisation being the first step to personal progression. With more than a week before Christmas there wasn't any great hurry, La Ceiba and the ferry to Utila lay only four days away, it was time to calm down and begin to enjoy the experience again. It was time to take a couple of days rest, to recoup my losses.

Making full use of the rest days, an excursion to the ancient ruins of Palanque was taken, a chance to see the past glories of a fallen empire. The bike was left relaxing in the shady courtyard, whilst I subjected myself to the suicidal escapades of a local minibus driver. A ten-hour return trip, for only two and a half hours at the archaeological site. Ten hours at the mercy of a madman who drove flat out all the time, overtaking round blind bends and into oncoming traffic. Rubber screeching around tight bends, horn blaring at everything anywhere near the road, traffic, animals or pedestrians, he wasn't about to slow down for anything. My fellow passengers gasped in horror at his antics, covering their eyes, incapable of facing each moment of approaching doom. Entrance to the national park was by courtesy of a nod and a wink, no money changed hands, no tickets obtained, the official on the gate literally looking the other way. I employed the same tactics when our driver tried insisting I needed an official guide, striding away on my own, bound for the forest's fringe, for less frequented realms of the site. Eventually only forty minutes were spent admiring the architectural wonders, my idea of fun had been getting lost in the rain forest, following the haunted calls of the howler monkeys. However bad the driving had been on the way, the return trip was infinitely worse! As a new group of passengers gathered (no-one else was repeating their ordeal with the same driver) so did a thick blanket of dark cloud, whilst the last door slid shut the heavens opened. And it came down in buckets, bouncing off the road like hailstones, collecting in huge swathes of groundwater, unable to drain away quickly enough for the falling torrent. If I'd thought it might have given us some respite from the demented driving I was sorely mistaken. He may well have driven a fraction slower, it wasn't noticeable if he did, but visibility was appalling, no doubt worsened by his drooping eyelids. For the second time that day I had a grandstand seat, up front, best view in the house, suspense and horror in full widescreen format. With a strange detachment I settled back and relaxed, I couldn't do anything about how badly the guy drove, though prodding him awake regularly was quite useful. Watching bullets of water rebounding off the tarmac, mist rising from its hot surface, I could only feel relieved at being in the confines of a warm dry vehicle, not astride my machine. Yeah, truly gladdened not to be out in such foul conditions, exposed to idiots driving at breakneck speeds. Exclamations of relief, exasperated sighs of pleasure broke the long silence on arrival back in San Cristobal. But these were nothing compared to the gasps of disbelief expressed at the driver's heavy handed hints at a tip, needless to say he left empty handed.

If I hadn't felt like a rest before the excursion, I sure as hell did after. Not that the drive had bothered me unduly, my fate was in his hands, it had just tired me out. Trust hadn't come into it, the driver was a reckless idiot, seriously risking the safety of a dozen people at a time. I didn't trust him as far as I could spit, and I'm real bad at spitting around corners. Sitting back and waiting patiently, for whatever might come my way, I was beyond caring about myself. To die in a foreign road accident would be unlikely to raise many eyebrows, at least being a passenger would quell doubts of any complicity in my own demise. Images of Cai laying mid-freeway, in pain, in shock, desperate for my arms to hold him, still haunted me. I'd been powerless to help, would gladly have given my own life to save his, and yet could only give him my love. How wrong it had been, my son to die before me, though neither would I wish to subject him to the pain I must bear. An easy way out wasn't sought after, I had no suicidal tendencies, but if death should have come my way, well, who was I to complain? I didn't dwell on such thoughts though, they didn't consume me, with a careless detachment I simply acknowledged them.

So a lazy day's exploration of the city ensued, chilling in shady pavement cafes, watching the world go by. A wealth of traditional Mayan costumes was flaunted everywhere, a huge variety of styles and designs. Thick, shaggy black skirts worn with simple cotton blouses, decorated with elaborate, heavy mantles of sequins, giving an effect of sparkling chain-mail, then edged with contrasting sequinned lace. Bright blue cotton dresses, overlaid by multi-layered mantles of lace, an apron of rich colour and design also worn over the skirt. Regional variations are normal among the Mayan world, minor differences marked which valley, village, or even family they belonged to. Their representation in the city was stunning, like the gathering of the clans, surely conveying the distance from which the indigenous women would travel to peddle their wares. And peddle their wares they did, plying the streets, burdened by bundles of hand woven goods, all too pleased to lay out their entire stock at the merest suggestion of any interest of a passing tourist. Even young girls could be seen hard at work, hustling the tourists with little straw dolls dressed in traditional garb, mini replicas of themselves. 'Meester, meester, you like?' Turning round I'd be confronted by two adorable girls, one no older than five years old, her sister little more than eight. So enchanting I had to have a photo of them, ye gods but they were sharp, 'Photo $2.' They weren't street urchins, unaccompanied for sure, but immaculately turned out mini Mayans. Of the men, little was seen, those who were to be found were, without fail, dressed in western style clothes. Whereas the young girls were dressed in impeccable fashion, the boys were scruffy, rag-tag lads, in need of a good wash and brush-up. They'd bear trays of chiclets, peanut brittle and other candies, also selling packs or single cigarettes. My heart went out to those Maya, once the all-conquering heroes of a rich culture, proud rulers of architectural grandeur. Now relegated to manufacturers of tourist tat, hustling the streets from dawn to dusk, slaves to the holiday whims of western wealth. The overall impression was of a race of peasants, second-class citizens within their own country, hardworking farmers condemned to a life of physical hardship. They seemed out of place in the city, ill at ease, rarely did I notice any expression of joy or humour. This was at odds with the Maya I'd come into contact with before, a shy, retiring folk, hardworking, but generally a happy, easy-going group. Was it purely a matter of being taken out of their natural surroundings? Did they, like me, find it denigrating to become a cultural curiosity, victim to the daily orgy of carelessly thrust lenses, cameras clicking in your face?

San Cristobel earns its highly recommended status, but pays the price. The very nature of its layout means little traffic congestion, making it a highly pedestrianised city. It's a delight to wander around, quiet little backstreets criss-cross main thoroughfares, many too narrow even for a pavement. Without shops or cafés they attracted no interest from visitors, tourists restricted themselves to the main attractions, the central plaza, the cathedral, large buildings of imposing colonialism. Swarms of western tourists filled those streets, seeming to outnumber the local populace. It was hard to tell what practical function the city held, aside from being a tourist trap. Captivated visitors had settled for many years, of these it was the tourist industry that sustained them. Guesthouses, cafés, restaurants, galleries and expensive craft shops, none at the lower end of the market, there were plenty of Mexican establishments for tacky tourism. However my cynical mind could find to label it, it still presented a very attractive picture. Everywhere I went the streets were clean, people friendly, and buildings painted. Rich, deep tones made a striking picture, strong but subdued colours, not bright and gaudy. The bright colours came from the beautiful fabrics woven by the Maya, the gaudy worn by groups of wandering Mariachi players. Sequins and frills, moustachioed men prowling the streets and food courts, instruments at the ready, some innate sense homing in on likely targets. They appeared comical, cheap reproductions of bygone days, of dashing Mexican heroes astride their magnificent steeds, fine embroidered jackets, tight flares, waving sombreros in the air. In reality, the Mariachos could actually have been wearing the originals, they were so faded and threadbare. Like so much of the city, they were a tourist enigma, giving a few moments of joy, a feeling of Mexico, how real it may be is neither here nor there. I preferred to spend my time surreptitiously taking shots of the Maya, for me they were the real Mexico; the indigenous population, not the Latino interlopers.

A couple of days walking eased off the stiffness in my knee interspersed with periods of inactivity the improvement was rapid. OK, it still looked twice the size of the other, but bent well enough to get on the bike normally. No longer having to hop up to the bike with my leg held out sideways, almost straight. Only four hours out of Mazitlan the knee support became defunct, it cut off the circulation whilst riding, causing more discomfort than without it! Taking it off was a bold move, but the correct one. Twinges of pain would only occur if exerting sideways pressure on it, I wasn't worried too much, hadn't I managed to push the bike five hundred metres uphill?

Chapter Twenty Seven

Rested and rejuvenated, my old routine of a leisurely breakfast fell quickly into place. Being keen to be off bright and early wasn't going to spoil breakfast for me, 9 a.m. was early enough. With a week left to Christmas, and about one thousand miles to go, there was plenty of time. Epic rides across far ranging lands weren't needed, only the breadth of Guatemala and the length of Honduras lay between Christmas and me. Two border crossings would hamper progress but it was nothing to worry about, simply a formality.

Few towns stood in my way to the border, as always the through roads were full of choking fumes and snarling traffic. I wasn't to be wound up though, when overtaking it was in plenty of time, without fuss. Steady progress was made, time taken to absorb the richness of people and land. Agriculture was purely maize, large swathes of the stuff, only within garden compounds was there any evidence of other food being grown. Countless benches, scattered along the road, offered whatever surplus the peasants had grown, meagre amounts of melons, papaya, cucumber, tomatoes, anything for the chance of a few extra bucks. Decent views were a rarity, the roadsides most often supporting dense vegetation, or housing. When seen, the hills were far off, never giving the impression of being within my grasp. And the slopes seemed impenetrable forest, no agriculture, no sign of habitation, a dense no man's land. The points of interest were the people themselves. I'd virtually dawdle through villages, delighted with the Mayan culture, eager to note variations in their dress. It also gave me a chance to admire some beautifully exotic women.

Chiapas is the border region of Mexico, in the heart of Mayan influenced lands, the indigenous population dominate the countryside. The rich diversity of textiles could easily be seen, also the regional aspect of styles, colours and designs. Regions tended to dictate the style of dress, each village seeming to have its own unique pattern of weave, sometimes slight variations in colour being the only discernable difference. San Cristobel had played host to a good variety, though one style was clearly the most common. In the surrounding villages, the thick, shaggy black skirts and decorated satiny blouses were the exclusive style of dress. A random selection of woollen cardigans, cord jackets and heavy shawls would be worn over the blouses, even in the midday sun, no wonder they wasted no effort with overt expression. Without travelling too far the styles changed, lighter weight clothing was favoured, gone were the heavy outer layers too. Cotton dresses replaced the cumbersome shaggy skirts, simple embroidered designs graced short-sleeved blouses. Further towards Comitan simplicity took over, voluminous skirts of subtle weave were loosely tucked under a bright red sash worn round the waist. Bands of bright primary colours, of a rough, home-woven material were stitched into a basic short-sleeved top, no buttons, no zips, no ties. Just the holes for arms and head, it was so much more utilitarian than many of the fiddly, elaborate designs of Mayan clothes.

Being a relatively short hop to the border at Ciudad Cuauhtemoc, I was there within a couple of hours. In my accustomed way, the main Pan-Americano had been avoided, having been led to believe that the bribes were cheaper at the smaller, more commercial crossings. Trucks queued for miles, at first I wondered if we should all join the queue, then thought better of it, swung out and carried right on to the immigrations buildings. Hey, no one stopped me, and if there's no one to tell you what you should do, then you do what you want. Of course, there are plenty of people happy to help explain the intricacies of crossing their border, if you speak Spanish, oops! Maybe that was the time to form a strategy to make the passage through easier. I knew the perfect strategy, play the bumbling Gringo who hasn't a clue what to do. Of course it wasn't how I set out to appear, but it became immediately obvious that was my predicament. Call them guides, runners, fixers whatever you will, every Latin American border seems to have plenty of willing hands to arrange the necessary paperwork. Dashing around, collecting the correct forms, photocopying vehicle documents, greasing the right palms with a little baksheesh. It's the name of the game and they play it well. '*Cuantos dineros, amigo?*' If he hoped I might be a bit wet behind the ears that probably confirmed it for him. But let's face it, with decent Spanish and a bit of local knowledge, assistance wouldn't be needed in the first place. And so entered Daniel into the den of lions!

I admit to getting totally bewildered with the flood of monetary requests they hit me with. Trying to mentally tick off each demand helped somewhat, trying to keep track of what I'd paid for and how much was a touch more difficult. Largely due to my own distrust, I escorted them to many of the relevant windows. There was $5 here, $5 there, $10 for this and $20 for that. A second lad would dash off for road tax, or possibly tourist tax, while we filled out the application for import tax waiver. And of course everything was written in Spanish, there were reams of paperwork and little made sense, was it really all necessary? To further confound me, it had to be paid for in Quetzals, with no bank on the border it meant using moneychangers. Waving fistfuls of currency they'd try and outshout each other for my custom, so I tried one at a time. How much will you give me for my pesetas? Letting them bid for my custom seemed the easiest way, I only had about $60 worth, just about the lot went on taxes, fees and bribes. It would have been easier to sit down with a beer and conduct business from the comfort of a bar, at least I could have got ripped whilst getting ripped off. In all fairness, they couldn't have fleeced me for that much, various taxes and import duties cost money. I won't insult their intelligence with claims that they didn't fleece me, but it was within reason. Even the moneychangers hadn't given a stupid exchange rate. There's too much competition, both sides of the border, hordes of guys waving bundles of money aloft. The whole border-crossing zone is manic, they can't possibly note who is passing between the two countries. Only vehicle papers were checked before the rather flimsy barrier was raised, pedestrians had free access.

A jovial, relaxed mood accompanied me away from the mayhem at the border, using the runners had been worthwhile, even as simple interpreters they'd earned their money. Almost dawdling through La Mesilla, I left the madness behind and greeted the rest of Guatemala with a pleasant smile glued to my face. Did this newfound serenity alter my perceptions? Was it possible an imaginary line not only separated two nations, but also delineated an abrupt change in topography? Maybe, if it had followed a natural feature of the landscape, a river course or range of mountains. But change it did, the vista and my immediate surroundings had a very different feel to them. There were no shady canopies overhanging my route, the views weren't obstructed by dense growth and fruitful *campesinos* lining the very edge of the road. They had a much more open aspect, giving far-reaching panoramas of trees and hills, steep sided mountains crowned by fluffy white clouds, the moisture laden atmosphere providing sustenance for the tree clad slopes, and the profusion of tiny farms eking out a living, wherever access could be gained to turn the soil. Large outcrops, walls of awesome rock, thrust from thick jungle, shrouded by yet more dense jungle growth. On distant hills clearings stood out from the surrounding jungle, with no sign of road or trail. I knew all about the isolated coffee *fincas*, privately owned plantations cut from the virgin forest, their Mayan workforce totally dependent on supplies from the company store. The only access for many of these places was by air, unless of course you're a worker, then days of trudging through inhospitable jungle might just get you somewhere worth being.

It wasn't that the character of the landscape itself changed dramatically. It was more the manner in which the land was used, the manner in which the roads had been constructed. In Mexico roads ran round the side of its mountains, dipping down and back up again to join between the various hillsides but remaining on the same flank of the hills. Guatemala was delightfully different, they appeared to wind gradually up one side of the mountain, cross over to the opposite side, then meander gracefully down into the next valley. Winding along the valley floor, the main byways serviced the larger communities, dirt tracks led off to reach the further flung homesteads, giving access to more remote mountain slopes. All accessible areas played host to a continuous stream of settlements, every centimetre of space occupied with the task of food production. Rather than cash crops, a rich diversity of food was cultivated. Of the homes themselves, they stood some distance away from the road, though food was grown right up the highway. Being the staple, maize was the most commonly grown, but only on small plots, never did I see vast areas given over to monoculture. Whilst Mexico generally practiced more modern methods of farming, the Mayan homelands were much more traditional in their methods, and the mountainous areas of Guatemala virtually ignored the invention of the wheel. Oxen were the beasts of burden, if a family had to choose between owning horses and oxen, the oxen won hands down. They were the sole method I saw of ploughing the land, the farmer standing atop the plough in an effort to dig deeper into the ground. And there was so much land to plough, as one stand of maize stood ripening in the sun, the soil was being tilled for the next crop to be planted. I assumed there was some form of crop rotation, with millennia of agricultural expertise they must have that one cracked.

Reaching the brow of the first mountain pass was a slow and purposeful exercise. There wasn't any need to hurry. I wanted to take in the pervading tranquillity of the mountain haven. As always, my route was to avoid the busy urban sprawl further south, forget the cities and tourist attractions, stuff the hustle and bustle. My way was to be the high way, not the highway! From Huehuetenango across a succession of Sierras, a gravel track beckoned, and if there's one thing I just can't resist its temptation. So I headed down into the next valley, squeezed between precipitous, scrubby escarpments. At the head of the valley (or is it the foot?) the land opened out into an oasis of green fertile land.

Hardly any of my attention had been given to the road itself, it had been almost deserted, devoid of traffic, towns or even villages. Quiet roads and lovely smooth tarmac lulled me into a false sense of security, though with growing frequency jerked me back to reality. This was Latin America, you can never take anything for granted, except, that you can never take anything for granted. Happily soaking up the serene vibes, a chasm opened up before me, the two halves of my lane ripped asunder. Ragged cracks ran up the road, though not wide they looked bottomless, the earth itself moving apart. Craters a foot deep also appeared randomly, not road damage as such, just unexplained depressions in the otherwise perfect tarmac. Frequent earthquakes would be the logical explanation for such road damage. Having witnessed the results of tectonic activity in the Rockies it was hardly a big deal. There was plenty to occupy the mind though, it didn't do me any favours to mull over the cause of any one particular road hazard. There was always another ready to catch me out. Over bridges tarmac gave way to cobbles which in itself is bad enough, when half the cobbles are missing it makes for a bone-shaking ride. But it was the sudden, complete absence of a tarmac surface I feared most, without warning, in the middle of a bend, the tarmac would come to an end and turn into a construction site. How glad I was the day found me in a mellow mood, that I wasn't pushing it to the limits. The broad switchbacks enticed me to thrash up the mountainside but the calm serenity of the scenery stayed my hand. It wasn't conducive to flat-out speeds, even without the unexpected hazards, the laid back atmosphere quelled any desire for excitement, a more harmonious approach was adopted. Without motorised mayhem all around, there was nothing to disrupt a sedate attitude to life, what could I do but settle into the placid pace of life in the Mayan heartlands? No gravel track presented itself, another failure on the part of US printed road maps, not that it mattered, I was worlds away from such concerns.

And there was plenty of life to be seen en route, too much at times. People walked cows on the end of ropes allowing them to graze the verges. A line of sheep wandered orderly, in single file, obviously adept at the Green X Code. Horses and cows, tethered, fed on the narrow strips between crops at the roadside. Again caution was called for, more than once I came round a bend to be confronted with a road full of animals, or a cart being loaded, taking up almost the whole side of the road. Domesticated animals were either attended to or tethered, yet how do you stop a herd of goats wandering across the road to munch their favourite fodder. Women with heavy, wide loads balanced upon their heads walked the waysides, their bundles of wood protruding into my path. Though it wasn't for my safety, a respectable speed was kept, the life around me was too precious. I didn't want to disturb the gentle balance, wanting to pass through leaving only ripples in my wake.

Man, woman and child pulled their weight, seemingly spending each and every moment, of each and every day, in the survival and proliferation of their families. Young boys herded the goats, girls as young as ten spent the day with baby siblings strapped to their backs, both were at the constant beck and call to fetch and carry whatever was needed. The adults undertook a succession of backbreaking tasks. Men assumed responsibility for the fieldwork, women for domestic chores, but life was much more convoluted than that. Either could be found carrying impossibly heavy loads, the women on their heads, where-as the men employed a carrying harness, a strap round the forehead, the load resting on their backs. In this manner they'd carry stupid weights, more than I judged capable of lifting in my own arms. Whatever the task at hand, however much they strained with a load, they always had a ready smile. Within the Mayan lands I never saw annoyance or anger displayed, unless it was by a Latino, aggression didn't seem to be in their nature, whether towards animal or human. Unlike the impression of Maya in the city, at home in the mountains they were a good-natured people, coy smiles always at the ready.

Shy by any standards, but warm and welcoming, it was easy to pique their curiosity and nigh on impossible to capture their images. Still amazed at the variations of traditional dress, attempts were made to catch them unawares and record their rich attire. If noticing my camera they vanished from view, confounding my most subtle endeavours. Close to Sacapulas, burgundy was the dominant colour within the weave, yet there the similarity ended, geometric designs highlighted in one example, another, simple lines of black or yellow barely discernable amongst the bold colour. In that area, without fail, the women wore white lacy blouses, flowery patterns and white bras almost disguising the transparency of the material. Sitting quietly for a few moments, I watched a small pocket of the Mayan world go about its everyday life. Beautiful young women, striding confidently down the road, gaily chattering, cheery smiles brightening my day. A fuller matronly figure standing in the middle of the road, leaning nonchalantly into a pickup window, casually passing the time of day, unconcerned about the buses passing inches from her elbow. And that was the general vibe, people were unconcerned with the rigours of life, they just got on with it and were happy to do so.

Through the mountains to Cunen less than two hundred and fifty miles of Guatemala were managed that first day, and to think that, before San Cristobel I'd entertained traversing Guatemala in one day. But I wasn't counting the miles, only the smiles. The antiquated little market town was hardly reminiscent of colonial splendour, a dried up fountain was the centre piece to a litter strewn plaza, the dregs of the day's market in the last throes of packing away. Narrow, cobbled streets led steeply uphill, there was little in the way of commerce, and with only one hotel and one restaurant, choices were unnecessary. I was treated like a celebrity, everyone wanted to say hello. Walking down the cobbled streets groups formed behind, having animated discussions as to why I was there. In the restaurant a gaggle of giggling girls took turns in coming to my table, they all wanted some involvement in serving me. Not a word of English was spoken and my Spanish was hard put to order food, let alone discuss anything. A shame in many ways, but it'd been a full eight hours of riding, I just didn't have the energy to comprehend a foreign language. I was asleep by 8 pm.

Within eleven hours I was off again, through a cloud-laden land already alive with teams of oxen hard at work. Like farmers the world over, there was no such thing as a lie-in, they started earlier than I awoke. As ghostly spectres in mist shrouded fields, they toiled, barely able to see one end from the other. Yet still they looked up, smiling broadly, surprised, but pleased to acknowledge my presence. I'm not sure who was more surprised, them or me. It wasn't even 7.30 am. I don't get far, whatever time of the morning, without shoving food down my gullet, or more importantly, hot coffee. Roadhouses are few and far between in the mountains of Guatemala, I'm glad to say, but it does pose a slight problem when you want breakfast on the go. Faced with the prospects of riding without my fix of caffeine, any lengths to find a solution will be taken. And as I often claim, the more effort you put in, the greater the reward.

Coasting along, I'd nearly passed a cluster of houses before a café cum store front was noticed, set off to the side about fifty metres. Too late to turn in, I slowed and did a U-turn, watched by pairs of wide eyes emerging from the corners of buildings. When I actually pulled in the kids vanished from sight, leaving not a soul to be seen. Ah, how cute! Some had gone in the store, again there was frantic scrabbling to vacate the place as I entered. From one end of the counter and the back door, three pairs of wide, round eyes peered at me, rapidly vanishing again should I glance their way. Absolutely comical, I might as well have stepped out of a UFO. For them I painted a similar picture, full protective suit, big bike boots, gloves with moulded knuckle protectors and flashy space-age helmet. Even without the monster bike with the barking exhaust, it was an apparition they were unlikely to have beheld before. They weren't about to be coaxed out of hiding either, the appearance of the storeowner didn't change that, though they were less inclined to stop their staring. In fact more curious heads peeped round the corner, more kids and a woman.

Well I could see a selection of pastries right in front of me so food was sorted, but did they have coffee? No, bugger! OK, it was a good job I came prepared. '*Tenes agua, por favor?*' Why, sure they did, all I had to do was make my own coffee, and then I could enjoy my morning's essential beverage. So out came the camping stove and pan. And out came a growing throng of villagers, curiosity getting the better of their shyness. From all directions they appeared, women and children, the latter remained hidden behind the skirts of the women, mesmerised by the spectacle. The travelling circus comes to town... roll up, roll up... gather round folks... see the magnificent *motocicleta*... marvel at the splendiferous spectacle... behold.... from the very belly of the beast... we have... FIRE! And I kid you not, whispered chattering followed my every move, questions passed amongst themselves, speculation ventured as to what I was doing. After pumping and priming the stove, gasps arose as the stove popped into life with in a ball of flame, settling down into a fierce, high-pressure hiss. Silence reigned as the water sat over the flame, wonder was shown at the sight of the *cafetiere*, even more so when I produced my Leatherman from its pouch and folded out the pliers. Not a soul interrupted the performance, and I loved every minute of it. By the time a hot mug of coffee stood before me, half the village was in attendance. A semi-circle of happy faces crowded the storefront, bright smiles shone forth, even some of the older kids had ventured forth. And now... for my next trick! Out came the camera, and with my sweetest smile, *'Por favor señoras?'* As if by magic, most of them disappeared, leaving only a small group smiling shyly for a photo, still with the young ones hiding within the folds of their mother's skirt. It fortified my spirits more than coffee and cakes ever could, such a lovely unspoilt people, such a privilege to share even such a small part of my life with.

Off into the misty mountains I went, smiling all the way. Smooth tarmac snaked sinuously up one mountainside, sweeping majestically down the next. Constantly doubling back on itself the road rose high into the clouds, only to falter, dip, and follow a fluid path, down the opposing flank of the mountain into the realms of another land. Always out of one valley and into the next, each new valley was a whole new world. Flowing down steep sided slopes, the road would twist and turn, spilling onto flat plains of rich agricultural diversity.

From on high the difference was plain to see, softly contoured hills rose gently from small, flat plains. A patchwork of greens and browns earmarked different fields for different crops, small-scale cultivation spread across the plains, creeping stealthily uphill in a series of terraces. More expansive lands grew larger crops of maize, harvests staggered to ensure a ready supply all year round. Traditionally the whole plant is used, corn for human consumption, husks and leaves for animals, stems would be utilised for their fibres. Differing varieties also satisfied different needs, a blander, white corn for grinding into flour, the more succulent yellow and red eaten off the cob.

Climbing high, the security of a good quality surface came into question, signs warned of falling rocks. On cue, rounding a bend, a slide of loose shale encroached into my path of travel, causing a brief heart-stopping moment. No more than a wiggle of the hips and the hazard was bypassed. Minor slides appeared with more regularity, taking heed, a slower pace was adopted. Fortuitously; for suddenly, on a sharp right-hander, half the mountainside had come crashing down, engulfing almost the whole road. It wasn't a thin spread of loose debris, but a huge pile of rubble. Maybe my speed was still a touch on the high side. Braking severely, as much speed as possible was lost, before reaching the landslide. Releasing both brakes at the last moment, I threw the bike over to the left, towards the cliff edge, snapping it almost immediately back and leaning it hard over to the right. And I sailed around, clearing everything with ease, no panic, no fuss, just the way it should be done. It could be argued that I was taking unnecessary risks, but riding a bike at any time is a risk, if you're not willing to accept that risk, don't get on the bloody thing in the first place! Meeting an approaching truck five hundred metres further on still failed to diminish my resolve. All too often death is simply a matter of being in the wrong place at the wrong time. Thankfully I lucked out and the truck was in exactly the right place.

If gravel track was what I expected, I got more than I bargained for. No wonder there was confusion between my map and the actual road, little wonder the road surface had been so lovely and smooth. It was in fact newly constructed. After only twenty miles that day the tarmac came to an end, replaced by on-going construction, and I don't mean laying a new surface. Diggers and dozers, were hard at work, excavating into the hillside, widening the single lane gravel track. No evidence of the track remained, loose mud hiding sharp, jagged rocks wound round one mountain, then down the next into Coban. The first holdup saw me waiting alone, while a trench across the road was hastily filled in to allow me through. At three metres deep, and loosely filled with moist mud, the way through was tough. Being so heavily loaded was a double-edged sword, initially it made us sink deep into the mud, then helped get traction to pull us out. The next holdup was marginally better, two cars went through before me compacting the soil and all I had to do was stay in the deep, muddy ruts. Forty miles worth of construction took over three hours, the worst part having to follow a line of trucks and buses, at 10mph, through deep slushy mud. Overtaking was out the question, banks of claggy clay lined the route, and at any passing places oncoming trucks pushed forward trying to bully their way through. At least when another complete closure came I got the chance to potter down to the front of the queue, then I was first out the starting gate, and made much better time. It was sloppy, slippery muck, one minute trying to bog you down, the next spinning the wheels from under me. But once clear of the pack, it got more pleasant. Sure my boots were clogged with muck, my trousers were caked too but it would all wash off. Getting mucky somehow makes you feel you must have had fun. I was still relieved to hit solid road again.

Junctions without signposts need checking on the map, the times you don't bother, you go the wrong way, sod's law. They're not to be sniffed at though, a minor inconvenience can lead to unexpected delights. My negligence at Sanarate took me down a long curving hill with gorgeous sweeping bends, on a bridge riding high over a deep ravine. Still keeping a semi-sensible head on, I cruised through it, noting the beautiful condition of the tarmac. A motorbike shop sat close to the bottom, heads lifted at my approach, arms raised at my passing. My attention was on an ox cart, plodded along at a snail's pace. It took me half a mile before deciding to turn around and get a photo. The lads from the shop were a bit dismayed to see me again, pulling a U-turn right by the shop. We all had a laugh when they realised I'd come back for the oxen, not the bike store. As a consolatory gesture the bike was left for them to ogle at, while I devoted all my time to admiring the oxcart. Poor lads, the dumb beasts got more attention than they did, at least they got to look closer at the bike before I roared off down the road again. Not for long, only until a signpost for Guatemala City gave me pause for thought. That was not the way I was meant to be heading, embarrassing or what? Yet again I had to U-turn and do a ride-by past the lads in the shop. What could I do but shrug my shoulders as I flew past? The pot of gold at the end of this rainbow was the ride back up the hill. I knew the tarmac was flawless, there weren't any tricky turns or hidden entrances, a perfect time to let rip. Boy didn't I hammer up that baby, I plain forgot about mellow and went for a quick dose of adrenalin instead. Hard and fast, all the way up, laying it real low, gunning it round the bends, exhaust note roaring with delight. And once the thrill of the thrash took hold there was no stopping it, it dictated the rest of the day's riding.

Up into the cloud forest I went, the misty heights damp and cold. No more distant views over fertile valleys, trees and traffic filled my view. Cutting through the cloud forest, both the cloud and the forest obscured what lay beyond. Lines of traffic streamed backwards and forwards, en route between Puerto Barrios and the capital. Commercial vehicles made up the bulk of it, ponderously slow, belching black clouds of diesel fumes, as usual. It's not big, and it's not clever, but hell it can be fun having a good thrash. When I'm in the right mood, there's nothing I like better than to mix it up with other traffic. Slow moving traffic just makes it easier, so with no malice or frustration I had a great afternoon's fun. My clarity of mind was exceptional, my judgement unimpaired and my attitude unflappable. Textbook manoeuvres all the way, nothing dodgy, no suicide missions, just making due progress. And what progress I made, stopping only for rice and beans, while admiring a young woman, in see-through black blouse and white bra. The contrast between olive skin, black transparent top and white undergarment was amazing, I only hope I didn't ogle too blatantly. Out of all the traditional dress I saw, it won hands down, though I can't seem to remember what the skirt looked like. Esquipulas, the border town, was far enough for one day. I preferred to hit the border early in the morning, allowing plenty of time for the crossing. Not all borders are open twenty four hours, getting stuck overnight isn't desirable, and officials have you at their mercy if it's approaching the end of the day.

A much better bet was to hole up in the nearby town and chill out for the night. Like a lot of border towns, Esquipulas was mainly a transit point, it saw little in the way of investment and the streets showed it. People slept haphazardly on the pavements, openly, on the brightly lit sidewalks rather than in the filthy, darkened backstreets. And who can blame them? Rotting fruit and veg clogged the gutters, mangy dogs picking through the decaying crap, spraying liquid shit amongst what they ate. Walking the unlit, deserted streets may sound daft, but it was fine, no one and nothing molested me in the slightest. Whoever I met simply expressed curiosity as to what I was looking for, again the assumption was that I was lost. Reassured that I was fine, just out for a walk, they wished me well and continued on their way. Not once did anyone suggest it might be unsafe. Street stalls left at the roadside still contained a host of goods, no locks were in evidence, just covered with a tarp and lashed down. People are not that stupid, despite the trappings of widespread poverty the only conclusion was a non-existent crime rate. And for me, the nicest aspect to see, was a multitude of bikes, almost all Japanese Trails or Enduros, blatting up and down the roads. Boy racers took the limelight, exhausts crackling as they whipped past, front wheel aloft. It made me grin, even though my serious side cringed at the lawless lunacy. Multiple lanes of solid traffic fought for space along the main drag, whilst the same youths went to and fro, popping wheelies between the sets of traffic lights.

Chapter Twenty Eight

The Pan-Americano highway stretching from Alaska all the way to Tierra del Fuego, the southernmost tip of Argentina, is referred to as "The Gringo trail". In my view it was more like a chicken run, police and officials lining the route, rubbing their hands in glee, waiting for the next Gringo to come their way. Corruption is rife in Latin America, honesty is not a requirement for positions of authority, nor is it expected. For the first time I was due to run that gauntlet, not a prospect to look forward to, so much effort had been put into avoiding it. In truth, the actual Pan-Am ran through El Salvador from Guatemala City, I was taking the main route up north to the Bay Islands, another busy tourist route, but it shared the same border crossing with the Pan-Am. Being the only land crossing into Honduras I was stuffed, before a chance meeting with an old Black American guy. He ran Illegals through Central America into the States, and was a veritable font of wisdom on border crossings throughout Latin America. There was actually a smaller border post, fifty miles back the way I had come at Frontera Florido. They were more lax, it could be said less corrupt, though I preferred to think less greedy, they weren't as used to the rich pickings of the main highway. Even better, the crossing lead directly to Copan, another renowned site of the ancient Maya, one I'd planned to visit on my way through.

What a laugh! A large, prominent sign displayed in the customs and immigration office, warned of corruption. It gave the *official* import duty and provided the phone number to report corrupt officials. One slight problem, a piece of card had been tacked over the official figure. When it came time to hand over the money, there was an unexplained sum, in addition to the figure entered on the document. So I queried it, and the explanation was simple, 'That is for me!' What can you say? 'But of course señor.' You can only admire such honesty. It wiped me clean out of my limpars, for the second time on the trot border officials had taken all my newly changed currency. Was I missing something? Were they in cahoots with the moneychangers? It wouldn't surprise me. They seemed to know exactly how much they could extort from me. Perhaps next time I wouldn't change any money, maybe then I'd get through for nothing.

Dehydration and a banging headache proved too much to consider a tour of Copan, the prospect of securing my bike gear, or carrying it all around the site, didn't appeal in the slightest. After the cool Guatemalan highlands it was unbearably hot, so hanging around wasn't a good choice. The town's ATM was utilised to full effect, I rested for half an hour and poured a litre of water down my throat. Other than that, the town held nothing of interest for me, in many ways it reminded me of a smaller version of San Cristobel, but poorer. A deadly mix of steep hills and broken, uneven cobbles put me off riding around anymore than absolutely necessary. The most pleasurable aspect of the town was reaching flat tarmac, as I left. Too drained to maintain the peace of mind I'd enjoyed through Guatemala, it was enough to make as much of a dent in the mileage to La Ceiba as possible. Beyond striking distance for one day, my mind was set on getting as far as I could, then enjoying a touch of luxury, a plush hotel with lashings of hot water.

Initially the scenery remained much the same as in Guatemala. Mountain vistas filled with tree-covered mounds, small-scale agriculture dotted about the hillsides, with a gorgeous twisty road winding between the mounds and cultivated land. Women still dressed in traditional Mayan fashion, the men in old-fashioned western clothes, still the same breed of peasant farmers. Though not immediate, the land soon changed completely in character. As the road wound down the mountain towards San Jeronimo, the forested mounds grew more distant, the land flattened out drastically and larger scale agriculture took over. Areas of pasture opened up, beef stock spread amongst acres of prime grazing. Banana plantations covered vast areas, too large to be catering for domestic consumption. This was commercial production, purely cash crops. Once prone to the exploitation of United Fruit, now masked under a plethora of other dubious investors, all chasing the elusive Yankee dollar. Winding slowly northeast, towards the coast, my route carried me past miles of date palm plantations, growing so dense as to leave a barren floor in deep shadow below. An abundance of palm crops gave a distinct tropical flavour to the countryside, only then did I register how different the highlands had been. Whilst supporting tropical varieties of food, they'd been a minority, maize had always dominated the fields, though the overwhelming habitat had been moisture-laden forests. But in Honduras, trees were mainly seen as thin lines on the horizon. Everywhere it stank of gross commercialism, gone were the self-sustaining, traditional methods of the Maya, this was a land sold out to the demands of faraway, foreign consumers. Whole banana stems, engulfed in plastic bags, hung waiting in the trees. I somehow imagined it as ready-wrapped production, destined from a tender age for foreign lands. Signed, sealed, to be delivered.

Each country seemed to consist of its own particular problems in highway hazards. Taking time to adapt was always a wise precaution, you could never assume major highway meant good quality road. Badly repaired pot-holes had been a hassle in Mexico, landslides a headache in Guatemala, frequent, deep potholes proved the main obstacle in Honduras, combined with rows of shiny metal hemi-spheres, imbedded across the road as traffic calming measures. The potholes were never huge, just deep, but they were enough to lose a wheel into. Not the sort of things to clip the side of, if you couldn't avoid them, aim straight for it and power over. Even when bottoming out, the rear wheel could handle it, having the front wheel drop into one was a bit like hitting a curb at speed, not pleasant. As for the metal balls, well, they couldn't be hit at speed, not safely anyway. Generally I could just about squeeze my tyres between them, with a slight pinch. If not, it was best to concentrate on the front end, taking it squarely over the top of one, otherwise the front wheel would slip. Not that there was too much chance of it pitching me off, it's just disconcerting when the front wheel slips or slides from under you. Normal speed bumps are much better which were also common in the few towns I had to pass through. Previous experience had shown these could be treated as a chance to get past a few more vehicles, without the angst I'd displayed before though. I was eager to make good headway, not take stupid risks. A bit too eager at times, hitting one whilst opening the throttle wide can have unexpected results. I assume those around me saw the massive wheelie as intentional. They must have thought I was a complete loony, or dead cool.

A few people had warned me about San Pedro Sula, you can't avoid it, but don't stop or stay there. One in particular advised me to keep going whatever, even if someone walked out in front of me, knock them down and keep going. It didn't look quite that bad, but I didn't fancy getting stuck there overnight. The city centre looked nice, architecturally, but the heavy police presence gave an unwelcome edge to it. Some cities just aren't meant to be stayed in, and I don't need much for me to avoid them, San Pedro definitely fell into that category. Anyway, my focus was further afield. I didn't think I'd make La Ceiba in one day, but it wouldn't be for the lack of trying. By 4 pm an eye was being kept out for the promised luxury of a plush hotel. The intention was to be settled before dark, bike parked safely and me safely ensconced in the lap of luxury. I well overshot the mark, gone 5 p.m. and all the road houses cum hotels were way behind me, none had met the standards set for that night, the next possibility was Tela. With over twenty kilometres to go at dusk, I didn't hit town until well after dark. The maze of streets was virtually deserted, there seemed a severe lack of accommodation, and I couldn't be bothered to waste time looking too long. Finding my way to a shabby promenade, the choice wasn't promising but there was a choice. One place offered hot water, but nowhere to secure the bike. Another could provide neither, so for the time being the bike was just left, while I went to find myself a flee pit to sleep in. I'd promised myself a spot of luxury, none was forthcoming, so I made do with a minging hovel, though decided not to take the optional extra of hot and cold running whores.

Tela was meant to be a seaside resort. It had a beach, though the title of resort, I thought, was being rather generous. Thatched shelters on the beach hid the suspicious stares of loitering malcontents, hushed disapproval followed in my wake, from their darkened depths it proved impossible to determine who was there, or what they were up to. One thing was for certain, they weren't about to make their presence known to me. Walking round the immediate neighbourhood was like wandering through a ghost town, it wasn't even 8 p.m. but nothing stirred. A handful of gloomy bars and empty restaurants near the beach were the only option of sustenance, I guess it was better than nothing but only just. Hell, I didn't care. I was only an hour away from La Ceiba and the ferry to Utila. After food and rest I'd be gone, unlikely to darken the delights of the town again.

Indeed, La Ceiba being only one hundred kilometres away was remarkably quick to reach, the ferry proved more elusive. Every time I tried to get directions they sent me to the airport, however many times I stressed, 'El Puerto del mar.' Three times I asked, all three times I was directed to the same place. Falling for it the first two times, they were, without doubt getting it wrong. The map didn't help, the town being depicted as standing off the actual coast by a short margin, which was utter crap. Going in and out of town, up and down the *Malecon,* and far beyond, there was no sign anywhere of a port or ferry terminal. Systematically trying every access road to the sea from one end of town to the other, was all that came to mind. Until, on the second approach road, an Internet café sowed the seed of enlightenment. Primarily thoughts of possible English speakers within had drawn me to their doors, no such luck though. Finally, turning to leave, shoulders drooping in despondency, a spark of life entered my numb brain. Of course, the answer to life, the universe and everything, and no (for the sake of Douglas Adams' fans), not forty-two, I mean the Internet. Even better, a printer, to send me happily on my way, map in hand. Somehow, I'd imagined there to be some roadside indication of where to find it. Sure enough, clear as day, there it was at the first crossroads the other side of town, about a mile further than I'd first ridden on my arrival, over an hour before.

Some days everything falls neatly into place, others, it's all a constant battle. Personally, I believe it's generally down to your own mind-set. If you give way to the demons of despair, it'll all go tits up. Remain chirpy, open to the infinite possibilities of life and everything falls into place nicely. Arriving just in time for the ticket office to open, things seemed to be going my way. The usual ferry wasn't running though, so they couldn't take the bike. Never mind, as one door closes invariably another opens, why not ask the skipper of an inter-island trading vessel? They already had a Toyota Hilux loaded and there was plenty of room for the bike, only delaying to pay port tax the bike was loaded and I was told to jump on too. And so we set sail, leaving the ferry still empty at the dock. Good fortune continued for the rest of the day, one hurdle after another failed to deter me. Never giving up over minor obstacles, they were all quickly overcome. The plans for my festive season fell neatly into place within hours.

By the time the ferry arrived, not only had a room been sorted for the night, but also diving and Christmas accommodation too. Riding up a crowded jetty and parking in the only crossroads, on a minute island, grabs people's attention, if only out of curiosity they are very obliging. Though dubious of the first available option, I genned up with Gina at the Captain Morgan Dive Store, checking out the prices of diving and local guesthouses. Having noted the common dive sites, a comparison of prices was wanted, so I set off along the single-track lane, towards the end of Utila, past a score of dive shops and hotels. The main street is only wide enough to allow a couple of bikes to pass, little else, it's hardly more than a broadwalk, hence why golf buggies are all the rage for tourists and ex-pats. Gathering information as I rode the main drag took all of half an hour, at the end of which I took a room for one night and finalised my arrangements. Ten minutes round the coast was a smaller island, Jewel Cay, where Captain Morgan's had a small hotel from which I could go diving whatever days I fancied, $5 a night. Hmm, doesn't fortune just blow your way? The only trouble was the bike. It could neither be taken over, nor used on the Cay. A couple more words, with a couple more people, and the manager of another dive shop agreed to let me store my bike, under his house in a locked compound. Yes, it really was blowing my way. In a mere two hours it was all in hand, hotel, boat to the Cay, dives and bike storage. Sitting contentedly in a bar, smiling into a bottle of beer, I watched the ferry heave to and dock, releasing the latest wave of Bay Island backpackers.

Utila hadn't turned out to be how I imagined, sun soaked beaches of golden sand didn't cut isolated swathes into the shoreline, and it was hardly a quiet, forgotten backwater. The leeward side of the island hadn't an inch to spare, not only were buildings packed tight together, land reclamation had robbed that side of all but one small area of public beach. Crammed full of people throughout the day, the central strip consisted of dive shops, bars, cafes, tour agents, hotels and general stores. It couldn't be accused of being the party capital of the Caribbean but it was lively enough. All day ex-pats and tourists crowded the busy cafes and bars and once the day's diving was done the denizens of the deep invaded, late night bars disgorging revellers into the early hours. Its reputation claims it as one of the cheapest places for diving there is, so it pulls in the crowds, dive centres offer free accommodation with courses, with about eighteen dive schools there's a lot of competition, per capita they must have more dive centres than I've ever seen. No way could it be described as hectic though, in that way the island was typically Caribbean, laid back and unhurried. In no other way did it fit in with my visions for Christmas though, bars and revelry was the last thing on my agenda, so it had to be Jewel Cay which turned out to be my home for the following ten days.

Chapter Twenty Nine

Glory days indeed, in a small low-key hotel on a small low-lying Cay. Less than two hundred metres long and fifty wide, the tiny Cay lay within a natural boundary of coral. Of the gorgeous sandy seclusion, there was no sight. The crowded Cay extended into the surrounding water, many houses built on pilings, accessible only along wooden walkways, barely more than a gangplank. But it was a small price to pay with a two-tiered sundeck at the end of our jetty. I could live without sand invading my every crevice. Slipping off the decking, into warm Caribbean waters, a couple of fin kicks carried me out amongst the coral. Each morning the dive boat arrived at 7.30 a.m. loaded up and took the day's willing participants out for two dives, returning at 1.30 p.m. No staff stayed in the hotel, we had it all to ourselves, traipsing all of one hundred metres into the heart of the Cay for food. Total relaxation, the most strenuous part of any day was lifting my dive kit onto my back. Now, that was what I went to Utila for!

And so I wiled away the days, without a care in the world. Or so it seemed to the other guests which is what I wanted, to detach myself from the grief, be a normal guy for a while. Friends and family were cast aside, I remained incommunicado, unwilling to let them upset my fragile balance. It couldn't have been less like Christmas, breath-taking sunrise, blazing sunshine, iridescent sunset and bright full moon glimmering across the water, a magnificent astronomical display. Christmas itself was heralded in by chaotic kids running rampage, setting off strings of firecrackers, dashing into the shops to buy more, and lighting them immediately outside. With demonic glee they'd throw them in your path, cackling manically to see tourists doing a hot-shoe shuffle to avoid the explosion. Local adults stood their ground, hurling abuse and threats at the backs of the delinquents. Only two houses sported decorations, full-blown displays of snowmen and Santas, the bright lights welcome targets for the teeny terrorists. However, it failed to invoke a feeling of Christmas, it just looked out of place, a dichotomy of worlds, and visions of a tropical paradise won over.

All three bars/restaurants opened as usual, breakfast of eggs, tortilla and frijoles could be enjoyed from 7 a.m. every day of the year. Slowly, over a twelve hour period, we gathered provisions in readiness for our evening's entertainment. Succulent tuna steaks, potatoes, tortilla chips & dips, rum & coke and a crate of beer. Not what you'd call a Christmas dinner but it was our way of a non-celebratory yuletide, a barbeque on the sun deck. And as a little something extra, fire dancing in the moonlight. Having procured some paraffin to light the barbie, I did my utmost to set the dive shed on fire with my fire breathing, and Mary Jo spirited up some fire poi putting my attempts at twirling with fire to shame. Half-cut and stoned, we stretched out under a brilliant moonlit sky, contented and replete. Glittering in the moonlight, the gently lapping waves caught my attention. At first I thought I'd seen a fire worm of some sort, but no, even better, the phosphorescent algae was in bloom. Charged with newfound enthusiasm, I was straight in the water, surprised when no one followed me. For shame, they were unsure of snorkelling in the dark, even armed with dive torches (courtesy of the dive shed) they proved reluctant. Having wasted enough time I just got on with it, spending over an hour in the water amongst the most profuse display of phosphorescence experienced. In total darkness the effect was staggering, the slightest disturbance of the water gave vent to incandescent swirls, sparkling from my fingertips. Singing through my snorkel, dancing with my hands. Nature treated me to the most spectacular light show to round off my Christmas Day.

Don't get me wrong, it obviously wasn't a day of denial in the physical sense, nor was it emotionally. You can't run away from bereavement, you can't hide from it, but neither do you need to wallow in it. I had my moment, a lump in the throat, tears in the eyes, that constriction of the chest to stifle an involuntary cry. Thoughts of Cai were all too clear, but as I swallowed my sorrow a different feeling engulfed me, that is was alright to take pleasure in life, without feeling guilty about it. And at that moment things took on a whole new meaning, I had to live my life, for my own sake. Of course it mattered what he would have wanted, but above all else he'd have wanted me to make the most of my life. So, with a sense of release, I allowed myself the freedom to do just that.

Any thoughts of getting rusty through not diving for a couple of years were quickly dispelled on the first dive. My buoyancy was perfect, grace and control maintained throughout the dive. Floating weightless has a serene quality about it, being able to adjust your depth by tiny increments by no more than a slightly deeper or shallower intake or expulsion of breath. What a joy to hang upside down, let out a touch more air, and sink gently between heads of coral, searching in tiny crevices for the most elusive of the underworld critters. Without flailing or kicking, disturbing nothing, it's truly feeling in tune with the natural environment. Little wonder I find it irksome to watch floundering novices, kicking shit out the coral, stirring up silt and turning the water into a murky cloud. No surprise then, that eventually my desire to share my underwater world with a steady stream of novices wore off. Each wave of fresh recruits subjected to the same series of dives, those of relative safety. It started to get repetitive for me, dives organised with trainees in mind, always far removed from those more suited to my wealth of experience. However enjoyable they'd been, when it comes to repeating a dive for the third time, the enjoyment starts to wear a bit thin. On New Year's Eve, both dives being repeats, I decided my diving days with Captain Morgan's were done. But what a grand finale, a pod of dolphins as a parting gesture. Thankfully the skipper had his senses about him, stopping people from plunging straight into the water and scaring them off. I was already slipping in quietly and striking out on my own. Five or six in a loose group, just passing through, barely slowing as they swept past, sending whoops of delight through my snorkel, as one surfaced next to me and another sailed by within an arm's length. In over ten years of diving it was only my second close contact with wild dolphins. Watching from the deck of a boat is so different, gorgeous, but all I ever want to do is jump in, be in the actual water with them. So I was ecstatic, whether or not it was only a fleeting glimpse, it made my day.

It would be wrong of me to call our New Year a non-event, everyone had fun, and we all got on well. Another barbeque took place, more rum and cokes, another crate of beer, I battled against a keen wind to breathe fire, managing to singe my eyebrows, yet miraculously nothing else. Yet again we went out for a midnight snorkel, the phosphorescence wasn't as spectacular as it had been previously but still nice. Being the only one left from Christmas, none of it was a novelty the second time round, it all had a repetitive ring to it. Try as I might, the genuine enthusiasm wasn't there, instead I had to make do with an alcohol fuelled exuberance. Unlike Christmas, my mind was full of thoughts and memories of Cai, for us Christmas had always been a bit of a non-event, New Year was the time to party. We'd shared the previous two New Years giving fire shows for the revellers, back to back fire twirling, stars of the show, like two peas in a pod. I missed him more than ever, but poured the booze down my throat, until I could hardly stand, then I could tactfully retreat to the sanctity of my bed.

Waking the following morning, homesickness plagued me more than the hangover, it wasn't that I wished to be there, just missed the way it used to be, a way I could never recapture. Of the folks who'd shared their time and jubilant natures over the festivities, I was extremely grateful. But they weren't my trusted friends, my stalwart supporters, offloading my crap onto them wasn't going to achieve much, probably only put them on a downer. Some had eventually been taken into my confidence, and been told the full story of the trip, but not many. To suffer in private had been the wish, if suffer I must. The hope had been more to step out of the realms of pain, if only for a short period. And I guess I had, but it came back with a vengeance.

Relocating onto Utila did nothing to bolster my dwindling reserves, days were spent twiddling my thumbs, waiting impatiently for a parcel from the States. Wanting nothing more than to be on my way, I'd wander aimlessly, sit for hours at the Internet, withdrawing further into myself all the time. Reading the last words of a dying friend tore me apart, had me considering a trip home. What do you write to a dear friend with only days to live? But he made his peace with life, with my blessing, I could only think to ask him to give my love to Cai, in the vague hope there might be something after death, some chance of companionship to help him on his way. Sifting through mementos that I carried; Cai's driving license, his death certificate, newspaper clippings of before and after:

Dad and Son plan ride… of 30,000 miles. Pair to Traverse the Americas. (Daily Post, May 19 2007) *A lovely picture of us both astride my Honda XL600 LM, Cai leaning out from behind me, both with huge cheesy grins.*

SON LAY DYING IN MY ARMS (Daily Post, July 7 2007)
The same excellent photo, with a whole new meaning.

And out slipped the most heartrending of all, the poem read at Cai's funeral:

Do not stand at my grave and weep
I am not there. I do not sleep.
I am a thousand winds that blow.
I am the diamond glints on snow.
I am the sunlight on ripened grain.
I am the gentle autumn rain.
When you awaken in the morning's hush
I am the swift uplifting rush
Of quiet birds in circled flight.
I am the soft stars that shine at night.
Do not stand at my grave and cry;
I am not there. I did not die.

Mary Elizabeth Frye

Memories of the funeral flooded my mind, making my speech to hundreds of faces, the throng filling the crematorium, spreading up the grassy slope outside, a sea of tears, my confusion, disorientation. Seeing all those faces, their open displays of grief, the admiration and support, if only they were with me to ease my way through life. Being transported back to that moment was bound to bring on a fresh onslaught of tears, and the earth crumbled from beneath my feet, leaving me in free-fall. Wracking tears reduced me to a quivering wreck. There was no panic, no fighting it, and there was no fear, just pure, unadulterated grief. Not a brief outburst either, more like a long, sustained deluge. A flash flood would have been welcome, I could have wiped away the tears and got on with my day. Maybe I didn't really want it to stop. I certainly didn't try very hard to stem the flow. I don't think I had the strength. Hiding in my room wasn't the answer either, that was just prolonging the process, even after walking a while and getting a beer I was still wiping away the tears. So it was no shock when I ended getting completely blathered, an evening of propping up a bar and talking bullshit to an anonymous American, once more the bold adventurer on his mega road trip. I didn't feel that way but the story has a life of its own, mine is not always a willing role.

A deep, morose despondency overwhelmed me, heightened by a mega hangover. I just wanted out of there, drinking myself into a stupor would not stave off the frustration. Stroppy youths squaring up to me and bellowing, 'W'appen foool?' did little to enamour me. I was livid and gave him heaps of verbal abuse, walking away from him left me almost shaking with rage. The confrontation had reached a point where I had willed him to get physical, wanted an excuse to pound him. Being in a situation where I was ready to brawl in public wasn't where I wanted to be in life. It was too much, the final straw, I had to make a move.

Despite the emotional hole I'd dug myself into I was resolute about continuing. That's what I was doing for myself by my own efforts, relying on my own strength and endurance. Realising the strength of support at home removed the fear and strengthened my reluctance to return home. A bridge had been crossed, a significant one at that. Freed from the apprehension to deal with life in Wales, the impromptu impulses to be with friends dissipated too. They were there, getting on with life, but ready whenever I needed them. And so they would be in a few months' time, or a year's time. Though feeling capable of tackling a return home, I wasn't ready to finish the journey, I wasn't satiated yet. While I was alone, most vulnerable, my strength was in my mobility riding in my own little bubble of reality. Waiting around, being inactive, was a real test of moral fibre, eventually leading to huge emotional upheaval when the grief caught up with me. It wasn't that I could outrun the pain, it was always there, on the road it blended in with the wonders around me, blurring the edges. It didn't capture my full attention. It wasn't my only point of focus, outbreaks of emotional trauma felt more like intense spiritual release. Being out there, doing something was uplifting. It counteracted the bereavement whilst heightening the healing process. And I still had a long way to go. It was way past time for more therapy.

Parcel or not, the island had outlived its usefulness, so I paid my bill and buggered off. The ease with which I got the bike on another trading vessel was a good omen. Unfortunately I had to take the ferry myself but it actually saved me from unloading the bike, which stood on the dockside by the time I arrived. Heaving one huge sigh of relief, I rode out the dock gates, yearning for the open road but being patient enough to stay overnight in La Ceiba. Though reluctant to waste time, I'd check one last time for the delivery of my power lead for the laptop, it was meant to be delivered to the DHL office in town. There or not I was setting off the next day, come what may.

Chapter Thirty

Local knowledge be damned! A promising track led south from La Ceiba through one mountain range, before spilling out conveniently close to another dirt road, again heading south. The majority of Honduras' northeast quadrant is mountainous, almost devoid of properly maintained roads, relying on these alone means long, torturous, zigzag, routes across the country. Access into the hinterland relies on a series of ever worsening, sinuous trails. By wiggling down over rough mountain passes it was possible to avoid the highways without resorting to any serious off road riding. Cratered tracks with washboard corners and loose gravel were all that had to be contended with. I'd been told in no uncertain terms that the track from La Ceiba was not passable. Of the two bridges one was definitely down, it had been for a few years and the track had not been maintained in the meantime. Bugger; that put a spanner in the works although I was tempted to try anyway, the eighty-mile detour by highway was only twenty miles longer than the track. A disappointing visit to the DHL office had taken most of the morning, I hadn't got away until early afternoon so I ended up taking the highway. But away I was, leaving all my worries and frustrations behind.

A loop carried me southeast then southwest through Saba towards Olanchito, which I inadvertently entered before realising I'd missed the track. That was back at a gas station I'd passed, providing a convenient place to fill up before hitting the hills. Two armed policemen on a Yamaha XT250 pulled in alongside, gesturing towards my bike, filling me with dread. Admiring smiles accompanied their gestures, indicating we should swap bikes. Yeah right. Pretending to consider the exchange I burst into laughter, closely followed by them. As we bade each other a hearty farewell it seemed only reasonable to give them a show of the bike's power, yanking the throttle open I was away, blaring exhaust and a rooster tail of dust in my wake. Was that maybe a touch irresponsible? Naaa, I like to believe it was appreciated.

The route along the highway had been rich in banana and date palm plantations, small domestic enclosures tucked alongside. It was poor country living, many houses were only of mud and sticks, a basic stick framework covered in muddy clay, odd shaped thatched roofs denying them any sensible shape or form. They looked a complete hotchpotch, every one different, without rational design. Was it only where fate brought the ends of the branches in construction that determined their final shape? More fortunate residents had homes constructed from homemade mud bricks, maybe they were just the more thoughtful and hardworking. The same materials were used but the process was more long winded, it needed more planning. The uniform construction of mud bricks also makes it easier to use corrugated iron for the roof, though some still seemed to prefer thatch. At the top of the housing market were square, block built homes. Enjoying either tin or tiled roofs, I guess the deciding factor here was money, ceramic tiles cost more and probably don't last as long in stormy weather, but they do display wealth. To complete the picture, these shows of wealth were more often than not surrounded by a walled enclosure with heavy padlocked gates. Inside would stand large 4x4 vehicles, with heavily tinted windows, giving the whole scene a more sinister outlook. Such luxuries weren't afforded the poorer folk, there were no vehicles at all standing outside mud houses, just a scattering of animals, maybe a rickety old cart or bicycle.

Small numbers of cattle grazed rough land, most enclosures contained goats, pigs and chickens. If families had transport it was likely to be a horse, farming was mechanised, oxen were unnecessary relics of the past. Even owning a cart was a sign of slight privilege, in a world where a horse is a more practical commodity than a cheap Chinese motorcycle. A soft, undulating, brown mass caught my attention. Overhead, vultures circled, spiralling down to join the throng. In a shallow ditch they formed a mound, with wings outspread, trying to protect their share of the spoils. Beneath the flurry of activity lay a dead horse, no doubt road-kill. Such a loss for a local family would be huge, easily taking them to the bottom of the poverty heap again. It doesn't take a genius to work out how drastic their loss would be, and they couldn't spare time to lament the loss, having to double the effort to provide for themselves. Survival level existence, where losing the family horse is a greater loss than a family member, what a far cry from our western ways. How lucky I was to lose myself in a prolonged period of mourning, how fortunate for the luxury to grieve. It hurt to recognise my own decadence in dealing with death, made me feel a complete drama queen for making such an issue over losing Cai. Not that it took away or diminished my pain, no one else's misfortune could detract from my own, I am after all, a product of that soft, pampered western world.

By the time the dust from my rooster tail had settled, tarmac was a thing of the past. So was any sign of cash crops. Though rural along the main highway, as soon I turned into the hills agriculture was distinctly marginal and so was the road. Typical of any mountain road, it was twisty, it was also loose and rough. The better corners had been swept clean of gravel by passing traffic, leaving them with washboard corrugations. Straight sections tended to be sandy gravel, often overlying barely noticeable corrugations. Badly cratered areas and deeply scoured ruts proved more problematic, they could spring up at any time, easily catching me unawares. Their favourite position was just round a corner, where vehicles had slowed, then got bogged down when the track was wet. If entering a rut that was where you stayed until it climbed back onto level ground. The sides were steep and the bottom was muddy, any attempt at steering unsettled my balance, it was best to sit there and let it pick its own course. A wrong turn took me through a particularly nasty patch on a steep hill, even worse lay ahead, thankfully I realised my mistake and precariously turned around on the hill, let loads of pressure out the tyres and turned tail. Soggy ruts beside the track were good for high-speed trail riding, after a while spent acclimatising. Washboard bends were best taken above 40mph to iron out the vibration. Slight back wheel slides were ignored; none were bad enough to lose the rear end entirely, if it went I'd just have to lay the bike down anyway. I must admit to a reluctance to purposely throw my bike down the road, but it wasn't my intention to come off, I was well within my limits.

Taking the terrain as it came was the only way. It could have been a long, slow process to ride worrying about where the next hazardous surface would pop up. It meant standing on the pegs and taking off into craters, the rear suspension bottoming out as I landed. Sudden changes going into gravel laden corners weren't clever, so a clean route needed picking quickly on the approach. The bike took a battering, and also took everything in its stride, even for the trickiest parts it pulled me through with barely a wobble. I did need to pay attention. The track was too poor to ride without concentrating fully. Being aware of beautiful scenery isn't really appreciating it, sometimes the riding is more important and the surrounding environment takes second place, it's always a shame to travel with such a blinkered attitude though. The mountainous interior of Honduras was more extensive than imagined, it always seemed such a small country, but not so when viewed from up high.

To the north, mountains barred any view of the coastline. Nearby densely wooded valleys vanished into shadowy depths, only to rise again as steep arcing ridges, incapable of supporting vegetation, marching in rows up the far flanks. Inland the slopes were impenetrable forest, only the northern facing hillsides thinned out enough to support scanty upland grazing, no sign of habitation or agriculture marred the picture, though the presence of telegraph poles managed to detract from the moment. Any track or trail that leads to a village has its accompanying lines of communication, if a vehicle can get there, so can telecommunications lines. Westwards, distant views showed only more mountain peaks, gradually blurring into the dazzling sun. Close by, sloping tabletops showed straight lines demarking different vegetation, clear signs of agriculture. Access seems improbable, yet faint white blurs in the nook of forestry, belied the illusion of total human abandonment. Apart from those nearest two clusters of peaks, bright sunshine and stark mountains combined to form a bluish-grey version of monochrome seemingly stretching into infinity, providing a surreal picture of landscape melded into the heavens.

According to my map the track was marked as a main road, two vehicles wide, as opposed to a gravel track. Whilst it was, indeed, two vehicles wide, my route saw not one iota of tarmac. Gravelled sections were a delight to meet, things were looking good when I hit gravel. Being the second best grade of road, I could only feel grateful I hadn't chosen "Other Trails" another two grades below. A couple of wrong turns had shown all to clearly how quickly tracks deteriorated, it may well have been fun to continue unabated, tackling ever worsening trails for the sheer hell of it. But the blinkers were on, my mind was set on the journey itself, once again it was full speed ahead skipper. I didn't feel desperate to get anywhere but neither did I feel like wasting time getting there. La Union was far enough for the day, midway point between highways, an expected journey time of five hours. I managed it in under four and got there as it turned to dusk. Miraculously there was actually a hotel in town, it came in the guise of a filthy farmyard with an old cowshed clad in hardboard. A faded sign hanging aslant at the entrance, would have made for a better partitioning wall. At least there was a bed inside, and I had mosquito repellent which was just as well as I still got bitten to buggery.

Of the town itself there was little, a road in, a road out, and a few hundred houses spread out in a grid pattern from the deserted town square. One or two bars hid in darkened side streets, cafés were more elusive. Finally, a house most closely resembled a likely venue to procure food. A steady stream of visitors ordered soft drinks and candy, families settled down in rows to watch TV. It seemed more a community centre, looked more like someone's oversized front room. There was no menu and no point in speaking English but there was no need, only a fool can fail to order rice and beans in Latin America. A strange atmosphere, an eerie silence, hung over the town, hardly anyone walked the streets, only a handful of lamps lit obscure corners, mainly at junctures of side streets or alleyways. And there were none in the Square, the only sign of life was the abode where I ate. I remain unsure as to whether it was actually serving food no one else ate more than a packet of crisps. My presence ruffled no feathers in fact from the complete lack of attention I attracted I may just as well not have been there at all. So no '*conquistador*' complex for me, no worship as a foreign, white god, riding a mythical beast, just nothing. Anyone would have thought they played host to passing adventurers every day, maybe they did, as there was little choice of direct routes between the coasts, stuck in the middle of the mountains it was the only transport hub en-route. Considering how cut off La Union appeared to be, and how poor the general area was, there were a surprising number of cars and pickups in town.

It wasn't as cut off as it seemed though, the road south painted a very different picture. Every ten miles or so another roadside village would appear, between villages, trucks and pickups provided the basis of a supply line. Provisions were brought in from the south from Limones and La Union was the area's distribution point, it was as far as the trucks could get. Which of course meant the track improved, the surface evened out, turning it into a maintained road of gravel. Much of it was washboard but at the speed I travelled at, it was irrelevant. A trickle of slow moving vehicles was all I encountered, passing was easy, and though sinuous the road was more than wide enough for two trucks and me to pass at once. Pickups provided carriage for villagers, each one loaded to the gunwales with peasants and their wares, from or to market. I got their attention. You could tell I was in cowboy country, nowhere else can you find such enthusiasm over riding hard and fast. Cowboy hats adorned many heads, especially amongst the peasants. Most pickup drivers sported baseball caps, but without exception, anyone riding a horse wore a cowboy hat. Village life once again favoured horses, as transport and work animals. They didn't have the affluence of La Union, cars were a rarity. Correlating recent events from the total disinterest of my being in town, to the joyful displays at my presence elsewhere, I'd be inclined to say the trappings of wealth detract from a simple, joyful life.

Cheers of encouragement weren't uncommon as I flew past other traffic, guys leaning over the side of pickups waving me on, grins plastered across their faces. The camaraderie was great, being egged on so enthusiastically was all I needed, my speed steadily creeping higher, until reaching normal cruising speed for the tarmac highways. A speck of dust far ahead turned out to be a youth on an XT250, it felt like forever before the gap closed, then I was past and gone in the blink of an eye. He eventually caught me up at the junction with the highway, giving my bike a big thumb's up and shaking my hand out of respect. Had he witnessed the bike slewing out of control, had he marvelled at the masterful way I fought and won against the track's attempts to woo me into a close embrace? Deep down my ego hoped so, what a waste to let such a display go unobserved.

Touching 70mph could be seen as overcooking it slightly, it didn't feel so. Visibility was good, there were no hidden obstacles, the surface was even and reliable, traffic was rare. Easing off the throttle for corners was enough, a drastic loss of speed wasn't necessary, so I didn't even need to change down from top gear. On each bend the rear end would slide a touch in the loose sand and gravel, I got to expect it, played with it a bit, respectfully of course, I'm no Evel Knievel. The wide-open track encouraged confidence, massively increasing the margin of error. Perhaps the drop to the left was quite steep, but I rode on the right side of the road, it was wise to keep a safe distance from the drop off. When the rear wheel stepped out from beneath me, it hardly registered until it had gone too far, then I was doomed to come a cropper. Theoretically, I should have let it go. In reality laying your bike down at high speed isn't the natural reaction, not miles from anywhere, a lifetime away from help, so I yanked it upright. From then on I had a fight on my hands, it was all-in wrestling as I fought for control but I was glued to that bike, no way was it going to shake me off. Bucking and bouncing into the roadside brush it went, with me hanging on for dear life. Hauling it back on course was only the first step, I may have got it steering in the right direction, but it was still throwing me all over the place. Perchance, the roughness of the terrain slowed me considerably and before I could comprehend exactly what was going on, I sat astride the bike, stationary, on the verge. And as the bike tried coughing into a stall, I snicked in the clutch, *And he makes it, YAHOOOO!* The next thought, in complete disbelief I'd not come off, was something along the lines of, *Fuck me!* I suspected the eager locals would have loved the show, I could almost hear their applause.

Each village was a one-road affair, little more than a staging post for passing traffic. Houses crammed ever closer as they neared the hub of village life, the pickup point for transporting goods and people between La Union and Limones. Cultivated hillsides seemed to spread out from these villages, on closer inspection, scrubby, uneven slopes formed almost bare fields, useless for anything but patchy grazing. What appeared as large comfortable houses, reeking of comparative wealth, were in fact semi- agricultural buildings made of block without even a lick of paint. Animals were left to roam free, foraging for that which their owners couldn't provide. Cows and donkeys were generally emaciated, bags of bones standing forlorn in the middle of the road, without the will or energy to move for oncoming vehicles. Even the horses could have done with a solid meal or two, but they fared better than many animals, cowboy culture ran strong in them there parts, your horse is your first priority. Pigs coped better still, capable of eating virtually anything, they prospered, a sow suckling a litter of eight looked fit and healthy, while the chubby piglets promised many a hearty meal to come.

Eighty miles of gravel track were on the agenda, before reaching the Nicaraguan border, and I loved every minute of it. It was a shame it wasn't more, an equal distance of highway had to be covered. But wherever I rode, it was the riding that enlivened me, most other things paled into insignificance. Though appreciating the surrounding environment, I paid it little notice, soaking in the whole vibe rather than being distracted with particulars. The near spill may have briefly curbed my excessive enthusiasm but not for long, 40mph just didn't do it for me, I may as well have been on a pushbike. Thrills without the spills was what I was after, so the track got my full attention, and I kept to a more reasonable 60mph. What speed and where was pretty irrelevant really, there was no hurry to get anywhere. Excitement was all I wanted, it felt good to push it a bit, the adrenalin rush swept away the blues. At least that was the theory, something had to lift me up from the depths of self-pity. Sparked by feelings of vulnerability, my future loomed large in my thoughts, and it scared me. A future alone, nothing left to love and cherish, for once it wasn't about Cai, it was about me and my life. Hustling along those gravel tracks gave no time for distracting thoughts, it took away the luxury of emotional outbursts, only the here and now mattered. From the relative safety of the highway my concentration would slip, tears would blur my vision, and miles would pass in a salty haze. No stranger to such circumstances by then, I rode through it, self-pity didn't rest as well on the soul as grief, but the symptoms were the same. So was the treatment, life goes on, good, bad or indifferent, you have to get on with it. I was getting to a stage where I could carry on regardless. It was just another potential hazard of riding, comparable to riding in wet road conditions.

Another occupational hazard was being prone to being accosted by the local law-enforcement officers. As notorious as Latin America is, I hadn't fallen foul of any baksheesh hungry policemen at that point. It certainly wasn't expected while walking down the street. Stopping briefly for an ATM, my bike only fifty metres away, two hick coppers barred my path. '*Pasaporte,*' one demanded. Then they wanted my license, registration documents, import papers, insurance certificate. A hilarious scenario played out, whilst initially angry and awkward, their incompetence brought only mirth, with an underlining of contempt. Unable to read most of the documentation, they hadn't a clue what to do with it. Making a point of radioing in my details, the two bit-part actors feigned concern, a problem with my registration papers. Whatever they hoped to achieve, the dismay on his face, when the return message was that their system was not capable of checking the details, was a sight worth seeing. Their cover broken, the two bungling idiots tried maintaining an officious, but hurt, air, exercising their right to be awkward to save face.

'Where you come from?'

'Limones!'

'Before Limones?'

'La Union!'

'Where you start?'

'Los Angeles!'

'How you bring moto to Honduras?'

'I rode it!'

'By air or sea?'

'I rode it!'

'You ride Los Angeles, here?' (Disbelief starting to show)

'To Canada first, the Yukon.'

'Where you go now?'

'Las Manos, into Nicaragua.'

'You stop Nicaragua?'

'No!'

'Where do you go after?'

'Costa Rica, Panama, Sud America.'

'En la motocicleta?'

'Si, Señor.'

Slow as the fools were, eventually, the cogs dropped into place, visibly! Comprehension fell across their features like the dawning of a new day, diverging into a slight frown of disbelief, before finally assuming a vacant stare, as though incapable of imagining the enormity of what I claimed. It left them speechless, then eager to confirm they'd heard correct.

'You ride from Los Angeles, to Canada, back through USA, then Mexico, Guatemala and Honduras, to Talanga?'

'Si, Señor.'

'Solo?'

'Si, Señor.'

I can only assume it was actually beyond their ability to fully comprehend, certainly not the reason why, *'Por la adventura!'* I mean, what else could they do but express amazement and offer the best of luck? In the space of five minutes they'd gone from bolshie pigs, to incompetent fools, awestruck innocents, then the fondest of well wishers. Unimpressed with the idiots, I gleaned directions for the next gravel track and left them to their stupidity. I started to understand the need for corruption in the police force. They don't have the intelligence to obtain money by their wits. No wonder I preferred the solitude of mountain trails, official imbeciles were a rarity. Amused at their antics I may have been, I still rode away leaving a string of profanities in my wake.

Over one hundred miles of those tracks allowed me to cut through the heartland of Honduras. They weren't particularly memorable, yet offered a constant panorama of empty hills, wild and unblemished mountain vistas. For me only the track, the bike and myself existed. Yes, I was blinkered, but calm and unhurried. I enjoyed my days of riding, though could recall little of the scenery, I was too cosseted in my own little bubble of reality. To describe them as nondescript would be unfair, they provided the headspace I needed, gave me an escape from my own emotional upheaval. The trappings of civilised society tore me apart, left me an emotional wreck, but the open countryside refreshed me, took me beyond mere thought. Highways were where I did my thinking, where countless miles could be ridden on autopilot while I mulled over my thoughts, worked with my feelings. Or allowed them to explode, to ride roughshod through the fallout, gathering strength from the experience. Whether by gravel track or tarmac highway, Honduras passed me by largely unnoticed, interactions with individuals marked my passage, left their impression. I remember fondly an old cowboy astride his horse, a young steer draped across the saddle, my envy at his simple existence. Those simple folk enthused me, egged me on, especially when standing on the pegs and blasting past them, spewing gravel behind, anyone would have thought it was a rodeo show. All in all they were a cheery people, relaxed and ready to enjoy whatever life threw their way. I may have started to get a touch blasé with my surroundings, but the interactions with plain country folk stimulated my faith in humanity.

Highways are by nature more impersonal. Interactions are with vehicles, not their human occupants, rarely do we penetrate the outer shell, communicate with the living, breathing entities encapsulated within. The metal boxes were no more than road debris, objects to manoeuvre around, get past without undue delay. They're little more than pieces in a game, throw a six, move four vehicles ahead, overtake truck. And riding along main highways can be as mindless as that, constantly aware of unfolding circumstances, but carried over great distances on autopilot. Being lost in thought, doesn't mean not being poised ready to take action, the mind is a many faceted organism, capable of multi-tasking. I didn't have to think about my actions on the road, it happened subconsciously. Having bypassed the busy route through Tegucigalpa, no other urban sprawls barred my way to the border. The road was the main thoroughfare into Nicaragua, but it was hardly busy. A thin, broken line of trucks plied the route, keeping average road speed at a minimum, making it quick and easy to overtake. Unlike other countries, the few towns encountered en-route were centred off the highway, they didn't cause bottlenecks, so it was plain sailing all the way to the border.

I sometimes wonder if borders are designed with the specific intention of creating total chaos, I fail to see how such mayhem could occur purely by coincidence. How many offices can customs and immigration utilise? Which does what? How do you know when to go where? It takes time and patience to suss it out, stamina and determination to carry you through, and always money to smooth the way. Alternatively use a runner, or fixer. Supposedly, for only a small fee, you can sit back and relax while they do all the work. That's what I'd deduced before. It had never cost me a fortune, and should have saved a lot of effort, if only I'd been a bit more trusting. You can be too trusting though, just how many officials are there to bribe. Aside from immigration and customs there shouldn't be much else, but numerous offices needed attending to, for every single form it required yet another visit to another official. You could say service was coin operated, the more you fed the official the less the delay in processing your details. My impression was that runners oil the cogs of the machine as standard practice. They butt in front of everyone, thrusting your paperwork under the nose of the official, both parties understood the game, and they played it well. The runner knew the score, wouldn't present your papers until everything was present and correct, he wasted little time, time was money. Knowing what you need and where to get it is invaluable, without signs or information on display it's pure guesswork to find the correct place and person to accomplish each task. Copies of paperwork are demanded, fresh copies, not my nice colour copies I'd brought with me. A natural reluctance to relinquish my passport and ownership papers into the hands of a stranger had to be overcome. If I was to pay for a runner I should utilise him fully, not run round after him checking each and every stage of the proceedings. So I did just that, it proved an expensive experience. The runner alone skinned me for $15, another $20 went to obtain a stamp to allow my exit from Honduras, with the various bribes, taxes and import fees I was down in the region of $80. Ouch, that would have given me bed and breakfast for a week.

You would never have realised a border had been crossed. There was no a distinct change in farming methods or house construction. Huts, houses and hills remained pretty much the same. Rundown villages still looked dirty and dusty, undernourished cattle still looked emaciated, country life still looked marginal. Few signs of wealth were evident out in the sticks, life was slow and simple, and I left quite a ripple in my wake. Dropping south towards the Pacific Ocean, from the border crossing at Las Manos, was still far enough off the beaten track to make me an oddity. Requests for where I could buy a road map were met with astonishment, as if such things didn't exist, which apparently they don't. Finally, meeting a couple of American residents, they confirmed that you couldn't get a road map for love nor money, and certainly not in Nicaragua. The Honduran map continued as far as Esteli, it was pushing it but I decided to reach that far before the end of daylight. Procuring a map could wait, it would be difficult to get lost on the way, just keep to the main highway, there was only one turn off.

Though few in number, towns spread a mile or more along the roadside, busy thorough ways packed tight with a host of retail outlets. Supermarkets stood back a discrete distance from the actual roads. On the very verge of the busy highway, tyre dealers vied for passing trade. Huge sound systems formed pillars each side of the entrance to their sales pitch. Banging dance music assaulted the eardrums and scantily clad, disco-dancing divas shook their "thang". Now it was my turn to stare in disbelief, it was only one step up from lap-dancing clubs, and there were four of them within a space of two hundred metres. But they went completely unnoticed, by everyone but me anyway, no one showed any interest, not even the dancers themselves, who woodenly went through slovenly imitations of dancing, boredom transparent. Welcome to the western world, all the trappings of decadence, without the wealth, a cheap buy off. This was definitely a different world than my mellow meanderings through the countryside. Señoritas in skin-tight jeans stood, hand on hip, hip outthrust, waiting with barely concealed impatience for a bus. A queue of J. Lo wannabes forced to endure third world deprivations, if they couldn't live the part they sure as hell could try and dress the part. Youths in baggy pants and tops, heavy gold chains hanging from their necks, baseball caps askew, emanating whichever rap star was currently in vogue. Billboards for Coca-Cola and Pepsi competed for people's attention, burrito and taco signs flashed in neon display. Pickups and shiny 4x4s are most commonly emblazoned with American logos. Yellow decommissioned school buses from the States form the bulk of the public transport. It could have been the Latin Quarter in many an American city, with the exception of the pedal-powered taxis. Only those belied the impression of total Americanisation, otherwise they were merely a couple of decades behind the times.

Reluctant to succumb to the vagaries of cheap western commercialism, only the plentiful supply of roadside food stands held any interest for me. An absence of hotels went unnoticed until reaching Esteli, with dusk falling the hunt was on, but neither vague wanderings through backstreets nor countless questions spirited up a solution. Finally, after extending the search far out of town, an educational centre/camp offered the only form of accommodation to be found in the area. Animal pits and cages decried the term 'educational', but dimly lit classrooms and canteen gave credence to the facade. Of children there was no sign, if fact there was no sign of anyone, anywhere. Two members of staff were the only evidence of life, nothing seemed open and a meal was out the question. Away from the reception and canteen area not a single light illuminated the way, nowhere could any other buildings be discerned. Eventually a torch lit tour through the grounds revealed a row of shabby rooms, hidden in a darkened hollow, isolated and deserted. A matter of take your pick really, but they all had beds and running water, all smelt musty and long unused, though the bedding was clean and dry. Once ensconced in my jungle home, it was only nature and myself left to enjoy a peaceable night in each other's company. No lights shone, no sounds disturbed the rustling, except chirps and croaks of night-time creatures. My supper of biscuits and a can of coke sufficed, munching and belching into the gloomy silence failed to entice any natural nocturnal wonders into the open, leaving me to concentrate on my own misgivings.

Emotional insecurity dogged my progress, feeling vulnerable I missed the support network awaiting me in North Wales, yet was far from ready to rush into their welcoming arms. Adrift and alone, I felt ready to accept the company of treasured friends, relished a time when I could happily return and face the music. Not having reached a satisfactory cut-off point, my destiny still lay on the highways and byways of Central America. Gone was the fear of returning home, replaced with a deep longing for familiar settings, valued friendships, and the security of my family. Whilst craving the immediately unobtainable, a stubborn refusal to crack under pressure kept me going, considering only the next part of the journey. Trying not to project my desperation into the future I dealt with each passing moment separately, each attack of trepidation put into perspective as it occurred. Thoughts of the future still frightened me, enhanced the doubts of coping in the long run but whilst journeying I could put off those fears. Bereft of companionship, my world must suffice, an existence of denial and control. Release came only through riding, the perfect conditions for clearing the mind and feeling at peace. Outbursts of tears still took me by surprise, without troubling me unduly they came and went, cleansing as much as hurting. They allowed a measure of sanity to remain, carrying away the hopelessness, sustaining my determination. When it all got too much torrents would spill forth, washing away the despair. Life had started to feel better after spells of profound weeping. It couldn't be described as happiness, but I was most content when riding. With my bubble intact many miles could be negotiated with the minimum of fuss, unconcerned with the world outside, taking everything in my stride. A trial of endurance had begun, where I was, my destination, my surroundings all took a back seat. My only motivation was to keep moving.

What direction to head in became a slight problem, without a map or knowledge of Nicaragua I felt pretty stumped. San Juan del Sur loomed foremost in my mind, a surfer's hangout, reportedly with an exquisite beach and quiet deserted bays close by. After Utila the sandy realms of a coastal paradise were sorely missed, a few days lying in the sand and soaking up the sun wouldn't go amiss. How to get there was the immediate problem though. Fate, fortune or pure coincidence led me to the nature camp. They couldn't help me get hold of a map, couldn't even suggest where one could be found, they did allow me into one of the classrooms though. And hanging on the wall, in full glory, a map of the country, for all I knew the only one in existence. Life would have been simpler if I could have purloined the damn thing, a convoluted zigzag route bypassed the capital, Managua, carrying me around a series of cities before joining the main Pan-Americano from which I could drop down to the coast and claim my share of Pacific paradise. Mayasa, Grenada, Namicne and Rivas, a list of these names were my sole means of navigating. They weren't much, but certainly better than nothing.

The main arterial roads were few, they were also the only ones with a decent surface. The majority of the country could only be accessed via a series of lumpy dirt tracks. Villages and towns consisted of rutted, dusty streets, all efforts focussed on maintaining the highways, no thought given to the appalling conditions of other roads. For the most part my route kept to the tarmac, as I turned first one way then another, winding my way gradually southeast. Smooth tarmac made the going easy, wide sweeping bends gave clear views ahead, overtaking was a doddle. Road signs were clear and precise, traffic was minimal, and progress went unhindered.

At Grenada I was ready to call it a day, despite having hours of daylight left, until realising the following day was my birthday. Did I really want to allow it to pass as just another day? Of course not. That spurred me on, pushing for the coast a new determination overcame me which even dollar hungry policemen couldn't quell. Welcome to the Pan-Americano, I was running the gauntlet after months of avid avoidance. Accused of an "infraction" at a road junction, I was having none of it. 'Ah, infracción Gringo!' And they were having none of that, insisting it was a genuine infraction. Apparently I'd stationed myself too far to the left of my lane while waiting to turn left at a T-junction, causing an obstruction. Outraged at my claims of them setting a Gringo trap, I further suggested it was a clumsy attempt to lighten my wallet, they weren't about to admit defeat. Eventually I bored of their shenanigans, 'Ok, how much is the Gringo tax?' I sure had the knack for rubbing those guys up the wrong way, they marched me back to the junction going to great lengths to explain. With better Spanish I would have understood more of their words, their meaning was clear enough though. It was a genuine traffic violation, not a fictitious claim to extort money from me, or so they assured me. Dropping the Gringo part, I enquired once more how much it would cost me, and burst into laughter at the reply. Two Hundred? It didn't matter whether it was dollars or pesetas, it was ludicrous and I ridiculed them over their attempts to rob me. One stormed off to catch another unwary foreigner approaching the junction, whilst the other took all my documents to record the transgression. When he dropped them back on his table and declared the episode finished, he shocked me, no money had changed hands. In disbelief I asked, *'Todos finito, Señor?'* and was waved away, dismissed with an exasperated sigh. I thanked him graciously and got the hell out of there. As the first interaction with Latin America's version of highway robbers I felt rather pleased with myself.

Forsaking the relative pleasures of the super smooth highway, an abysmal track bore me away from the Pan-Am and towards the coast. It was the only access road to that part of the coast and more closely resembled a moto-cross track. Rough and badly broken through its entirety, trucks and buses slowly ground along, constantly switching between one side of the road and the other. As they edged over the lips of craters, chassis grating, gears grinding, they edged around the obstacles inexorably slowly. The vehicles themselves were the obstacles to me, I'd ridden worse at higher speeds so, barely bothering to slow I'd whip past the cumbersome monsters, spraying them with road debris. Giving the impression of being in the back of beyond, the neatly paved streets of San Juan del Sur brought me back to reality. A congested grid of hotels, surf shops, Internet cafes, restaurants and bars filled the town, spilling out onto a gorgeous crescent of golden sand. Secluded hideaway it was not, yielding neither the isolation nor solitude I sought. It definitely wasn't what I'd had described to me, there was no temptation to linger, or explore further, I wanted the quiet life. A kindly surf shop pointed me in the right direction, praising me for my choice and guaranteeing that I'd not be disappointed.

Hours of light remained, my birthday venue was only half an hour away, I thought it was plain sailing. Full of myself I went for the shortcut, across the beach, through a shallow river and up a slippery gravel slope. Being weeks since any cut-out problems with the bike, the last thing I expected was for it to cough and splutter to a standstill, right in the middle of the river, BITCH! But it started at the push of the button, carried me further into the river, then cut-out again. I was flummoxed, it wasn't as if a wave of water had engulfed the engine when I stormed through the water, but it was obviously a water specific problem, not one restricted to heavy rain. Any number of times I sat, stabbing my finger onto the start button, and any number of times it failed to start. I managed to push it part way up the gravelled slope, nigh on giving myself a hernia before collapsing in a heap. In a last desperate attempt, I turned off the fuel tap and emptied the system of fuel, my supposition being that I'd probably flooded the engine with the continuous attempts to start it. And as the sweet sound of my exhaust note broke forth, I didn't care about cut-out problems, the bike was running again, further investigation could wait.

Directions had been simple, culminating in a ride over a steep hill and taking the first track left, for the beach parking area. And what a hill it was, steep was an understatement, near vertical would have been more accurate. Stopping at the top I could only stare in disbelief, during the rainy season it must be a cascading torrent, scoured clean down to bedrock. The passage of traffic along the dirty, dusty trail had carried bucket loads of sand and gravel, filling the pockets and crevices amongst the rock, resulting in smooth, shiny protruding rock interlaced with loose aggregate. It was daunting, and took a few gulps of air before easing myself down its long slippery slope. Locking up the rear wheel wasn't the best start. I was being too cautious, needed to allow power to the rear end, not freewheel in trepidation. I tried again. Let the clutch out all the way, covered the rear brake, and kept the revs low. I made it all of three metres and over went the bike, any attempt to lift it only sent it crashing down again, the best I could manage was to hold it up enough to stop the fuel draining out. Then along came the friendly neighbourhood Norwegian who had to stop because I was blocking the way. He also had little choice but to help for the same reason, not that he minded, he was very good humoured about it, even holding the bike still while I climbed aboard again. Wasn't I glad to pull alongside a ramshackle beach café, everything intact except my pride? Even my dented pride dwindled into insignificance when I stepped onto the beach. Awestruck by the beauty, I knew it was a place I would appreciate, a place to lounge around and spend my birthday, a brief respite from the rigours of the road. In truth, I'd only spent a few days on the road since leaving Utila, but there was no turning my back on that sandy haven, it had me hooked the minute I set eyes on it.

As the day-trippers slowly drifted away, and the sun sank into the golden haze of dusk, a quiet tranquillity descended, leaving me alone on a totally deserted beach. There were no lights to dispel the illusion of isolation, only the moonlight illuminated my twilight world. Sparkling lines of luminescence rippled below the breaking surf, flashes of brilliance highlighting the waves. At my feet a white, foaming residue lapped gently, while its soft wash of sound lulled me into the realms of a contented peace. I'd regretted the lack of a good beach over my Christmas break, but I'd found one to make up for it. With my birthday to wake up to, I determined to appreciate the scenario while I could.

Chapter Thirty One

Forty-eight years old, adrift in Central America, lonely and lost, with no faith in the future, I'd had better birthdays! Raucous greetings of, 'HAPPY BIRTHDAY' rang out each time I approached the surf shack, they at least showed determination for it to be a happy event. It proved the ideal way to get to know the beach bums who masqueraded as surfers, everyone loves a birthday, loves to join in with a drink for the birthday boy. And so I slotted right in, without the stigma of being a non-surfer, I was the dude on the bike, peaking everyone's curiosity.

Half the day I sat and marvelled at the antics in the water, amazed at the majesty of mastering the waves. Ragged lines of boards cruised behind the break, waiting, endlessly, for their dream ride. Wave after wave was ignored, some proved too tempting for the keenest but only elicited a half-arsed response from the serious guys. They'd not waste their time until being certain of a good ride, always searching for perfection. For those in search of real adventure there was the left break, rearing high, it would roll in, crashing with ferocious force onto jagged rocks. Excitement surged through the ranks to see a bold challenger lining up for that break. Out would come the binoculars, people squinting through the lenses to identify the fearless contender. It was where the real adrenalin junkies hung out. Within two metres of the rock, with the surf smashing onto their tails, they'd race along the break, weaving up and down, attempting to gain more speed, more time. Hats off to 'em, they gained my respect.

Away from the crush of surfboards bearing down from behind, I forgot everything in a frenzy of body boarding, throwing myself into the crashing waves, whooping in childish delight. Beyond the day trippers, beyond surf-able realms, the beach was empty, an expanse of fine white sand leading down to a choppy but steady surf. Warm water and scorching sun was the ideal combination, I made the most of it, determined to appreciate the occasion. But birthdays are also times for reflection, not that I needed a special day for that. My only companion to witness the tears was a bottle of rum and coke mix which I took with me to seek solitude, or solace, they amounted to the same thing. Nothing specific brought on the deluge, the confusion of alcohol, memories, grief and fear was plenty to contend with, and it was too much to contain. So I blubbered into my booze, cried myself dry throughout the afternoon, only wobbling back towards the surf shack as the sun neared the horizon. Over evening beers the main talk was of surfing. The energy and excitement with which they spoke was invigorating, I had to have a taste of that and vowed to book a lesson the next day.

Surf's up! Minging hangover aside, I surprised myself by getting onto my feet and riding through the spraying foam a few times. It wasn't quite like riding the crest of a wave, more like teetering at the head of the spume. But it was on my feet and I managed to steer clear of a couple of people's heads, how cool was that? Cool enough to pack up my tent and take a shared room in the surf shack, a couple of extra days would cap it off. The idea was to gain enough proficiency to be able to pick it up again at a later stage, I liked surfing, thought it might provide another direction, a new obsession.

And so the days marched on. It only took another two before I rented a board for a week, payment in advance. Trying to make the most of my money the days were filled with surfing, between sessions I'd stuff my face with fairly crap food, refuelling, keeping up the energy reserves for the next session. Early mornings gave a chance to enjoy empty waters, only about a dozen people actually stayed on the beach, the chosen few. We got it all to ourselves until about 9 am, then it cleared again an hour before sunset. I could be up and out there before breakfast, shake off the hangover, and be back in time for the café to open. As the first pickups and minibuses arrived the bland, tasteless stodge they called food was being shovelled down my gullet. As long as it was washed down with a cup of nice, strong coffee it went down almost unnoticed. Of the coffee, I'd brought my own from a local supplier, one of the perks of having a camping stove and cafetiere.

When the surf was really up, the hordes were out in force. At first it was a pleasure to play in the small stuff, away from the frantic scrabble, the fight for each wave. But there's only so much of pansying around I was prepared to do, once capable of getting on my feet and gaining basic control it was time to go and mix it with the big boys. It was a daunting prospect, and that surf looked real heavy from where I stood. In it came, line after solid, rolling line, crashing down in an impenetrable wall, time and time again. And there was only one way out to the relative calm beyond the pounding surf, straight through. With board in hand, thrust into the roiling wall, punch your way through, before it breaks upon you shattering any false sense of composure. By the time I'd come up, spluttering and mounted the board, the next wave would be bearing down on me. Gaining ground was desperate at times, robbing me of all my energy before I even got out to the decent breaks. What a relief to be able to lay there and catch my breath, suss out where's good, where's crowded and best avoided. I hear surfers are very protective of their space in the water. Easing nearer the break line, I rode the swell on a couple of incoming, judging the point at which I'd launch myself into action should I go for them. The line thinned as a few rode what was available, other eyes were still out to sea, waiting patiently. Grumblings could be heard from various directions, heads were raised, a ripple of expectancy spread down the line, a growing swell gathered force, its shoulders lifted clear, leaned forward. This one looked promising! People started turning their boards, lining themselves up, watching over their shoulders. Heart's pounding, we waited. The wave loomed behind and everyone started paddling frantically. I was aware of no one else, only the rushing wall of water and my desperate attempt to get caught in its maw. As the board was lifted into its churning embrace, I sprang valiantly to my feet, just as the tip of the board was sucked into the swirling vortex. Limbs, body and board flying every which way, I was driven into the very jaws of death, tumbling wildly out of control, not knowing up from down, when it was going to stop. But it did, eventually. Kicking towards the light, I surfaced, covering my head as I did so, and pulled in my board. Wearily, turning seaward, a barrage of breaking surf barred my way, daring me to try again. But I did, back out through the pounding surf, time and again, for days.

Each morning I woke aching from the battering of the previous day, yet still I was up for the challenge. Those few times, when it all came together and you copped for a decent ride, it was pure ecstasy. Getting on the board at the right time was hard enough, keeping it together once there was even harder, most of the time I was instantly plunged into the inky darkness of the roaring tube of water. Now and again I'd get my feet planted, only to tumble and become engulfed into the roiling foam. On rare occasions, it did come together, seeing me upright with my brain in gear, adjusting my weight to maintain balance, almost long enough to start steering. And those, oh so few, magical moments, getting to ride the board all the way in. Only upright, under power can you get a feel for the board, distribute your weight correctly and start playing. If it had only happened the once it would have been worth it, I was luckier than that and got a good feel for surfing, I still hadn't got far enough with it to be hooked. The constant pounding I took was too tiring, being battered beyond belief daily began to have an adverse effect.

After five very long days I was exhausted but kept throwing myself into the maelstrom, caught unawares I held on as my board got ripped from my grasp while battling the oncoming waves. The tendons in my shoulder shouting in protest, I just scrabbled back onto the board and threw myself into the next tempest with considerably less conviction. I'd not viewed surfing as a sport for sustaining muscle injuries, had only considered the perils of drowning and being slammed into rocks and reefs. Nearly knocking a local lad off his board shook me, made me feel a liability. He was up and running by the time I got to my feet, driving fast along the bore, stumbling to my feet I barely saw him as I tried to launch myself into the void. I damn near took his head off. Taking a metaphorical step back I adopted a more cautious approach, restricting myself to only two sessions a day. Early mornings and late evenings felt more relaxed, gave me more time to concentrate on the water rather than other surfers. I'd succumbed to a frenzy of surfing, got off on the excitement, and embroiled myself in a whole new world. I'd welcomed the hard physical exertion, it had cleared the mind, offered a release. Nursing an iffy shoulder snapped me out of my reverie, it broke my rhythm, made me reassess what I was doing; gain a broader perspective on my life again.

For ten days surfing filled the void, occupied it entirely, leaving little thought for much else. The bike stood forlorn, virtually ignored, providing little more than safe storage for my valuables. I lived, breathed, walked and talked surfing, absorbed it by osmosis from my environment, it simply oozed surfing. In fact it got very close to drawing me in, our small community was cosy, friendly, devoted to the sport and all serious contenders. The camp followers tipped the balance, the hangers-on, malcontents, spreading ill will and distrust into whichever nest they fouled with their presence. By association we copped for their flack, they weren't even staying at the surf shack. They used a low-key hotel complex, the only other possibility for food and accommodation, hidden from our view and fifteen minutes walk away at the far end of a darkened beach. A standoff between machete wielding tourist and gun-toting local stirred up a hornet's nest of international discontent. We were all caught up in the backlash. Helpful, polite restaurant staff turned belligerent overnight, their establishments out of bounds to associates of their antagonists. It made for an uncomfortable trip down the beach, treated with suspicion, as intruders, as unwelcome trespassers into the twilight zone of tourism. Our alternative to the shoddy attempts at food served at the surf café, snatched from our grasp, and the guy had the audacity to come and bitch to us about being shot at. It doesn't matter where you go, there are always undesirables, you have no control over where or when you encounter them, but encounter them you will.

I moved off the beach, into the local town of San Juan del Sur. Without the distraction of surfing the thoughts closed in again, probing, questioning, doubting. Freeing up more time saw me writing again, catching up on the blog in the local internet cafes, which in turn brought the journey to the forefront of my thoughts. Despite feeling cut off and alone it wasn't over yet, to finish still wouldn't feel right, I'd reached no conclusion, hadn't done enough to satisfy myself. Craving the company of friends and family was reassuring, again no fear tainted thoughts of returning home. I knew it would eventually prove a traumatic event, knew someday I must face those demons, but that was yet to come, my path lay before me, and it led towards South America. The drive to continue was for myself, so I could feel content, proud even, of my efforts to ride the Americas. It mattered that I could hold my head up high, feel I'd achieved something, which I was no longer doing on Massella beach. At the end of the day I had to live with myself, I had to be my own Judge, jury and executioner. Finding evidence of a yacht, sailing between Panama and Colombia, proved too strong a case to ignore, the verdict was a foregone conclusion, and I was destined to continue. The blinkers were going back on, thoughts of friends thrust aside; everything else could wait, there were no longer reasons to delay further.

A blast through the Desert - Baja Peninsula, Mexico

Typical stunning sunset - La Paz, Baja Peninsula, Mexico

A quick breather on 'The road of a thousand turns' - Mazatlan to Durango, Mexico

Highland pass - Nr Huehuetenango, Guatamala

*Cowboys, both modern and traditional - Nr La Union,
Central Honduras*

A peaceful end to a day's surfing - San Juan del Sur, Nicaragua

Indigenous inhabitant, typically non-plussed with the world -
Panama City

Chapter Thirty Two

In a final show of contempt that bloody hill spat me off again, taking the rear end out in a power slide and spewing me onto the gravel. Perhaps a full frontal assault wasn't the most expedient method of approach. It was a damned good try though. Three times I'd ridden up, twice it had spat me off, never again though. Handy help had me up and running immediately, from a couple of guys busily trying to improve the track. They did a fine job of holding the bike, both upright and from sliding backwards, as I clambered on. Being much too steep my brakes wouldn't hold me, I relied on those guys. I couldn't hold it on my own. My only other choice would have been to drag it, on its side, back to the bottom and start the whole process again. You just can't lift and hold a heavily laden bike on a steep hill, not on loose, lumpy terrain. What a start, not the most fortuitous, depending on which way you look at it. Get the falling off bit over with and you can relax into the ride better, it's out of the way then, isn't it?

At 8 a.m., an abysmally battered, torn up and cratered building site type road can be quite fun, being almost deserted. Not quite a rip-roaring ride, a mellow mood prevailed. It was nice to be on the move again. Hopefully with a place reserved on the Yacht 'Stalleratte', I'd be sailing to Cartegene from Panama on February 15, giving me more than two weeks for a mere four day journey. I had all the time in the world. With only a short way before hitting the Pan-Americano, there was certainly no rush. I'd run out of alternatives, it was the only through route to Panama. The PA would carry me diagonally, northwest to southeast through the length and breadth of Costa Rica. I savoured those moments bouncing and sliding through a perpetual bombsite, I was at peace, content. Mentally and physically prepared to continue, I had no doubts as to my ability to do so, I knew I could tackle the travelling, however long it took, however extreme it became. I knew I could stave off the loneliness, if by no other means, than by the act of riding itself. I felt committed and strong, full of myself. As I rode along sitting tall and proud, I came to realise that I believed in myself. After so many months and so many miles, it actually came to pass, I had taken stock of my achievements and, at long last, believed in myself. And while a little longer to appreciate the momentous occasion may have been nice, there was a border looming along the road. Once more into the breach my friends.

For the first time a photocopy of the Title of Ownership for the bike was not acceptable, or so I was told. Surely there are ways around such problems, it was Latin America after all. Sure enough, there was, a straightforward bribe. $100 gets you over the border, after that you take your chances. Welcome to the Pan-Americano, if that was the best a runner could do I'd have to take responsibility for my own problems. In my best halting Spanish, I explained to the official where the original was and why I didn't carry it with me, a simple matter of security. Understanding my predicament, he apologised, and directed me elsewhere. It took four hours and numerous visits to numerous offices before I could present satisfactory paperwork. Riding freely around the Costa Rican town, I'd been directed to one office after another, waiting patiently at each until a Public Notary finally stamped my photocopy, validating it as a satisfactory replacement for the original. Why, I even saved myself a grand total of $50, and felt quite proud as I tucked my last $50 bill safely back into my wallet. But whatever way you looked at it, I'd been screwed over yet again. It may be part and parcel of flitting between one country and another, in that part of the world at least but it still doesn't come easy, I still detest the hypocrisy of bent officials.

Being pulled for speeding wasn't clever, not under the circumstances. A radar trap stationed on the way out of a small town, the most obvious place for them to be. Worst of all, I knew I was about 20mph over the limit. How I hate those radar guns. What can you say but fair cop? And they obviously thought so too, with oily grins smeared across their faces, partially hidden by 'tashes drooping over their top lips, they bade me a good day and asked for my license. Oh fool of fools, I deftly whipped out my wallet and produced my nice new Photo ID license. As I handed it over the sudden thought flashed through my mind, *Hang on, why am I giving him my proper license?* I possessed an old paper copy of my license, a sacrificial license to dispose of in just such circumstances, my means to deny them a bargaining tool. Now, unable to deny the offence and with my license held to ransom, it was a matter of damage limitation, time to eat humble pie, no point taking the piss here. They offered a simple solution immediately, pay $80 on the spot, without a ticket, or my license goes to the local court, where I can pay my fine of $120 the following day. My Spanish was being pushed to the limits that day, I had to explain I couldn't pay them $80, I just didn't have the cash, otherwise I would gladly do as they suggested. That didn't wash at all, my only choices were to hang around for court the next day or cough up $80. Then it was my turn to plaster an oily smile on my grimy face, as I slid out my last $50 bill, rolling my hands to show there was no more, '*Señores, por favor?*' And like the true gentleman they were, they graciously accepted my meagre offer. With oily smile intact, I thanked them profusely, and rode away, slowly!

Great care was taken through Costa Rica. I kept an eye on my speed, ensuring it was reduced substantially through built up areas. Sure enough the police presence at the roadside was prolific, radar traps within town boundaries were commonplace. They proved effective, vehicles queued to take their turn in being processed; speeding must be the national pastime, a very lucrative business for the police indeed. As luck would have it, I ran afoul of no more, the majority being set on the opposite side of the road. National speed limits were only 50mph on single carriageway roads, at the approaches to schools a mere 15mph. Looking at the queues, there must be a large number of residents who, like me, feel these speeds are a touch conservative. However, the law enforcement officers were having a field day. A couple of cars stood parked, an officer zapping one vehicle after another and pulling them over, another three or four officers processing the culprits, I wondered what ratio of bribes to fines they maintained. Of all the Latin American countries, I'd been led to believe Costa Rica was the most hospitable, few problems were likely to occur, corruption was minimal. To all intents and purposes though, the country only had one major highway, it was a doddle to patrol, and it was, "The Gringo Trail".

Slow moving trucks ground painfully up long, steep, winding hills, queues of traffic formed impatiently behind, engulfed by belching black clouds of exhaust fumes. Major road or not, the Carretera Inter-Americana (as they called the Pan-Am) failed to materialise into more than a single carriageway road, only through towns were multi-lane sections found. Which was a blessing, it didn't plough straight through the countryside but wound up and down the hillsides offering many a good view, and gathering huge tailbacks as it went. No matter how many queues I passed there was always another just round the next bend. But I was the fortunate one, the only one to ease past almost unhindered. Fully utilising the bike's power and dexterity, I needn't wait in line, I got to play with the traffic. Cautiously, as my wallet held no more examples of the cherished Yankee dollar, and the cost of corruption was at premium rates there.

Nicaragua had displayed the first signs of widespread westernisation, south of the US border. Raised kerbstones demarked the roadside in its towns, sidewalks provided a measure of safety for pedestrians. Cheap, tacky commercialism, reeking of the western world, lined the crowded streets. A growing show of affluence gradually spread from the urban conurbations into rural areas. Alongside dilapidated mud huts and wooden shacks stood well maintained, block built housing. Fancy 4x4s graced the driveways within gated enclosures. So recently wracked by civil war, it was obvious which nation had come to their rescue at the cease of hostilities. Maybe a more accurate term would be Americanisation, rather than westernisation. I can't recall many European cities with the same extent of glitzy tat despoiling the cityscape. Whilst trying to emulate American culture, Nicaragua fell well short, suffering a lack of wealth and investment to rebuild itself into a modern, mercantile nation. The decorative veneer was no more than icing without the cake. Costa Rica has no such shortcomings.

Ramshackle hovels, falling into disrepair became the exception rather than the norm, most rural homes were modern and well-constructed. Throughout the countryside, housing was generally of good quality, some homes could have done with a lick of paint but appeared structurally sound. Subsistence living took a back seat, as did the production of food. Rose gardens ringed well-maintained premises. Detached houses sitting prettily inside three-metre high protective barriers of spiked iron railings or concrete blocks.

Wrought iron scrollwork, a popular form of decoration, barred open access to both the windows and doors. Subdued pastel shades softened the harsh outward appearance of these mini-fortresses. Yet the blackened windows of the family people carrier smacked more of death-squad kidnap vehicles than family saloons. Latino versions of middle-class suburbia, such properties were strung along the highway between towns, within commuting distance. Everything is more modern once you hit the cities. Malls and shopping centres, bland concrete monstrosities occupied the centre of San Jose. Much of it is unimaginative, featureless and seemed to serve no practical use, there was more concrete than commercialism. But that was only the view from the throughway, from there it looked so ugly it could have been a prison but not all of it. At junctions to the highway, glittering facades of darkened glass hid the plush interiors of glitzy hotels, uniformed doormen and bellboys waiting eagerly to step forward and welcome new arrivals. Tasteless neon towers, in gaudy colours and clownish design, tempted punters to the Roulette and Blackjack tables. Light flooded the night from fast food joints and convenience stores but these are only pockets of light, close to the highway. Within two blocks the buildings crumbled, the façade of wealth vanished squalor and decay hid just around the corner. The riches only spread so far, there is never enough for everyone, and those who have it are reluctant to share it with the have nots.

If I'd been travelling on a budget, the hundreds of dollars for a swanky hotel would have been beyond my means. I wasn't, but I still wouldn't contemplate their exorbitant prices. Arriving any later would have forced my hand, darkness was descending as I entered the metropolis, and after a long day I hadn't the inclination to start a prolonged hunt for a room. By sheer coincidence I backtracked along a side street, having reached the far side of town, and chanced upon a 'Pensión'. A cheap alternative to hotels they may be but only when compared to the hotels locally. At $25 a night, they more than doubled the usual cost of accommodation. Prices were sky high, this was Costa Rica, playground of affluent Americans, home of many ex-pats. Comparative wealth was high for Central America, tourism was well catered for too, if you could afford their prices. After a $25 meal in a rather relaxing Italian restaurant, I was satiated, not by the minuscule portions they served, but by Costa Rica itself. It stank of America, the attempts of glitz and glamour, tasteless attempts to entrap the unwary, big bold signs assaulting the eyeballs. Crass commercialism, imported straight from the States, built with American money, for American people. Even the ethnic mix reflected the extent of outside intrusion. Of any indigenous peoples, there was no sign, neither by dress nor genetics, a bygone culture lost forever. If there had ever been a slave trade it didn't show, Black Costa Ricans were thin on the ground. White blood, North European or American showed clearly throughout the country, prevalent amongst the Latino masses. And it wasn't only denoted by skin colour, western features were common amongst the old and the young. How much was integration, how much immigration? How long had our westernised culture been nurtured there? It was definitely the prevailing one, and it didn't suddenly appear overnight.

Endless beaches line the Pacific coast, all reported to be gorgeous, the surf a delight. Amenities are plentiful, awash with tourist resorts and hotels there's plenty of choice with accommodation. Inland, National Parks and Protected Zones abound, any place of geographical or natural significance has been denoted as such and protected, it is renowned for its eco-tourism. Rain forests, wetlands, volcanoes, rivers and lakes, just some of the variety of habitats set aside for preservation. Biological reserves are liberally strewn along the coast and throughout the hinterland, protecting anything and everything of even the slightest interest. Seen as a conservationist's dream, it's a destination of international repute, a place with easy opportunities to truly appreciate nature. A country in which to lose yourself in a wealth of natural glories, if you have the material wealth to afford it. The statistics should have impressed me, the opportunities should have tempted me, but all that came into focus was the overpriced commercialism. Their conservation efforts may have been commendable but it wasn't exactly priced to be accessible, I doubt if a high proportion of their nationals could afford what was on offer.

Huge areas of the country were accessible only by seasonal tracks, the timing was right but I wasn't inclined to loiter. My mission lay in Panama, boarding a yacht called Stahlratte. With marginal tread left on the rear tyre a spot of shopping was needed before departing for Colombia. If there was time to dither, I'd do so later within the confines of Panama's borders, where living was considerably cheaper. As you can tell, I wasn't enamoured with Costa Rica, I wasn't in a rush but neither was I inclined to linger.

Already being about mid-way through the country, I should clear the border the following day.

Clear of the city environment, the highway resumed its winding path ever upwards. Steep and bendy was fine by me, it caused plenty of tailbacks though, lines of trucks crawled along without respite from the constant gradient. Too twisty to overtake, patience was called for, unless you were on a bike, then you could hustle past. And I did bully my way through when needed, maintained an ominous presence close to their rear wings, in overtake position, encouraging them to pull in slightly to allow me past. Sitting out wide, so the drivers could see me in their mirrors, I'd flash my headlight, then indicate and fly past at the slightest opportunity. OK, I also overtook on bends, against oncoming traffic, over double centre lines and through towns. My temperament remained placid though, my mind clear. I was on the ball and making due progress, not once doubting my judgement calls.

What a miserable day it turned into though, the sun had barely raised its head above the tree line when the road tightened and snaked up, steeply, into the murk of the cloud forest. The forest closed in, we rose into the misty depths of cloud cover and the world became a surreal existence of woods and water. An eerie silence pressed inwards, only the outermost trees were visible, the rest hidden by dense fog. Any trace of sky was obliterated, and the road opened a mere twenty metres ahead, closing immediately behind me. Visibility was awful. Truck rooftops scrape the very roof of our world, the cloud was all around, heavy, moisture-laden cloud. It got in everywhere, gathered, ran off me in rivulets. From the gloom above hung Bromeliads, floating tendrils, dangling before me, sinister, menacing. An eerie silence enveloped everything, even deadening my raucous exhaust. Wisps of mist rose from the tarmac, swirling around my tyres, making it hard to discern the multi-coloured blotches of spilled diesel. This called for a more cautious approach to riding, or should I say an even more cautious approach. Hit a patch of diesel at the wrong angle and it's like trying to ride on ice, it'll take your wheels from under you before you have a chance to react. Pushing carefully past the laboriously slow traffic was the only way to do it. Costa Rica probably has the best medical care in Central America, but I didn't want to put it to the test. Conditions took a turn for the worse with the onset of a steady drizzle, further reducing visibility. It made for a long hard slog up and over those hills. Where I was or what lay ahead was unbeknownst to me, all I knew was that the front end pointed up. When the road finally pointed downwards there were no awesome panoramas to behold from mountains high, just another tunnel of mist, still wet, still spooky. I preferred pointing upwards!

Abruptly emerging from the cloud, a clear blue sky lit up my day and the valleys below sprang into view. Succulent leaf stems sprang from below the road, fighting with banana plants for space. An impenetrable canopy cascaded down the hillside, revealing my first panoramic view in the country. Plunging from the roadside, the steep forested slopes quickly evened out. Thick forest prevailed, yet parcels of cleared land supported small-scale agriculture. Tiny tracks threaded their way between the trees, veering round rocky escarpments to the remote communities above. Behind, the hills faded into a hazy mist, the blanket of cloud lay thick just above my head whilst before me brilliant sunshine paved the way.

Dry roads and warm sunshine beckoned, a chance to dry out and make the most of the well-maintained *Carretera*. Traffic eased up as conditions made it easier for vehicles to filter past the trucks. Strange, I hadn't seen a single policeman when it was wet and horrible, once it was dry they were positioned at almost every town. Miraculously, they all seemed determined to hassle traffic from the opposite direction, not a single speed trap was set up on my side of the road. And I didn't even take advantage of the fact, being only half a day from the border meant there was no rush. There's no point hitting the border at the end of the day, when the offices are due to close bribes get expensive, and I didn't fancy spending a night at the border. The day could be enjoyed. The border was tomorrow's problem. I could just sit back and relax. Hustling around the bends was delightful, gorgeous tarmac, even cambered in the right direction. It wound steadily down towards the coast, seeming to change from a rainforest environment to being more tropical at lower altitude. Broad expansive vistas of valleys and far mountaintops gave way to wide, sweeping rivers, lined by craggy outcrops of rock and darkened woods. Date palms and coconut palms appeared. The roadside seemed more sand than soil, the sun was out, the sky was blue, I thought I was heading for balmy weather as I swung closer to the coast.

Sweeping out of the hills behind, the deluge engulfed me, it came down in buckets. Before managing to get my waterproofs on

I was soaked, the heat made it like sitting in a steam bath. True to form, the bloody bike spluttered and died. As an instant reaction I switched to reserve, weird, it coughed back into life again, I was nowhere near reserve. So back onto main tank it went, without the slightest protest. Mere miles down the road the same happened, with the same result, and again I sailed through the tempest, slightly bewildered but heartened by not coming to a grinding halt. But if the rain gods want their wicked way with you, their wicked way they shall have. Third time lucky for them! Bleurghhh, the bike lost power yet again, I switched to reserve and gave it a handful of throttle, bleurghhhh, back to main, bleurghhhh, and stop. Waggle the bike, fuel sloshes noticeably from within, stab the button, no joy. Same problem, same symptoms, same thoughts. It had to be fuel, it felt like fuel starvation, couldn't be the filter, I'd eliminated that possibility. After half an hour sitting in the pouring rain, I was still none the wiser, but stabbed the button again, for the umpteenth time. And we had liftoff! I was flummoxed, doubted my prognosis, it always seemed fine after being left for a while, I was at a loss as to what it could be. I refused to believe it was an electrical or ignition fault, maybe I was a bit hung up over fuel starvation issues but it sure felt like that. What do you do though? Once it starts there's no problem, so how do you find the fault? As there's no longer a fault, you ride on, at least I do, albeit with nagging worries at the back of my mind.

Pushing on through a light but steady downpour, darkness caught me unawares, it had been so gloomy I hadn't realised dusk had fallen. Road signs declared the border to be only thirty kilometres away, a number of motels had been passed, there seemed no shortage, and within a few kilometres a rather unattractive, fenced compound claimed itself to be a hotel. The gate was shut, no outside lights were on, but there were vehicles parked inside and lights shone from one of the buildings. Letting myself in caught their attention, by the time the bike was parked and my helmet was off, they were there with a stony faced welcome. Sure they had a room, they didn't seem to care whether I took it or not. Yes I could get food, yes I could get beer, and no I couldn't get a better price on the room. In fact when I went in to pay, the price had gone up $5.

All in all, Costa Rica hadn't given me much in the way of a good experience. I'd gone expecting the worst and not been disappointed. From one end of the country to the other, one thing after another tainted my perception of the place. From one border to the other, it'd failed to impress me, the bike cutting out hadn't helped but it was much more than that. Only seeing life along the Carretera InterAmericana was a distorted view, it may have shown some gorgeous hills and river sceneries but it also passed through all the main towns and cities. They were ugly, loud, asphyxiating hellholes, with too many people and not enough humanity. For me, they represented Latin America at its worst. But it went deeper than that, the officials were corrupt and officious, people looked at you with dollar signs in their eyes, you represented nothing more than how much they could deprive you of. How I wished to have ventured into its nether regions, though permits into national Parks didn't come cheap either. It stank of commercialism. I was bound to dislike it.

Chapter Thirty Three

Panama, on the other hand, welcomed me with open arms. The entrance to the border post was carnage, as I approached passers-by and truck drivers waved me on pointing me in the right direction for a quick route to the border post itself. A simple exit stamp from the Costa Ricans and I was through, amongst the throng battling their way through the bureaucracy. For a change it was quite orderly, a window clearly signed, "Imigración" was my first stop. Turning down the services of a runner, who'd given me the order of windows to visit, he left me to offer his services elsewhere. It went like clockwork, often pushed to the front of queues, officials would deal with me as a priority, politely and with a smile. There was no import tax, tourist tax, road tax, custom's bond, baksheesh or any other excuse to grab my money. A measly $6 bought me legit road insurance, if I understood correctly, it was only *advisable* to buy it, and I already had the import documents in hand. Bubbling with enthusiasm for such open hospitality, I actually tipped the customs guy who, barely glancing to confirm there was a fully laden motorcycle outside, stamped my form. Who knows what he thought about the smiley Gringo, who gave him money after being allowed through. It tickled my sense of humour though.

What a distinct pleasure to have sailed through the whole border crossing process without bribery or hindrance. That was a first! With bright sunshine, clear blue skies and a whole new country before me, a chirpy mood was inevitable. It was carnival week in Panama, the city was expected to host a big carnival parade, and it only lay a day's ride away. Hotels would be fully booked, roads choked with snarling traffic, sections blocked off and people everywhere.

A better proposition was a nice spot on the beach, then bus into the city when I needed. A promising start had been made and patchy, ill-repaired tarmac stretched out in front of me. The road looked grim, but the outlook was bright.

Poorly paved and tediously straight, the two-lane highway bore me directly towards Panama City. A succession of towns slowed the proceedings down, as traffic thickened it became a free for all. On the open road I was generally alone, no one else in sight, large distances passed between towns. With the extra wide road cruising at 80mph was a breeze, traffic was never so heavy as to bar my way through. Being so hot and humid, the faster I went, and the faster the moisture was wicked away, the better. It was stifling in all my gear. Though preferring to crank round the mountain roads, I'd take it as it came, one day wet but windy roads, the next hot and monotonous. Despite the boring road, the scenery was lovely. Open land of low, green hills, lots of open vegetation, and only a few heavily wooded areas. It was sparsely populated, towns and homesteads stood far apart. Most housing was well-constructed, fairly modern in design, rickety shacks were the domains of animals, not people. Cattle ranching dominated the agricultural scene, fairly small herds but plenty of them, small-scale beef production. Sugar cane appeared to be the only cash crop but many home enclosures produced a healthy variety of food and veg. Space around houses wasn't wasted on rose gardens any longer, people grew food, not flowers. The emphasis was back to working the land, maybe rich pickings for some wealthy landowners, but it was subsistence living for many farmers.

For the poorer farming folk, less cared for thatched blockhouses tended to stand within farm enclosures. Farmyards cluttered with junk, converted army trucks and rusted tankers, scraggly kids playing barefoot in the dusty yard, but they were happy and healthy. Curiosity brought another bunch of kids, peering down from a roadside embankment. In pristine clothes, cuddly toys in hand, they watched, whispering, as the strange Gringo photographed the weaverbird nests. Four button shaped faces, filled with wonder and awe, fingers pointed at the bike, surreptitious looks in my direction. As the camera swung their way they adopted sheepish grins, caught in the act. Exchanging guilty looks they agreed to a photo. One stared wistfully away, trying to hide a smile, another peered from behind the safety of her teddy bear, the two lads bravely sported awkward smiles, almost grimacing with the effort. Only fifty metres away from each other, the two groups of kids are miles apart on the social ladder. They don't beckon or call to each other, make no effort to acknowledge each other at all. With only a road to separate them, they were worlds apart.

No doubt about it as the main arterial road of the country, the Pan Americano was in an atrocious state, but it was maintained. It may have been a patchwork of concrete, tarmac and tar banding, with only the faintest suggestion of road markings but it was consistent. Constructed decades ago, it had obviously received countless repairs and reconstructions. It was a real hotchpotch of surfaces. The important thing was that they gave a reasonably flat riding surface, it wasn't broken, it wasn't potholed, it was reliably consolidated. It just looked awful. Road noise and vibration was at a peak, the less than perfect surface was anything but smooth. At higher speed it eased off which suited me fine, if only the local law enforcement officers felt the same way. I was sheepish on the Pan-Am. I had good reason to be. Approaching towns I slowed considerably, only wrenching the throttle open once checking the exit road was also clear. From 80mph, even 60mph feels a lot slower, and I wasn't keeping too close an eye on the speedo. I swear I saw a speed restriction for 60kph and dropped my speed accordingly. There should have been no cause for concern. So when the policia stopped me it was obviously another shakedown by greedy, corrupt coppers. And I was having none of it.

In many ways, I loathe false sincerity, to be greeted cordially when you know the person is about to stiff you big time. But I kept it formal and greeted them pleasantly, not exactly refusing to hand over my license, only questioning why they should want my license when I'd done nothing wrong. Aha, so suddenly the speed limit is only 40kph, or so they claimed. I claimed they were wrong, convinced the correct speed was displayed just along the road. I was wrong about that one, a long hot walk proved as much, a walk I did alone, as they waited in the shade of an overpass. Again my license was requested, again I questioned why I should give him my license. Give the guy due credit, he was very patient with me, 'I am policia! License por favor?' It was a very good point, one which I conceded to, assuring him he was correct, and would he please forgive me for not being immediately co-operative. Really, I don't know what gets into me at times. As an explanation I described being stopped in Nicaragua and Costa Rica, of bribes, corruption, having my license held as ransom until paying. Apparently, I was in Panama, and the police are not corrupt there. And to prove a point he handed back my duplicate licence, advised me to keep my speed down, and bade me farewell. A glowing example of positive policing, or maybe a quick recovery after realising I was onto him. The jury was out on that one.

More bemused than angered, I pretty much continued as before, clocking up the miles on the open road, slowing within urban environments, speed restrictions around towns were treated with a lot more respect though. The nearer to Panama City the more police patrols there were, traffic my direction may have been light, but streams of cars poured out the city. All headed for the coast, to spend carnival week on the beach. It hadn't dawned on me, the celebration was countrywide, not just the city, were the beaches going to be more crowded? I found a lovely beach, tucked away on a quiet stretch of coast halfway between the border and the city, and sure enough it was heaving. All the rooms were full, at whatever price. Bars and beach were packed, and new arrivals kept on coming. It was party time, and this little party pooper didn't want to play. I wasn't about to camp on the beach, didn't want loud music and drunken shenanigans, only wanted to exist, undisturbed, in my own sweet world. More places were tried, not so close to the beach but still within striking distance of the city. Only one had any spare rooms, at $55 per night, with free entertainment each evening, as if that were a bonus for me. What became clear was the advantage of the mass exodus, carnival or not, the city would be deserted. I'd rather take my chances in the city, so I turned tail and ran for La Carretera, my lifeline to *Ciudad Panama*.

Towns huddled closer the nearer I got, traffic got much heavier, all of it beach bound. Tailbacks stretched for miles approaching urban intersections, traffic lights and police created severe bottlenecks. The lights weren't programmed to handle the one directional flow of traffic, and the police stopping scores of cars only compounded the problem. It took attention away from me, or so I thought. I probably shouldn't have even looked at them, let alone nodded acknowledgement to them with a beaming, 'can't catch me' smile. As it happened he did, by radioing another traffic cop. I got pulled as I rode out the other side of town, by a bike cop. Panamanian police could teach the modern British bobby a lesson or two, he welcomed me, enquired as to my well-being and actually shook my hand. He hadn't a radar gun, and I was close to the speed limit, what else could be wrong? Which is when he informed me of the radio call, how a fellow officer reported me speeding through town. I should keep my smugness to myself it only entices people to see it wiped off my face, especially when they have the means to do so. Call it an abuse of power if you like, detaining a person against their will, for personal pleasure or gain, isn't it only corruption under another guise? Purely to prove a point, a point of power, I'd been pulled over, and I had a feeling the best they could do was inconvenience me. No argument, best establish the facts, together. What speed did the officer believe me to be doing? Having no recorded speed left them in a poor bargaining position, personally I couldn't see it posing a problem for me. Using Spanglish to the best of my ability, my appeal went something along the lines of: "Señor, this concerns me. An officer thinks my speed is too high, while I make every effort to remain within the legal limit. I was confident my speed was not excessive. It is a great surprise to be accused of speeding". I think he got the point. Of course, he had to take the word of his compatriot, don't they always? But for the second time in one day, I received only friendly advice to be more careful with my speed. It wasn't even a slap on the wrist, and certainly couldn't be seen as a deterrent. Though it worked, instead of setting off oblivious to their ineffective policing, I slowed right down, and stuck to the imposed speed limit wherever I rode.

Slower speed means longer journeys, in this case, it meant not reaching the city. Headlight on and squinting blearily into the near darkness, still short of Panama City by fifty kilometres, and desperate for a convenient hotel, I wasn't about to be choosy. And then I passed one, standing well back from the highway, a hundred metres down a gravel track. An unimaginative square block of nondescript colour with no outstanding features, and no concept of design, as if it had just been plonked there. Unable to label it as ugly, it was at best, utilitarian. Seemingly deserted, the subdued lighting and unlit hotel sign did nothing to boost my confidence. It didn't look particularly run down, maybe a touch seedy. Actually, it didn't really look as if it was even open. But it was open, and they were very obliging. Of course they had a room, would $20 be alright? Strange, for two nights I'd begrudged paying $25, now all of a sudden twenty a night was a bargain. But would my bike be safe from the road? 'Of course Señor, there's an underground garage, kept locked at all times'. They couldn't provide food and there was no restaurant close by, but there was coke and biscuits in the vending machine, and they'd be only too willing to change a banknote for me.

Bare concrete stairwells led to central corridors, a line of indistinguishable doors running their length, the only sound was our footsteps echoing through the emptiness. Not much was expected, nor was it needed, I merely wanted to rest my weary bones for one night. A bed, bog and running water were fine. How luxurious to discover a pile of soft white towels, crispy clean sheets and a spotless bathroom waiting, the king size bed was icing on the cake. And the cherry was the lashings of hot water, it was my first hot shower in two months, I cherished every single one of the thirty minutes I blasted myself with almost scalding water. Squeaky clean and ravenously hungry, I settled into bed with my packet of biscuits and can of coke. Gone were the days of camp cooking, fresh stew every night, gazing at the stars before bed. I guess I was travelling in comparative luxury, it felt more a state of deprivation. The wider world passed me by, consciousness restricted to my immediate surroundings, the road, the bike, and my own thoughts. This was the world through which I came to exist in, withdrawing more and more from outside influences, digging deep, finding the fissures to my soul, and smoothing over those cracks.

Progress had been a long, drawn out process, one that escaped my notice, I hadn't reached a point where I recognised it as such. Accepting the loss of Cai was still difficult, but my mind no longer went into spasms of denial, it just hurt. I felt alone, out on a limb, though felt confident this was not an issue to deter me from future decisions. What I had managed to accept, was the inevitability of returning home. That was the closet in which my skeletons hid, sooner or later I must return, and lay them to rest. Whenever this came to pass I was ready, the eventuality was no longer tinged with fear, my thoughts no longer recoiled from that possibility. Bolstered by a newfound confidence, I could proceed, not driven by fear or anxiety, but encouraged by my strength and fortitude.

Early Sunday morning and the city was hauntingly quiet, the streets disturbingly empty, a virtual ghost town. Entering the suburbs, grimy tenement blocks cried out of urban decay. Once white facades were blackened by soot and road borne pollution, city filth etched into their very fabric over decades. Amidst aging degradation, a bright, shiny Shell station showed the only signs of modernity, and the only signs of life. Life in the American fast lane, fast food and prepaid petrol pumps, armed guards and ATMs. Normally I steered clear of guys with guns, but I wasn't given the chance, the security guard was on my case with no delay, in the nicest possible way. Where was I from, how had I travelled to Panama City? What brought me to Panama, what was I looking for, did I know my way? He proved a wealth of information, giving concise instructions to the city's hotel region and dire warnings of the high crime levels on the streets. Don't carry valuables openly displayed, keep your wallet in an enclosed pocket and avoid the streets after dark, above all else, trust no one. Welcome to Panama City eh?

Needless to say, it put me on my guard. Leaving my bike unaccompanied was a risk I wasn't willing to take. I kept it in my sights at all times, not even venturing into hotels unless it was in plain view. Actually, few of the hotels interested me except as a means to getting directions. I knew they were out of my price range, even the more mediocre of them. Without a guidebook information was scarce, hotel staff were either reluctant or unable to point me towards a hostel or Pension, as if it were below them to possess such information, to know of such places. I had a hostel name and an area but they all claimed ignorance of either. Finally, an American ex-pat who I accosted on the street pointed me in the right direction. Unsure of actual names, he at least got me to the area it was purported to be in. Trawling haphazardly round the empty streets found me none the wiser though. Riding around in widening circles, indistinct signs would catch my attention as I passed a side street trapped in a one-way system, I'd have to loop a long way round to double check. In this way I found a couple of alternatives but no trace of the reputed 'Biker friendly' hostel. OK, the empty roads made riding round easier but I was getting nowhere fast, only dizzy in the process.

Deciding to bite the bullet, the bike was ditched, locked securely, but left to fend for itself all the same. Empty streets made navigating by foot far easier, giving more time to scrutinise each and every street, it also made me stick out like a sore thumb which attracted attention, from one of the reputed untrustworthy locals. Tim considered himself an American Panamanian, he drove one of the service buses from the provinces into the city. He was my guardian angel, concerned to see me wandering the streets, looking lost, he took me under his wing, took it upon himself to escort me to suitable lodgings. He also gave strict warnings of safety on the city's streets. I'd be safe in that particular area, providing I didn't wander too far afield. He accompanied me, interpreter, guide, up one street then down the next, the rare times we met anyone else he questioned them as to hostels. Failing miserably to find that particular hostel a number of others were recommended. One Tim advised against without even entering the doors, claiming it likely to be a brothel, how he could tell I'm not quite sure, I didn't see any notices declaring hourly rates, but maybe he knew something I didn't. In reality I waited for the sting, convinced he was setting me up for a scam, that he'd eventually spring the trap. In another place, it was simply too much to charge for a basic room, in his mind an inflated price because I was a tourist, he didn't want to see me get ripped off, not to worry there would be more close by. That allayed my suspicions slightly, if he was playing games he was playing them well. I suspected he might be touting for one particular hotel, expecting to find myself taken to a stupidly priced shit hole down some filthy back street. We passed low key hotels, they were for the wealthier tourist, he was sure there were more suitable places for my budget. And so we came upon the Pension Palmeras. It wasn't the Ritz, but it was cheap and quiet, the bike could be parked off the street and it was only $10 a night. It would suffice for the time being while I organised for my departure to Cartagena.

Chapter Thirty Four

Desolate city centres have an ominously surreal quality about them. It just doesn't seem natural, like walking through a post-apocalyptic remnant of human existence. Everything, everywhere was closed, shops, banks, restaurants and offices, all premises shuttered and locked securely. Occasional fast food joints and hotel bars were the only source of sustenance, a single Internet café my only point of contact with the outside world. How frustrating, a place that still respected the Sabbath day as a day of rest. Except it wasn't merely one day of rest, not in the religious sense. Worship and prayers of forgiveness were not the determining factors, it was carnival time, not a time to rest and reflect on the grace of the divine, but a time to party. There were no flocks of the faithful lined outside the churches, bells did not toll to welcome the sinners into the churches forgiving folds. Panama's citizens had gone forth to multiply, in a drunken orgy on sun kissed beaches. The city was on shutdown for five days!

The hustle and bustle of cities normally grinds me down. There are too many people, too much noise, and way too much pollution. So I was in my element, only an occasional car passed me by, almost no other pedestrians graced the sidewalks to molest or otherwise disturb me, I could explore, wander to my heart's content. Along palm-lined avenues stretching to the shore, past unoccupied driveways, uninhabited homes. Through prestige shopping precincts, deserted arcades devoid of humanity. Between soaring skyscrapers, gleaming glass towers, abandoned save for gun toting security men barring entry. Multi-laned highways swept through the city, connecting various districts, the old colonial hub, the commercial sector, the tourist centre, each an island surrounded by waves of empty tarmac. But the tide was out, the city held its breath, and I let out a sigh of relief. It was a bizarre pleasure to wander at will, relaxed and unperturbed by the rigours of normal city life.

First my fingers did the walking, then my feet, telephone directories and a city map my able guides. If they could be trusted four bike shops lay within walking distance, two even advertised as tyre specialists. I must have walked a good thirty miles a day, under a crucifying sun, in search of likely suppliers of tyres. Whilst being exhausting work, it kept mind and body busy, I hadn't succumbed to lethargy, everything that could be done was being done. Even had I wanted one, taxis were in short supply, apparently even taxi drivers joined in the festivities, and it never entered my mind to use the bike. That was parked securely, awaiting some TLC before being thrown wholeheartedly at the South American Sub-continent. My place on Stahlratte had been confirmed, we sailed on 15 February, giving me ten days to prepare, to find a tyre and give the bike a thorough service. Plenty of time really, though at the end of three days I was gagging at the bit to get on with it. Five promising suppliers had been located, two were main motorcycle dealerships selling similar style and size bikes to mine. Surely one must have a suitable tyre.

In the meantime, I wandered aimlessly, seeing what the city had to offer, checking the lay of the land. But appearances proved to be deceiving, not all had fled the city, not all could. Other hostels were found, chock full of bored backpackers, engorging themselves on culinary delights with a distinct European flavour. In transit, like me, they probably hadn't known of the festivities before arriving. Now, frustrated at the closure of travel agents, they wiled away their time, counting off the hours before being able to procure tickets before possible release. Also present, at the lowest end of the social spectrum, came the poor and destitute, for them there was no release, no means to flee and no reason to celebrate. Without the masses to hide within, they stuck out like a sore thumb. People fed off the street, literally, crusts of bread picked off the sidewalk and shoved straight into their mouths. From a hotel skip a guy scooped handfuls of rice into his mouth, discarded leftovers, scraped onto assorted waste. There was no delicacy in the operation, he shovelled it into his mouth as quick as possible, glancing furtively about in the process. Bin bags lay in the gutters, disembowelled, their entrails strewn down the road. And then there were the ghettoes, filthy, squalid places, yet far from deserted. Loud and lively, life carried on as usual amongst the carnage, plenty of folk loitered and mingled, music spilled onto the streets, rap was alive and doing well. Youths in wife beater tops, jeans dragging below their arses, sauntered jauntily down the road, past fat middle aged women, hair big with supersize curlers, blubber hanging over their waistline. Poor housing, poor diet, poor health and no doubt, poor education. People living in obvious poverty, yet half the youths were dripping in gold, who says crime doesn't pay? Even the police wouldn't walk there alone, patrolling from the relative safety of marked cars, they'd pluck unwary tourists from the slum areas, returning them to their hotels and warning them to steer clear in the future. Small ghettoes were to be found isolated between other sectors of the city, pockets of crumbling old buildings, overcrowded urban degradation, merely one or two blocks from the colonial splendour of the old city. Rows of ugly concrete tenement blocks, an island amidst a profusion of spaghetti like overpasses, the passing traffic marked the passage of time, the grime of airborne pollution deeply ingrained into everyday existence, the buildings, the lines of grubby washing strung out like bunting to celebrate the carnival.

The ethnic mix threw me. The lines of demarcation appeared so inflexible, making a travesty of the concept of racial harmony. Almost without fail the Panamanians I'd met on the road were Latino, the queues of cars driven by Latin Americans, police officers of typical Spanish/Indian mix. Once delving into the heart of the city, it became obvious the remnants of the population were predominantly Black. Rundown sectors, inhabited by those of African descent, the homeless denizens, every last one of them, Black. Waiters in restaurants would invariably be Latino whereas staff in cheap fast food outlets, tended to be Black. Not one Black police officer crossed my path, not a single Black security officer stood guard outside the numerous banks, hotels and offices. The disparity of wealth seemed plain to see, if your ancestors had arrived in chains, the future looked bleak, if they'd slaughtered, subjugated and bred with the indigenous population, opportunity knocked. Ironically, few of the Latinos can boast Spanish descent, their genetic code, portrayed by their physical features, betrayed the richness of indigenous blood coursing through their veins. Yet standing proudly separate were the true indigenous population, easily distinguishable from the Latinos, and still worlds apart.

Everywhere the iconography boasted of the all-conquering heroes, the bold Spanish who decimated their lands, raped their women and exported their natural wealth. Little wonder independence was so widely celebrated, it was not solely a Spanish or Latin American enigma.

But the celebrations in February were not tainted by the past atrocities of colonial power. They fell between Ash Wednesday and Shrove Tuesday, and despite their debauched nature they are actually of religious significance. Claimed by some to be a mix between New Orleans Mardi Gras and the Rio de Janeiro Carnival, the Panama Carnival is reputed to be a wonderful spectacle. Loud and raucous reggae echoing through the city streets, with an endless parade of wonderfully decorated floats brought alive by energetic, flamboyant dancers cheered on by joyous crowds of celebrants. It somehow managed to pass me by almost unnoticed. The tail end of a meagre parade was all that I encountered, half a dozen dismal floats, bedecked in tinsel and crepe paper. Characters smeared in body paint, gaudy costumes aflutter with listless gyrations, half-heartedly vying for attention. Pitifully small crowds attended, the whole kit and caboodle was over and done with in the space of two hours. It was a far cry from the week long parties carrying on along the coast. I envied those sun seekers, soaking up the rays in gentle sea breezes while I melted in the hot, humid city environment. But I felt glad to be missing out, the pressing throngs, the pounding music and chaotic celebrations, it was the last thing I needed. All too soon the hordes were due back, and I wasn't looking forward to sharing my city with its full contingent of inhabitants.

Milling crowds packed the streets, rushing hither and thither, oblivious to the lone Gringo carefully picking his way through their midst. Snarling traffic, streams of it, sprang without warning from every which way. Crossing roads took on a whole new dimension. It was downright hazardous. Walks of fifteen minutes took twenty-five energy sapping minutes, constantly battling through heaving crowds, dicing with death at every intersection. A dormant city sprang to life overnight, our quiet leafy lane grew raucous, road pollution rose to asphyxiating levels, and the streets were wall to wall with the press of humanity. From out of every nook and cranny emerged the destitute, dragging bags from bins, spilling their contents onto the sidewalk, rifling through the discarded debris. Drunks stinking of piss hustled for money, beggars shook their tins or held out their hands, the crowds were back, and the pickings were rich. City life was back with a vengeance! Rare sightings of indigenous Panamanians showed how under represented they actually were, their presence at street stalls selling traditional craftwork to tourists suggested, like the Maya, they only ventured into the cities for commerce. Angular facial features held a distinctly noble bearing, the look of a people who remembered days when they were beholden to no one. In cheap floral print shorts and blouses they'd sit beside their wares, wearing bright coloured leggings of tiny ornate beads, strung together in geometric designs. On their arms, sleeves of similar design and colour yet a less complicated pattern, complimented the effect. Never flustered, never hustling, these fair folk always appeared self-contained, even aloof. With a detached acceptance as if the city held little of interest for them, they patiently endured the ordeal.

At only a dollar a pop, taxis were a more relaxed option than walking. Better still were the city buses, for only a few cents you could jump on and jump off at will. The whole city moved at a relentless pace, walking against the flow of people was a nightmare, and whichever way I turned I never seemed to be going with the flow. On the other hand, traffic was constantly on the move, a half hour walk could be overcome with a five-minute bus or taxi ride, so long as you knew where you were going. Jumping on a bus was easy, there were scores of them, knowing where they went was slightly more difficult. If they didn't take a turn where I wanted, or turned off when I didn't, I got off. When not on a bus route I hailed a cab, often arguing over a realistic price. Being white meant being wealthy, at least in their eyes, a fair price didn't come into it, only how much they could extort from you. Since I'd pounded the pavements to my hearts content while the city was deserted, I knew where to go and how to get there.

First port of call was a Suzuki dealer, they sold DR650's, whose tyres are the same as the KLR650. Alas, they didn't stock that size. They had slightly wider tyres with a higher profile, the tread design and wheel size were fine, it wasn't good enough for me though. It also meant going back to Dunlops with a life expectancy of only three thousand miles. I guess striking lucky first time was too much to ask for, so I trawled around all the places I'd stumbled across on my wanderings. There were a lot of very friendly and helpful shop assistants, they all had the utmost confidence that the tyres they stocked would do the job, shame none could provide what I actually wanted. Too fat, too thin, too Chinese, whilst admitting it would be best to buy a good quality tyre, of the correct size, they all assured me I'd be fine with the one they offered. Determined to exhaust all options first, I doggedly visited place after place. By the time I'd exhausted those options, I'd also exhausted myself. It wasn't with a smile on my face and a tyre under my arm that I finally dragged myself back to my room, but I was satisfied that all alternatives had been explored.

An acceptable choice of tyres was available, there were any number of tyre fitters in the near vicinity, and plenty of time before setting off to rendezvous with Stahlratte. Boarding was to be at Carti, a small coastal town on Panama's north coast, as I understood it the track was a humdinger. An unmaintained jungle track, involving immense hill climbs and non-ending loose and muddy dirt.

Scaremongers claimed it impassable, 'Well I heard of some guy...'

Right, so it was only hearsay, they didn't actually know. As the story went someone had attempted the track on a fully loaded BMW 1200GS, a big heavy brute of a bike, suitable for little else but highway riding. He'd apparently hurled himself at one particular hill a score of times, each time loosing traction on the treacherously muddy incline and sliding all the way back down, eventually giving up and returning with his tail between his legs. My KLR650 was nigh on half the weight, it had got me nearly sixteen thousand miles and only one hill had proved problematic, though not impossible. Even such big heavy BMWs had managed this impassable jungle track, having met such a group in Honduras, I knew. So scoffing at the harbingers of doom, I was not to be put off. As far as the Stahlratte was concerned, well, they weren't concerned. They regularly transported motorcycles between Carti and Cartagena, it was a well-travelled route. Besides, a guy in a jeep would be travelling the route to take supplies to Stahlratte, he'd provide backup, just in case it might be needed. And then there were three, a Danish biker took the last place on Stahlratte. There'd be two of us on KLR650s making the sailing, and the jungle ride. Everything had fallen into place nicely, it looked like it was full steam ahead for Cartagena.

An air of satisfaction prevailed; despite the claustrophobic oppression of the heaving metropolis my days had all been productive, if for nothing else then as fact-finding missions.

Amazingly, I'd settled in rather well, helped by the camaraderie of my fellow guests and newfound friends. Tim would come and go, stopping to chat, checking I was OK. I think I'd hit a soft spot, tears glistened in his eyes as I told him the story of losing Cai. He stopped by every couple of days, often dropping a small packet of weed into my hand, a little something to lighten the emotional load. Another two-wheeled adventurer booked in, the Danish guy on his red KLR650, the sight of my bike parked out front enticing him in. Four Argentinean lads travelling north also crowded into the biggest room they could afford, they waited while their '61' Ford Falcone cleared customs before continuing their journey of Latin America. We formed a happy little community, a band of bold adventurers whiling away the hours together, all resting before their next push forward. The company was refreshing, regardless of language barriers, hours were spent in a haze of dope smoke, as the four lads strummed a guitar, singing an endless host of Spanish melodies. Sadie, a Hungarian ex-pat with his pretty young wife joined our fold. He fawned on the attentions of his wife, keeping her happy with countless shopping trips while he conducted business in Panama. The setup was slightly strange, with the reception desk safely behind a secured wire cage and expectations of paying our bills on a daily basis. It was more reminiscent of a knocking shop than a homely Pension. But we made it a welcoming place, hanging out on the front steps, greeting new arrivals and casual passers-by alike, adding warmth and friendliness to the rather austere interior we inhabited.

I had my reservations about setting off with another companion. The last riding partnership had left a lot to be desired. Without doubt it was convenient, for the jungle ride especially. Colombia's reputation was daunting, it could well be dodgier riding solo, but that was worlds away, who knew what could happen in the meantime? It wasn't worth concerning myself with such worries. It went deeper than that though, images of riding together, red and black KLRs venturing into the big wide world, played on my mind. The intention had been for it to be Cai and me, father and son conquering the world together. How could anyone hope to fill that gap, how could I hope to fill that gap? Memories of our dreams, the times we'd shared, sprang to mind. What an amazing adventure he'd missed, how much he would have enjoyed it. There was a lot of life to reflect on, much hinged on the pain so deeply etched into my soul, although most of it consisted of happy times, of good memories. No companion could fill that void. It would be unfair to expect such miracles.

Feeling remarkably calm and relaxed, composed even, the process of putting my life and Cai's death into perspective began, with little conscious contribution on my behalf. While gazing across the road at the 'Hospital Nacionale' and hijacking their Wi-fi, I realised how lucky we were, under the circumstances. What would Cai's accident have been like somewhere like Panama? How much more traumatic would it have been for all concerned? It didn't bear thinking about, just as once I couldn't bear to think of losing him at all. I got to flicking through photos of him on the Laptop, smiling at his happy face, glad for everything we'd shared, how good our life together had been, happy to have such memories. My sense of loss hadn't diminished in the slightest, I realised it never would, yet it was easier to bear. A stray tear might escape at such times, rolling gently down my cheek, more often than not a smile interrupting the flow, easing away the pain. Rather than being tormented by visions of him lying close to death on the highway, or his lifeless body laid on the hospital trolley, I filled my mind with thoughts of the joy we'd shared, the fullness of our relationship. Many people spend a lifetime without the closeness and pleasure we'd shared, no relationship is faultless, but ours had been pretty damned close. If all the miles, the countless tears and immense emotional upheaval had all been to gain that one moment of insight, the effort had been worthwhile.

Chapter Thirty Five

February 8 2008, it was a bright and sunny Panamanian morning. Opening my eyes and breathing deeply, a clean, morning freshness suffused and lifted my spirits. I felt refreshed and relaxed, my heart and mind clean and clear, neither emotions nor hang-ups clouded my thoughts. I lay motionless, aware of little more than breathing and being alive, savouring the gentle pleasure those simple insights brought. Gone was the weight of the world from my shoulders, no longer pressing them into the grubby mattress below, delaying the inevitable need to rise and face another day. No constrictive mantle bound my heart, how comforting to feel the welcome glow of love without the anguish of loss, to relish the warmth of life without the cold grip of fear. Raising my head off the pillow, a new found sense of liberty overcame me.

Stepping beyond the realms of conscious thought, there was no need to decipher life's multifaceted foibles. Call it an epiphany if you must, but there was no blinding flash of light or fanfare of trumpets, no celestial beings descending from up high to herald the dawning of a revelation. Though divine inspiration failed to lift me above mortal realms, a subtle shift occurred removing the self-imposed strictures of coping with bereavement. Freed of worries and fears, pain and turmoil, a whole new world lay ahead. A world within my grasp, to bend and shape to my own will, to become master of my own destiny, rather than a victim of circumstances.

For seven months, sixteen thousand miles, the journey had been my redemption, my salvation, the only point to my life. Through the USA and Canada the immensity of the wilderness had blown my mind, the beauty of nature captured my heart. The enormity of the Rockies had soothed my troubled mind and quelled my raging emotions, filling my soul with awe and wonder, overwhelming the depths of despair. I'd driven myself hard for those two months, pushing myself ever onwards, determined to give meaning to Cai's death, not wanting it to be for nothing. My whole existence hinged on what I envisaged he would have wanted, what he'd have approved of. Barely a minute passed without being consumed by grief, only the magnitude of my environment could contend, could stave off a never-ending downward spiral. Once into Mexico the emphasis had changed, I had attempted to ease back from the relentless force driving me on. Hoping to placate the all-consuming grief, my plan had been to take time out, partake in other pleasures. And I did, but it never really had the desired effect. No matter the nature of activities, how genuine the people I associated with, I could never quite let go of my grief. The longer I spent in one place the more disenfranchised I became with the rest of humanity, the petty lives they lead. All too soon the compulsion to lose myself on the open road would rear its ugly head. Riding became an escape, a way to maintain my own little bubble, cut myself off from the rest of the world. Pig-headed determination had kept me going, initially in honour of Cai, but always due to a strong reluctance to return home. But that didn't faze me any longer. The only question left remaining was what did I want to do with my life? No matter how far I rode or how hard I pushed myself, it would not bring Cai back. However harsh, however painful, life goes on! We must all be responsible for our own lives, for our own choices, whether we like it or not. Those choices may seem limited, we might wish for more, we might bow to external pressures, but the choices we face are ours to make.

And for the first time in many months I acknowledged that I had choices. The blinkers were well and truly off, and there were options. Crossing to South America had been the goal for so long, but I no longer felt I must continue. I felt no need to return home, though maybe more important, I felt no reluctance to return. I felt free to go home, or free to carry on, no pressure and no guilt either way. Any thoughts of giving meaning to Cai's death had deserted me, all my efforts had merely been to give meaning to my own life. It may have helped to think it was all for Cai, but at long last I realised it was for myself it must be done. And I felt I'd done enough. I'd come a long way, far further than can be measured in miles. I'd achieved more than could have been imagined, I could face the new day without wanting to scream in anguish. The future didn't make me recoil in horror; it was always there, for better or worse. I couldn't escape that, but I could mould it, I had the ability to shape it to suit my own needs. I wanted to get to grips with the rest of my life. It was about time I went home and faced the music.

Epilogue

In any other circumstances this would have been the ride of a lifetime, I guess it still was, but at too high a price. I think in the end it more resembled a scramble for survival. Noble sentiments filled my thoughts as I steeled myself for the grand return, I certainly wasn't kidding myself it would be an easy transition. But I had faith in the world, and in myself! How sorely that faith was tested, how far I fell when I finally got to Wales. Another roller coaster ride began, emotional upheaval kicked back with a vengeance.

My quiet little corner of Wales would never be the same. The initial turmoil hit me hard, everything I passed, every tiniest little detail brought forth memories of life with Cai. Grief came crashing down on me, leaving me in a no man's land of quiet despair. No amount of self-control was going to stop the deluge that washed me away. Whether or not I maintained a façade of calm tranquillity, my head was going round in circles, tearing my heart apart. With no sense of purpose every day became just another period of daylight to muddle through. Every passing moment was filled with sorrow for the life I'd lost. Simple walks would take hours and emotionally drain me. One moment of reflection, while gazing at a river flowing by, could find me emerging from my hypnotic daze an hour later. The world I'd once known and cherished was lost to me, replaced by an alien world where I found no joy awaiting.

Life does indeed go on, while I'd been cruising the highways and byways of the Americas everyone at home had been getting on with their lives. For most the tragedy of death was far behind, many months of savouring the joys of their own parenthood had passed. Often seeing those happy families nearly made me run away again, to seek solace in private. Single male friends were easy to handle, we could fall back on easy camaraderie and drunken exploits. Friends with families proved so difficult to deal with, they only served to remind me just how much I'd lost. Almost instantly patterns were set, it quickly became apparent with which friends I could talk about the on-going trauma, with whom it was simpler to pretend life was as it always had been. Too many people were afraid of upsetting me to initiate conversation regarding Cai or his death, even to the extent of awkward silences when I mentioned him. That in itself hurt, as if denial of the facts could make it better. Not only had I lost my son, also gone was the joy of sharing precious memories. I felt cut off and alone, despite the presence and support of many friends. For those at home little had changed, for me everything had.

Without transport I was doubly lost, my bike was due to take at least six weeks before reaching the UK. I felt totally lost without my personal freedom. Friends and family were spread far and wide, and public transport wasn't the solution. That was a situation I couldn't cope with overly long. So within a week I travelled down to South Wales to buy a fairly new Triumph Daytona 955*i,* gaining a new lease of life in the process. I'd only once treated myself to a comparable sports bike, that had still been of vintage stock, not a modern Sports Bike pulling about 165bhp with a top speed of over 160mph. Did I really need such a monster, was it really the bike of best choice? Certainly it wasn't but I wanted a toy, something different, something to have fun with.

So as the weeks went by I settled into an empty routine of odd jobs and selective socialising. I picked my moments for meaningful talks about Cai and life without him, chose carefully those whose levels of compassion could deal with my intense emotional state. Drunken get togethers proved a ready source of forgetfulness, often ending with quiet tears as the alcohol eventually stripped away the last visage of self-control. Requests for work came slow but sure, it didn't bother me, the last thing I wanted was to slope back into a life of boring drudgery. Physical exercise and my new monster machine became my forms of release. Hours in the gym would wear me ragged, it may have been hard to motivate my frequent trips there, but the effort was always worth it. Once the endorphins kicked in emotional pain eased off too. I'd love to claim a healthy body leads to a healthy mind, but the attitude of many muscle bound morons, testosterone fuelled idiots, makes a mockery of the statement.

To deal with my frustrations there was the bike. Its awesome power was plenty to get the adrenalin flowing, I used it and abused it relishing the totally irresponsible attitude it induced. Let's face it, there is only one reason to have a bike of such power, to go fast. And so I did, regularly reaching speeds of over 140mph. But it wasn't purely the thrill of flat out suicidal speeds, the bike was well balanced and quick to turn, acceleration was phenomenal. I hustled around the roads with impatience and intolerance, giving no quarter, taking liberties at every opportunity. It wasn't that I'd turned kamikaze, I wasn't looking for that final release, only wanting to feel alive. As it happened I wasn't going at breakneck speed when the demise of my pristine Triumph finally came to be. At little more than 40mph, on a fairly quiet dual carriageway, a council worker in front swerved to miss some road debris. I merely maintained my speed, and picked my way through the jumble of shredded truck tyre. No sooner had the obstacle been passed when the council van swerved back onto the main carriageway, straight into my front wheel. Being shunted across both carriageways should have been terrifying, I felt strangely detached. Ploughing into a wire central barrier could easily have flipped me into the opposing traffic, miraculously we both bounced back into the outside lane. The bike was a mess, a write-off without the least shadow of a doubt, I could see that the second I scrambled to my feet. The biggest surprise of all was my own condition, though not coming away completely unscathed, I sustained only a broken wrist.

In my mind the accident couldn't have come at a worse time, the KLR had recently arrived home and had only a couple of simple changes for type approval and full UK registration. I was gutted and, deprived of my independence, sank into an alcoholic stupour. It wasn't prolonged nor was I heading for alcoholism, my attitude merely reflected a desire to while away the weeks until my plaster was removed. I didn't throw serious amounts of booze down my throat, wasn't rolling around drunk, although I drank freely during the afternoon and evenings, relying on friends and hitching rides to maintain a social life. Mornings were filled with cumbersome attempts to write, typing isn't too easy with a plaster caste but I persevered. I had a story to tell and wanted the world to hear it. Being partly incapacitated was nothing but a temporary inconvenience, to an extent it took away the distractions, gave me time to think. No, the real spanner in the works came a mere three weeks after my caste came off. Returning home from my last session of physio on my newly registered KLR, the wrath of doom reared its ugly head and crashed upon me with full fury.

Joyous to be re-united with my old friend, eager to enjoy its familiarity, I flipped it through the first few bends on my favourite country road, the back road between home and town. How I loved to hear the exhaust bark its throaty roar, how natural it felt to push it hard through the gears. But caution forestalled me, a nagging feeling at the back of my mind, *relax, there's no hurry.* So I dutifully eased off the throttle and continued at a more sedate pace. I'm well versed in the procedures for progressive riding without excessive speed, and felt a need to refresh myself of those procedures. Having had enough time to realise the risks I'd been taking on the Triumph, it was now time to put into practice a more responsible manner of riding. Every bend on the road is a blind bend, each was approached maximising visibility, giving myself the best chance to see anything approaching from the opposite direction. All went well until the last bend before the village a couple of miles from home. Coming cleanly round the preceding bend a battered Landrover parked on the opposite verge encroached into the road, right on the entry point to the bend. Obviously any approaching traffic would be coming round wide, to miss the Landrover. So I eased off the power even more and took the inside line, close to the overhanging hedge. You should never be surprised to see oncoming traffic, you should ride expecting it. Maybe you get a touch blasé on a bike, there are very few instances when an approaching obstacle can't be negotiated round. But as I came out the bend a huge John Deere tractor bore down on me, angled across the road, blocking it completely but still trundling on. A sedate 30mph or not, it still takes an average twenty or so metres to stop; I had about six. It wasn't possible, so I didn't bother. Instead my reactions took me towards the smallest of gaps, a hope that fifteen centimetres might increase enough to allow me through in the time it took to get there. It didn't.

Losing consciousness would have been a blessed relief, but I wasn't to be so blessed. All I had at first was the sense of flying, colliding with something solid, and landing with a heavy thump half propped against a stonewall. My mind raced, pain screaming throughout my body. For once there were no thoughts for the condition of my bike, the pain was too intense, my only concern was how bad the damage was to me, I knew immediately it was serious.

Excruciating pain threatened to overwhelm all sense of anything. Trying my damnedest to blot out the agony I systematically took stock. With my visor closed it was hot and steamy, I couldn't see much, it felt claustrophobic inducing a sense of panic. A figure loomed over me saying an ambulance was on its way, it was the farmer. I yelled instructions to get my helmet off, I could at least move my head without adding to the pain wracking my body. It seemed that whatever else I moved hurt, it was so hard to decipher exactly where any specific problems lay. My right forearm jutted out at an impossible angle, moving my hand wasn't an option, that hung useless from the wrist. The fingers on my other hand were clenched into claws, the hand itself bent and crooked. Moving either arm caused massive jolts of fresh pain, it had to be done though. Using my elbows I eased my body into a more comfortable position, and screamed in agony as my right leg dragged across the ground. I managed to move my left leg without suffering, somehow that gave me some form of reassurance, at least I wouldn't be a quadriplegic. It took an awful amount of verbal abuse before I could get the farmer to undo my jacket, I was burning up in my full wet weather protective gear. And then the paramedic arrived.

Help was at hand, or so I thought. I only recall how foul some of my language was, and how desperate I was for pain relief. First of all my condition had to be assessed, they wouldn't take my word for it, systems had been designed for these situations, and procedures must be followed. The emergency services wouldn't even listen as I tried to tell them they were trying to cut through the protective armour of my suit. It took forever, they cut it off in chunks. In fact, they cut off every stitch of clothing, leaving me naked on the side of the road. Not that I cared, I was in a hurry for them to expose a vein, then I could have a shot of morphine. But even the morphine and constant nitrous oxide (gas and air) failed to alleviate the pain, especially as one of the ambulance men stumbled, kicking one of my arms as he recovered his balance. That elicited the foulest stream of abuse I could muster, and every time that particular guy approached another pored forth. My fury at the farmer hadn't abated, he'd been the target of earlier abuse, only the actions of the bumbling fool had turned my anger towards my saviours. It took forever before we set off for hospital, I guess there was a lot for them to consider before moving me. As they did so a wave of nausea swept through me, and my whole body started shaking. It's shock, I told myself, but it was scary. As they slid me into the ambulance doubts as to seeing the inside of the hospital crossed my mind. For some strange reason I didn't find that disconcerting, any release from the pain was welcome.

Along with two shots of morphine, I sucked dry two bottles of nitrous and was halfway through a third by the time we arrived. Pandemonium greeted me, teams of doctors and nurses crowded into the reception area clamouring to get at me. I'm sure someone did actually take control of the situation, but questions came thick and fast, from all directions. Total confusion took over, I could only lay there and try to siphon out the requests for information from the general hubbub. However bad the pain had seemed before, the manipulation of my left wrist was beyond endurance, I nearly passed out. Pumping me full of morphine was fine by me, knocking me out with a mallet would have been preferable but regulations must be adhered to. In all honesty they wasted very little time getting me into theatre. I was so drugged up and disorientated it passed in a flash, for me there were no queues, no waiting times. They rushed me through all their procedures at double speed, I'm sure they informed me of their findings but it was only the following day that I was coherent enough for it to sink in.

Two plates held my right forearm together. One, the length of the forearm, to support a completely shattered ulna. The second, on the inside of the arm, was for a fairly straight forward break to the radial. My left wrist had also shattered, the manipulation had been to release the nerves and ligaments the collapse of the carpal tunnel had crushed. That had been emergency treatment, it also needed the addition of a titanium plate to secure the many fragments in place. My right leg had concerned them, a huge gouge from my thigh suggested a broken femur, the chances of rupturing a major artery were high. Fortunately the femur wasn't broken, but the complicated break of the tibial plateau was not a job they wished to tackle immediately. It was encased in plaster, pending future interaction. So far the extent of injuries and the nature of them was pretty much as I first thought lying at the roadside. There was a surprise in store though, that was my left knee, I'd severed three of the four ligaments in it. That, they sadly informed me, would take the longest to reconstruct and heal.

Boy what a sorry state, both legs encased and immovable, and both arms useless. I had in effect become a quadriplegic, albeit temporarily. I couldn't feed myself, take a drink, have a pee, even pull myself up in bed without help. Of course there was also the pain, much diminished by then but still accompanying any movement. Frequent, large doses of morphine helped, it didn't so much deaden the pain itself, mainly improved my ability to deal with it. Being able to do little other than lay there and think proved difficult, acceptance of such limitations were harder still. It took days in coming, but by fighting and fumbling with the utensils I quickly got to a stage of feeding myself. There were still many hours of nothing but lying still, with nothing but my own thoughts to occupy the mind. Though still furious with the farmer I'd managed to accept the incident as par for the course, these things can happen on a bike, whether or not you're at fault. Funnily it was my ability to walk again that most concerned the hospital staff, for me it was how I'd cope with riding again.

It could easily have been the straw that broke the camel's back. Since returning home I'd struggled to see any point in life, found that little stimulated or motivated me. In effect I was going through the motions of living, while my spirits were at an all-time low, and rising above this had proved beyond my ability. If it were excuses I needed to give up completely, this was the perfect one. But it just didn't pan out that way. The overwhelming opinion was that my days of motorcycling were over, I couldn't accept that, it got my goat. Why should I give up the longest standing pleasure in my life? Why should I allow the incompetence of one farmer to take away my future? So lying broken and busted, with not a single limb functional, I vowed I would become strong enough to ride again. Realising just how much I did value my life, I determined to recapture the chance to give it meaning once more. I wanted my life back and nothing was going to stand in my way. I would regain my strength, I'd rebuild my trusty KLR and when I did I'd know I was fit to ride again.

It was the end of August, the doctors predicted up to six months being stuck in hospital, but I was having none of it. With a fierce determination I fought every minute of every day to regain the independence I'd lost. Every morning I did multiple sets of sit-ups, starting with fifty at first and working my way up to two hundred. I had to build up my strength rather than let my muscles atrophy. After three weeks they hoisted me from bed and into a wheelchair, they thought it would do me good for visitors to be able to wheel me out the ward. My elbows bled using them to propel myself along, my arms couldn't take the strain at first, and I wasn't about to rely on other people to get around. It didn't take me long to manage the pneumatic hoist myself, securing myself into the transfer sling, operating the controls, only needing someone to fetch the equipment for me. Pushing ever harder I soon managed to transfer myself without using the hoist. It was an awkward and precarious undertaking, but it gave me my first degree of true independence, I could come and go at will. Struggling with the simplest of tasks, I none the less refused to rely on the medical staff for my every need. Fortunately they never saw the struggle of transferring myself from wheelchair to toilet, I refused the ease of a commode. My fight for survival hardly abated, but there were plenty of tears, my grief never left me for a single moment. Emotional trauma was over shadowed by bloody-minded determination though, I wouldn't give up, I wanted my life back.

Eventually I spent eleven weeks incarcerated in hospital. It was like a sentence, I even referred to my future discharge as my release date, complaining that prisoners were at least given a release date. I kept my mind on the final goal, full mobility, smaller increments of progress didn't concern me. I applied myself wholeheartedly to achieving this, feeling strongly that progress was often hindered by the professional paranoia of the medical staff. Miraculously the splintered remains of my tibial plateau hadn't displaced, they'd knitted together well, after two months the specialists had high hopes that no medical intervention would be necessary. It still took ten weeks before they'd risk allowing me to exert any force through it again though. But they were magical moments, when I finally set my feet upon the ground. Rising to my full height almost put me into a dead feint, as the head rush hit me with full force. The physiotherapists pleaded with me to take my time, but I was having none of it, cursing them for the physical support they insisted on giving. I wanted to run but couldn't even hobble unaided, a mere five metres had me trembling with the effort. They wouldn't leave the crutches in my possession, I may have earned their respect, but apparently not their trust. They'd worked with me for months, they knew how pig-headed I could be, and felt that I needed to take things slower then I'd allow myself. So progress was at their whim, twice daily excursions, I always pushed myself further than asked, increasing my distance every time. Who knows how long they would have kept me given the chance, but I was getting stir crazy, I wanted out of there. I wasn't about to discharge myself, so I had to convince them I would not be at risk in my own home. I put forward a strong case.

Despite being able to cope for short periods on crutches, I was still pretty much confined to a wheelchair. It apparently wouldn't fit through the door leading into the rear of the house, in effect cutting me off from the kitchen and bathroom amenities. So they rearranged my home, turning the front room into my bedroom, and equipped it with numerous aids to ease the transition. A commode and washable urine bottles were the solution for my sanitary needs, provided a carer was on hand to empty and wash them out. I assured them my brother was staying, to cook and clean, to care for me as long as necessary. I guess I neglected to inform him of that proviso. Where there's a will there's a way, I managed to negotiate that impenetrable doorway, and only removed a minimal amount of plaster off the wall on my way through. I never once used the commode either, regardless of how tricky it proved to access the bathroom. Using the crutches took a lot of effort, put a lot of strain on my arms, I desperately wished to take giant leaps forward but was restricted to taking one halting step at a time.

Within weeks of leaving hospital I discarded my wheelchair altogether, refusing to rely on it any longer. The crutches weren't far behind them either, less than four months from the accident I was back on my own two feet. As soon as I'd regained my sense of balance it was simply a matter of strength, which I worked on constantly. Once I could walk I made the most of it, every day ended by me flaking out on my bed, utterly depleted. I had little else to do, and nothing that was more important to me. All my hopes and aspirations hinged on my mobility, my emotions remained in tatters and there was little I could do about that. The psychological and physical battle for a full recovery took my undivided attention, which was probably a blessing in disguise. Half my weeks were spent at the hospital, either in physio or appointments with one of the specialists. They were still keeping close tabs on me, neither my treatment nor rehabilitation were anywhere near.

Further surgical reconstruction of the ligaments in my left knee was necessary, they needed to wait six months before this was possible. Walking without a full compliment of ligaments was precarious, with each step I could feel my lower leg part company with the upper limb. But it had to be done, a certain level of mobility was essential before that final operation. A magic degree of bend of the knee was required before they'd put me under the knife again, and that was a minimum. The more use I regained beforehand the better the final outcome would be, which was enough for me to religiously exercise every morning and every night. I walked, I swam, I bent and I stretched, I never missed physio, I never missed an appointment. I lived on painkillers and relied on the professionals to keep track of progress. Eventually I surpassed that magical figure, it was over six months since the accident when I was admitted back into hospital. Using a section of my hamstring to replace the ACL was to be the final procedure. It wasn't a nice one, they drilled diagonally through the knee to insert the donated section of hamstring, securing it each end with surgical pins.

Waking up in a hospital ward, in an anaesthetised stupor, had become an all too familiar experience. I fell into old habits without fuss, utilising the self-medicating morphine feed to the maximum permissible limits. It had taken me weeks to wean myself off morphine towards the end of my previous stay, I wasn't about to go through that again. A limit was set, two capsules, enough for the first twenty four hours, enough so I could float through the initial pain. The hard work would start soon enough, at least this time I had one decent leg to rely on. Physio turned out to be more regimented the second time round, there were prescribed time periods to limit what abuse I could put my knee through. They wouldn't even let me start for six weeks after the surgery, the closest I got to exercise was gentle manipulation of the joint. When I did join the leg class again they really laid down the law, these and only these exercises are to be done for the first period of rehabilitation. After a set number of weeks I could extend the variety of exercises, but only to another predetermined limit. It had me gagging at the bit. When they finally gave me the all clear my efforts increased exponentially. Painkillers went out the window, I wanted to gauge progress myself, to feel how far I was pushing myself, not mask the pain. And I excelled, I threw myself wholeheartedly into every session of physio, making seemingly rapid progress.

However hard I worked my legs, whatever progress I made, the injuries to my arms impaired my ability to work. I couldn't lift heavy objects, manipulate work tools effectively, or even raise myself off the ground with any level of decorum. A year after the final surgery my legs were as good as they were going to get, the only time they were a problem was on rough ground and under heavy load. It would be pointless to say I could live with that, there was no choice in the matter, I had to. I also had to see to what extent I could use my body, if I wasn't capable of rebuilding my motorcycle by that stage I never would be.

Over the preceding months a thorough inspection of my battered bike had been made, for all the obviously damaged components I'd already bought replacements. A damaged headstock, the frame part that houses the steering assemblage, had a hairline crack, so the whole frame had to be replaced. If it hadn't been for that it would have been a simple job, only requiring the replacement of periphery items, it had become necessary for a complete rebuild. It was a job I'd previously have relished, taking the opportunity to make upgrades to the standard bike. In theory my thoughts were still on the same track, but doing the work was physically difficult. Lowering myself onto the ground was awkward, getting back up even worse, twisting at odd angles for tricky bits of work was clumsy. Many times I just thought sod it, often got so frustrated I was nearly in tears. In previous years such a task could have been completed in a few weeks, from start to finish. After one month I'd only just stripped everything off the old frame and prepared the various bits for the rebuild. But rebuild I did, slow and painstakingly working every day, often late into the night. Spanner work caused problems for my arms, I began to rely on painkillers again. But as it began to take shape my enthusiasm increased. I discovered methods to overcome the lack of force I could put through my arms, learnt I had to use a torque wrench rather than rely on my own innate ability to gauge how tight bolts were. I was indeed still capable of building a motorcycle, maybe not as quickly, maybe not as effectively, but it could still be done.

Two months later I struggled to prise my newly rebuilt KLR from the barn I'd used as a workshop. It started with ease, sounded as good as ever, and looked a completely different machine. The moment of truth had arrived, now I had to ride it. Looking across a soggy, overgrown and lumpy field, I gulped. Before I could even get to a road I had to ride across two fields and a mile or more of bumpy gravel track. Elation overcame fear though, a sense of achievement filled me with pride, the memory of my hospital bed was still so vivid. Trepidation filled me as I swung my leg over the beast, it felt taller than I remembered, on tiptoes I barely reached the ground. It was like my very first time on a bike, all over again, tentatively letting out the clutch, millimetre by millimetre. As the bike started to rock forward I paddled with my feet, reluctant to commit myself to balance alone. That wasn't the way to do it, it was poor riding practice, which I abhorred. After another couple of hesitant attempts to pull away I'd hardly moved, I wasn't getting anywhere fast. With a deep breath the throttle was gently rolled on and the clutch carefully let out, I was determined not to bottle out again. Planting my feet firmly on the foot pegs, I eased forward feeling very shaky, uncertain of what would happen if I had to take the weight of the bike on my legs suddenly. I was my own worst enemy, filling my head with paranoid nonsense. Quiet reassurance calmed my mind, I settled into the seat and chugged carefully up a bumpy slope. I had been sitting bolt upright, rigidly so, until finally with a huge sigh of relief, I let the tension go. And with it went all the doubt and anxiety, the bike felt balanced, poised for my every command. A quick blip of the throttle smoothed out the lumps and bumps across the next field, relaxing me even more. Halfway across, stamping on the rear brake, I locked the rear wheel on purpose, just to get the feel of it again, further reassurance. So I could ride a bike, the only question left to answer was to what effect.

Apparently I'd exceeded all expectations, though I fell way short of what I really wanted, a full recovery. Neither my arms nor legs would ever be what there were before, but my job at that stage was to discover what I could achieve, rather than dwell on what I couldn't. A stubborn refusal to quit had me back on my feet, back on a bike, given me back some semblance of life. All that was left was to make the effort worthwhile, to make the most of the mobility I'd regained.